PERSPECTIVES

Understanding and Evaluating
Today's World Views

by
Norman L. Geisler
and
William D. Watkins

PERSPECTIVES

UNDERSTANDING AND EVALUATING
TODAY'S WORLD VIEWS

NORMAN L. GEISLER And
WILLIAM WATKINS

HERE'S LIFE PUBLISHERS, INC.
San Bernardino, California 92402

PERSPECTIVES:
Understanding and Evaluating Today's World Views
by Norman L. Geisler and William D. Watkins

Artwork by Jeff Yutaka Amano,
used by permission.

Published by
HERE'S LIFE PUBLISHERS, INC.
P.O. Box 1576
San Bernardino, California 92402

ISBN 0-89840-073-2
Library of Congress Catalog Number 84-70487
Here's Life Publishers Product Number 950972

For More Information, Write:

L.I.F.E. —P.O. Box A399, Sydney, South 2000, Australia.

Campus Crusade for Christ of Canada—Box 368, Abbottsford, B.C., V25 4N9, Canada.

Campus Crusade for Christ — 103 Friar Street, Reading RGI IEP, Berkshire, England.

Lay Institute for Evangelism —P.O. Box 8786, Auckland 3, New Zealand.

Great Commission Movement of Nigeria—P.O. Box 500, Jos, Plateau State Nigeria, West Africa.

Life Ministry —P.O. Box/Bus 91015, Auckland Park 2006, Republic of So. Africa.

Campus Crusade for Christ Int'l. —Arrowhead Springs, San Bernardino, CA 92414, U.S.A.

To our wives,
Barbara and Pamela,
who have been most encouraging
and
patient companions
throughout this endeavor.

CONTENTS

Preface 9

Chapter 1. An Invitation to Other Worlds 11

Chapter 2. Theism: A World Plus an Infinite God 21

Chapter 3. Atheism: A World Without God 43

Chapter 4. Pantheism: A World That Is God 69

Chapter 5. Pan-en-theism: A World In God 99

Chapter 6. Deism: A World on Its Own Made by God 137

Chapter 7. Finite Godism: A World With a Finite God 165

Chapter 8. Polytheism: A World With Many Gods 195

Chapter 9. Choosing a World View 231

Appendix: Chart on World Views 243

References 247

Indices 253

Glossary 265

PREFACE

What is it that everyone has, no one can live without, every important decision in life is made with, and yet most people do not even know they have? Do you give up? It is a world view. A world view! What is that? It is what makes a world of difference in how you view your life in the world. It is the framework through which you see and the basis on which you decide.

A world view is all-important and yet most people are not even aware they have one. What is worse, most persons never stop to think about one. You are different. Otherwise you would not have read this far.

There are many world views. Which one you have is of the greatest importance in your life—and death. Anything of this importance demands intelligent comparative shopping. It is for this reason we have prepared this catalogue of world views for you. In it we have outlined the seven basic world views people hold. We have presented them in such a way that you can compare and contrast—and count the cost. Which one you buy into will make a world of difference in your life. It is our hope that you will carefully consider all your options and then intelligently decide, even if it means discarding the world view you now have.

Socrates said, "the unexamined life is not worth living." And the unexamined world view is not worth living by.

9

1

An Invitation
to Other Worlds

Why is it that two people looking at the same ink-blot can see entirely different things in it? How is it that some star-gazers can see bears, birds and giants, while others can scarcely see the "Big Dipper"? The answer is that each person is looking at the same event through different "glasses." And one's "glasses" will color what he sees. Through red glasses everything looks red.

I.   What is a world view?

A world view is a way one views the whole world. And since people have vastly different views of the world, depending on the perspective from which they view the world, it is clear that one's world view makes a world of difference.

A world view is a way of viewing or interpreting all of reality. It is an interpretive framework through which or by which one makes sense out of the data of life and the world. There are a number of ways this can be illustrated.

A.   A world view is like a pair of colored glasses.

As has already been suggested, a world view is like a set of colored glasses. If one looks at the same object through green colored glasses he will see it as green. While another looking at the same object through red glasses will see it as red. This is why people with different world views will often see the same facts in a very different way. For example, an orthodox Jew looks at the Exodus of Israel from Egypt as a divine intervention. That is, he sees it as a miracle. A naturalist, on the other hand, would view the same event (if it really happened) as an anomaly, that is, as an unusual natural event.[1] Both could admit the same fact and yet come to entirely different conclusions as to what that fact *means*. This is because they have different world views. World views make a world of difference, even in how one understands the same fact.

There are some differences, however, between a normal pair of glasses and a world view. For one thing world view glasses are worn continually. They are the enduring lenses by which one interprets everything he sees. A world view is not put on the bed-stand at night. One even dreams within the framework of his world view. It is, in fact, the integrating center of one's entire personality.

This raises another difference: one not only "reads" (i.e., interprets) through his world view "glasses" but he also *lives* by means of them. For a world view is really a world and *life* view. That is, it includes within it value indicators or principles by which one makes value judgments.

There is a third difference between normal glasses and a world view: a world view is more dynamic and flexible than are ordinary glass lenses. Like living organisms it is capable of changing yet it remains substantially the same. In this way world view glasses are more dynamic and adaptive than physical glasses. So one's world view is capable of minor changes and adjustments.

Further, one set of world view "glasses" can be exchanged for a different world view. In science this kind of major change is called a "paradigm shift."[2] In religion it is called a "conversion." That is to say, from time to time people do discard one world view for another. However, metamorphosis from one world view to another is not an everyday occurrence. It is a more radical and rare event, often occurring no more than once in a lifetime. For most persons it never occurs.

There are other ways to describe a world view. One is to think of it as a scientific model.

B. A world view is like a scientific model.

In science a model is a way of constructing the observed data so as to make sense of it or to use it for some human purpose. The same data can be explained by different models, sometimes equally well. A model then is a framework given to the known facts so as to unify or construct them. For example, a phylogenetic tree is a construction by evolutionary biologists to illustrate how to see the branches and limbs between every living species. There are, of course, different phylogenetic trees because different biologists draw the branches in different places. That is, they model them in different ways. In fact, non-evolutionists see no tree at all. Some see each leaf (life type) as a special creation of God.[3] This model is obviously different.

An even more simple example of a model would be that of dots and lines. Suppose the following eight dots represent bare facts and the lines represent the interpretive framework or modeling of those facts. It is obvious that the lines can be drawn in many different ways. For instance, ⦂⦂ ⦂⦂ could be interpreted as ⊓ N or N ⊓ . It all depends on how one draws the lines. So it is with world views. One world view may draw the "lines" of meaning on the facts of life in one way and another world view will draw the lines in a different way. Anyone who has tried to "see" the lines which astrologers have drawn in the night sky often have difficulty seeing much beyond the "big dipper." There are other ways to draw the lines. One religious writer even concluded that God's way of salvation can be seen spelled out in the stars![4] Unbelievers, however, do not see this. It seems obvious enough from this that not all meaning is being read "out of" the facts; world views also read meaning "into" the data.

There is an important difference between a world view and a scientific model. The world view is a *macro*-model; it is a model that attempts to explain *all* of reality, not just some aspect of it. Scientific models are generally aimed at some particular aspect of reality or relationship within the universe.[5] A world view, on the other hand, is designed to explain *all* relationships of all things and/or events in the *whole* of reality. This leads to another way to illustrate a world view.

C. A world view is like a picture on the puzzle box.

Anyone who has ever put together a complex puzzle knows how handy the picture on the cover is. The picture serves several functions. First, it provides the overall picture of the whole puzzle. Secondly, it gives helpful clues as to where individual pieces fit into the overall picture (by showing where certain patterns of color are). Consequently, one is enabled to put the whole picture together much more quickly. In a similar way a world view provides the overall picture of reality into which one can fit all the pieces of life and the world. Without it life would be as complex and confusing and mixed-up as are the individual pieces of a difficult puzzle. A world view acts as the guiding pattern which enables one to integrate all the parts into a meaningful whole.

There are, of course, some drawbacks with this illustration. World views actually "shape" some of the pieces of the puzzle; they do not merely fit existing shapes together. Also, not all the pieces of life are neatly "precut" for one and only one place in the whole. Different pieces may fit in different places in different world views, whereas in a puzzle there is only one piece for one place. In this respect the pieces of a world view are more like those of a mosaic where the same piece could be used in an entirely different picture. Nonetheless, a world view is like the picture of a puzzle in that it serves as an overall guide for all of the particulars of the world and life. It is a general framework within which one can fit all the facts.

In summation, a world view is the structure with which one molds the "stuff" of experience. It is the mold into which the "clay" of reality is cast. A world view is like a plot that holds the "play" of life together. It is a pattern superimposed on the "cloth" of the world by which one knows where to cut the fabric of experience. And it goes without saying that one's structure, mold, plot, or pattern will be the determinative factor in understanding the facts of the world. World views will make a world of difference in how one views the world.

II. What are the differences between the major world views?

Historically, there are seven major world views. Each one is different from the other. No one can consistently believe in more than one world view because the central premises of each are opposed by the others. That means that logically only one world view can be true; the others must be false.[6] The seven major world views are as follows: theism, atheism, pantheism, finite godism, panentheism, deism, and polytheism.

14

A. Theism: An infinite God is beyond and in the universe.[7]

Theism is the world view that says that the physical universe is not all there is. There is an infinite, personal God beyond the universe who created it, sustains it, and who can act within it in a supernatural way. This is the view represented by traditional Judaism, Christianity and Islam.

B. Atheism: God does not exist beyond the universe or in it.[8]

Atheism says the universe is all there is. No God exists anywhere, either in the universe or beyond it. The universe or cosmos is all there is or ever will be. It is self-sustaining. Some of the more famous atheists were Karl Marx, Friedrich Nietzsche and Jean-Paul Sartre.

C. Pantheism: God is the universe.[9]

For a pantheist there is no creator beyond the universe. Creator and creation are two different ways of viewing one reality. God is the universe (or, the All) and the universe is God. There is ultimately only one reality, not many different ones. Pantheism is represented by certain forms of Hinduism, Zen Buddhism and Christian Science.

D. Pan-en-theism: God is in the universe.[10]

This view says God is in the universe as a mind is in a body. The universe is God's "body." But there is another "pole" to God other than the physical universe. It is His eternal and infinite potential beyond the actual physical universe. This view is represented by A. N. Whitehead, Charles Hartshorne, and Schubert Ogden.

E. Deism: God is beyond the universe but not in it.[11]

Deism is like theism minus the miracles. It says God is transcendent over the universe but not supernaturally active in the world. It holds a naturalistic view of the world while insisting that there must be a creator or originator of the universe. It is represented by men like Voltaire, Thomas Jefferson, and Thomas Paine.

F. Finite Godism: A finite God is beyond and in the universe.[12]

Finite godism is like theism, only the god beyond the universe and active in it is not infinite but is limited in his nature and power. John Stuart Mill, William James, and Peter A. Bertocci are examples of this view.

G. Polytheism: There are many gods in the universe.[13]

Polytheism is the belief that there are many finite gods in the universe who influence it. They deny any infinite God beyond the world such as in theism. They hold, however, that the gods are active in the world in contrast to deism. The chief representatives of this view are the ancient Greeks and modern Mormons.

III. What difference does a world view make?

It is obvious from the foregoing discussion that world views can make a radical difference in several very important areas. Two of them are of note. Others will become obvious when each view is discussed in particular.

A. A difference in meaning.

World views are different interpretive frameworks. Each has a different view of what is ultimate and of how all else relates to it. Some say the ultimate is finite; others claim it is infinite. Some believe it is personal and others not. Some call it "God" while others prefer Nature, All, or Cosmos. As such, different world views attach different meanings to the events of the world and life. Ultimately these meanings are not only different, but they are opposed.

Let us examine some specific areas. What is the meaning of death for a theist as opposed to an atheist? The former believes in personal immortality and the latter generally does not. Hence, for the theist death is the beginning of eternal life. For the atheist death is simply the ending of one's mortal life on earth. And for the pantheist, death is the cessation of one life and the beginning of another leading to reincarnation and ultimate merging with God. These are three radically different meanings of the same event. World views provide vastly differing meanings for life's events.

Another example would be the different meaning assigned to a virtuous act by various world views. A theist views an act of compassion as an absolute obligation imposed by God and one which has intrinsic value regardless of the consequences. An atheist, on the other hand, views virtue as a self-imposed obligation which men have decided upon because of the good they perceive it may bring. The act of compassion, however, has no intrinsic value apart from that which men give to it. Here again the meaning of the same act is radically different between these two world views.

B. A difference in value.

There is also a great gulf between different world views with regard to the nature of values. For a theist certain things have ultimate value because God has so endowed them. Human life, for example, is sacred because God made it in His own image. This means that there are divine obligations to respect life and absolute prohibitions against murder. For an atheist, by contrast, life has only the value man gives to it. This value is not sacred or divine, it is simply humanistic. It is not absolute but is merely relative. Usually the atheist believes an act is good if it brings good results and evil if it does not. A Christian believes that certain intended acts are good within themselves regardless of their results. So there is a radical difference in the value of the same act in these two systems.

There are of course many other and important differences between world views. These will be discussed in due course. It is sufficient to note for now that world views do make a world of difference not only in how one thinks but in how and why one acts.

In the following chapters each of these world views will be discussed in turn. Both representative proponents and the main principles with their implications will be explained so that the reader may come to understand and evaluate each view. In the last chapter suggestions will be made on how to choose a world view.

In summary, reality or all that exists is either the universe only, God only, or the universe and God(s). If the universe is all that exists then *atheism* is right. If God is all that exists then *pantheism* is right. If God and the universe exist then either there is one God or many Gods. If there are many gods then *polytheism* is right. If there is only one God then this God is either finite or infinite. If there is one finite God then *finite godism* is correct. If this finite God has two poles (one beyond and one in the world), then *panentheism* is right. If there is one infinite God then either there is intervention of this God in the universe or there is not. If there is intervention, then *theism* is true. If there is not, then *deism* is true. In short, there are seven basic mutually exclusive world views. Only one can be true.

This book is a catalogue for the world view shopper. Study it carefully. The one you buy will make a world of difference in your life. The possible combinations yield seven different world views.

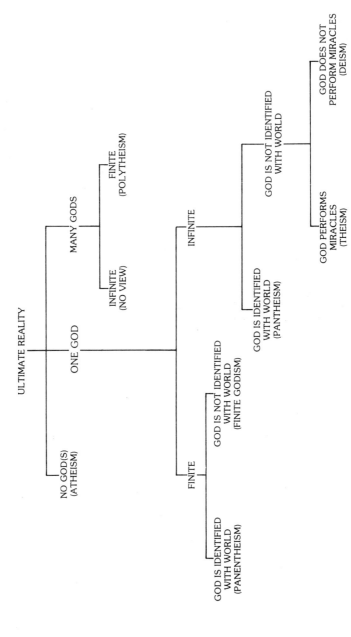

SEVEN MAJOR WORLD VIEWS

ULTIMATE REALITY

NO GOD(S)
(ATHEISM)

ONE GOD

MANY GODS

FINITE
(POLYTHEISM)

INFINITE
(NO VIEW)

FINITE

INFINITE

GOD IS IDENTIFIED
WITH WORLD
(PANENTHEISM)

GOD IS NOT IDENTIFIED
WITH WORLD
(FINITE GODISM)

GOD IS IDENTIFIED
WITH WORLD
(PANTHEISM)

GOD IS NOT IDENTIFIED
WITH WORLD

GOD PERFORMS
MIRACLES
(THEISM)

GOD DOES NOT
PERFORM MIRACLES
(DEISM)

NOTES

1. See Chapter 3 for a naturalistic interpretation of unusual events.
2. See Thomas Kuhn, *The Structure of Scientific Revolutions* (Chicago: University of Chicago Press, 1962), pp. 147, 149.
3. See Wayne Frair and Percival Davis, *A Case for Creation* (Chicago: Moody Press, 1983), chapters 1, 2.
4. Ethelbert W. Bullinger, *The Witness of the Stars* (Grand Rapids, Michigan: Kregal Publications, 1979, first published 1893).
5. See Max Black, *Models and Metaphors* (New York: Cornell University Press, 1962).
6. Of course some world views (for example, pantheism), do not believe ultimate reality is non-contradictory. This too will be discussed in chapter four.
7. See chapter 2 for a discussion of theism.
8. See chapter 3 for a discussion of atheism.
9. Pantheism is discussed in chapter 4.
10. Panentheism is discussed in chapter 5.
11. Chapter 6 is devoted to deism.
12. Chapter 7 is devoted to finite Godism.
13. See chapter 8 for a discussion of polytheism.

2

Theism: A World Plus an Infinite God

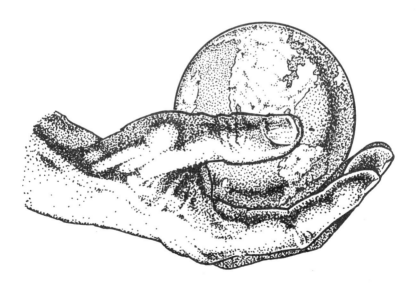

I. Introduction.

Theism holds that there is more than the world—there is also an infinite God who created it. Furthermore, there is a radical distinction between creation and Creator. Many great religions are theistic, for example, Judaism, Islam and Christianity.

Classical theism—theism proper—is represented by St. Augustine (d. 430), St. Anselm (d. 1109) and Thomas Aquinas (d. 1274). In the modern world, Descartes (d. 1650) and Leibniz (d. 1716) are two of the more noted defenders of theism. Perhaps the most popular exponent of theism in recent times is C.S. Lewis.

II. A typology of theism.

There are many ways to distinguish one kind of theist from another. One of the most helpful ways is to note the perspective from which they approach God. For example, there are *rational* theists (such as René Descartes and Leibniz[1]) *existential* theists (such as Sören Kierkegaard), *phenomenological* theists (such as Peter Koestenbaum), *analytic* theists (such as Alvin Plantinga), *empirical* theists (such as Thomas Reid), *idealistic* theists (such as Bishop Berkeley), *pragmatic* theists (such as Charles Sanders Pierce) and many more. All of these are distinguishable by the method of philosophy through which they approach their belief in God.

Theists can also be distinguished by what they believe about God and His relationship to the world. Most believe that the material world is real, but some believe that it exists only in minds and ideas (Bishop Berkeley). Most theists believe that God is unchangeable, but some (generally influenced by panentheism) believe that God can and does change in some ways. Some theists believe that the created universe may have always existed (such as Aquinas), while most theists believe that the universe must have had a distinct beginning (St. Bonaventure). Perhaps the most important difference among theists is that many—such as orthodox Jews and Moslems—believe that God is only one person (monotheism), while others (such as orthodox Christians) believe that God is tripersonal (trinitarianism). For the purpose of this chapter we will concentrate largely on what classical theists hold in common.

III. Some representatives of theism.

In the Western Christian tradition, two of the greatest traditional theists of all time are St. Augustine and St. Thomas Aquinas. In the contemporary English-speaking world, C.S. Lewis has immense popularity. For these reasons we will discuss these three.

A. St. Augustine (A.D. 354-430).

St. Augustine began as a near-pagan who made his pilgrimage through Manichaean dualism (the body springs from evil, the soul from good) to neo-platonism (pantheism) and finally to Christian theism. His great mind and immense literary output place him in a unique position among theists. He is considered the greatest theist of the early Middle Ages.

1. God.

For Augustine, God is the self-existing "I AM WHO I AM." He is uncreated substance, immutable (unchangeable), eternal, indivisible and absolutely perfect. God is not an impersonal force but a personal being. In fact, He is tripersonal: Father, Son and Holy Spirit. In this one eternal substance there is neither confusion of persons nor division in essence.

God is omnipotent (all-powerful), omnipresent (all-present) and omniscient (all-knowing). He is eternal, existing before time and beyond time. He is absolutely transcendent over the universe and yet operates in every part of it as its sustaining cause. Although the world had a beginning, there was never a time when God was not. He is a necessary being who depends on nothing, but on Him everything else depends for its existence. "Since God is supreme being, that is, since He supremely is and, therefore, is immutable, it follows that He gave being to all that He created out of nothing."[2]

2. The world.

According to Augustine, the world was created *ex nihilo* (out of nothing). "Out of nothing didst Thou create heaven and earth—a great thing and a small—because Thou are Almighty and Good, to make all things good, even the great heaven and the small earth. Thou wast, and there was nought else from which Thou didst create heaven and earth."[3] Hence, the world is not eternal. It had a beginning, yet not in time but with time. That is, time began with the world. When asked what God did before He created the world out of nothing, Augustine retorted:

> For whence could innumerable ages pass by which Thou didst not make, since Thou are the Author and Creator of all ages? Or what times should those be which were not made by Thee? Or how should they pass by if they had not been? Since, therefore, Thou art the Creator of all times, if any time was before Thou madest heaven and earth, why is it said that Thou didst refrain from working? For that very time Thou madest, nor could times pass by before Thou madest times.[4]

23

The world is temporal and changing, and from those facts the theist concludes that there must be an eternal and unchanging being who made it. "Behold the heavens and the earth are; they proclaim that they were created; for they change and vary." However, "whatsoever hath not been made, and yet is, hath nothing in it, which before it had not, and this it is, to change and vary. They proclaim also, that they made not themselves."[5]

3. Miracles.

Since God made the world, He can intervene in it. In fact what we call nature is simply the way God regularly works in His creation: "...when such things happen in a continuous kind of river of ever-flowing succession, passing from the hidden to the visible, and from the visible to the hidden, by a regular and beaten track, then they are called natural." However, "when, for the admonition of men, they are thrust in by an unusual changeableness, then they are called miracles."[6]

But even nature's regular activities are the works of God:

Who draws up the sap through the root of the vine to the bunch of grapes, and makes the wine, except God; who, while man plants and waters, Himself giveth the increase? But when, at the command of the Lord, the water was turned into wine with an extraordinary quickness, the divine power was made manifest, by the confession even of the foolish. Who ordinarily clothes the trees with leaves and flowers except God? Yet, when the rod of Aaron the priest blossomed, the Godhead in some way conversed with doubting humanity.[7]

4. Man.

Man, like the world, is not eternal. He was created by God in the image of God. Man is composed of a mortal body and an immortal soul. After death the soul awaits reunion with a transformed body in either a state of conscious bliss (heaven) or of continuous torment (hell). And "after the resurrection, the body, having become wholly subject to the spirit, will live in perfect peace to all eternity."[8]

Man's soul, or spiritual dimension, is of higher value than his body. Indeed, it is in this spiritual dimension that man is made in God's image and likeness.

5. Evil.

Evil is real, but it is not a substance. The origin of evil is the rebellion of free creatures against God. "In fact, sin is so much a voluntary evil that it is not sin at all unless it is voluntary,"[9] wrote Augustine. Of course, God created all things good and gave to His moral creatures the good power of free choice. However, sin arose when "the will which turns from the unchangeable and common good and turns to its own private good or to anything exterior or inferior, sins."[10]

By choosing their own self-serving sense of good, moral creatures brought about the corruption of good substances. Evil, then, is by nature a lack or deprivation of the good. Evil does not exist in itself. Like a parasite, evil exists only in good things as a corruption of them.

> For who can doubt that the whole of that which is called evil is nothing else than corruption? Different evils may, indeed, be called by different names; but that which is the evil of all things in which any evil is perceptible is corruption. So the corruption of an educated mind is ignorance; the corruption of a prudent mind is imprudence; the corruption of a just mind, injustice; the corruption of a brave mind, cowardice; the corruption of a calm, peaceful mind, cupidity, fear, sorrow, pride.[11]

Thus, evil is a lack in or distortion of good things. It is like rot to a tree or rust to iron. It corrupts good things while having no nature of its own. In this way Augustine answered the dualism of the Manichaean religion, which pronounced evil to be a coeternal but opposed reality to good.

6. Ethics.

St. Augustine believed that God is love by His very nature. Since man's obligation to his Creator is to be morally God-like, man has a moral duty to love God and his neighbor, who is made in God's image.

> For this is the law of love that has been laid down by Divine authority. "Thou shalt love thy neighbor as thyself," but, "Thou shalt love God with all thy heart, and with all thy soul, and with all thy mind:" so that you are to concentrate all your thoughts, your whole life, and your whole intelligence upon Him from whom you derive all that you bring.[12]

All the virtues are defined in terms of this love. Augustine said, "As to virtue leading us to a happy life, I hold virtue to be nothing else than perfect love of God. For the fourfold division of virtue I regard as taken from four forms of love." For these four virtues, Augustine added, "I should have no hesitation in defining them: that temperance is love giving itself entirely to that which is loved." And "fortitude is love readily bearing all things for the sake of the loved object." But "justice is love serving only the loved object, and therefore ruling rightly; prudence is love distinguishing with sagacity between what hinders it and what helps it." However, "the object of this love is not anything, but only God, the chief good, the highest wisdom, the perfect harmony." Augustine expresses the definitions thus:

> that temperance is love keeping itself entire and incorrupt for God; justice is love serving God only, and therefore ruling well all else, as subject to man; prudence is love making a right distinction between what helps it toward God and what might hinder it.[13]

In summation, for Augustine, God is absolute love, and man's absolute obligation is to express love in every area of his activity, first toward God and then toward his neighbor.

7. History and goal.

In his classic, *The City of God*, St. Augustine wrote the first major Christian philosophy of history. He said that there are two "cities" (kingdoms): the city of God and the city of man. These two cities have two different origins (God and Satan), two different natures (love for God and love of one's self, pride), two different citizens (believers and nonbelievers) and two different destinies (heaven and hell). History is headed for a goal, a completion. At this end of time, there will be an ultimate victory of God over Satan, of good over evil. Evil will be separated from the good, and the righteous will be resurrected into a perfect body and a perfect state. The paradise lost by man in the beginning will be regained by God in the end.

History is His story. God is working out His sovereign plan, and in the end He will defeat evil and accomplish the perfecting of man.

> Hence we have an answer to the problem why God should have created men whom He foresaw would sin. It was because both in them and by means of them He could reveal how much was deserved by their guilt and condoned by His grace, and, also, because the harmony of the whole of reality which God has created and controls cannot be marred by the perverse discordancy of those who sin.[14].

B. St. Thomas Aquinas (A.D. 1224-1274).

Two of the greatest theists of all time, Augustine and Aquinas, stood at either end of the Middle Ages. They were separated by 800 years but by very little difference in their basic views of God and the world.

1. God.

For Aquinas the basic attribute of God is pure actuality—"I AM WHO I AM" (Exodus 3:14). God *is* existence, pure and simple. Everything else merely *has* existence. God is pure act; all else is a composition of act (actuality) and potency (potentiality). That is, God is a necessary being—a being which cannot *not* be. All creatures are contingent beings—beings which *can* not be.

> Therefore that God gives being to a creature depends on His will; nor does He conserve things in being otherwise than by continually giving being to them, as we have said. Therefore, just as before things existed, God was free not to give them being, and so not to make them, so, after they have been made, He is free not to give them being, and thus they would cease to exist. This would be to annihilate them.[15]

Since God has no potentiality in His being (that is, He is all that He ever will be; He will not become anything more), He cannot change. For change is moving from a state of potentiality (wherein one has the capability to change) to a state of actuality (wherein one has actually changed). Since time is a temporal change, and God cannot change at all, God therefore must be eternal. God has no befores or afters; He is the eternal Now. God is also indivisible, having no composition or parts. He is infinite because He has no potentiality to limit Him. In addition to these metaphysical attributes, God is a personal (tri-personal) and morally perfect being.

> Although the things that exist and live are more perfect than the things that merely exist, nevertheless, God, Who is not other than His being, is a universally perfect being. And I call *universally perfect* that to which the excellence of no genus. is lacking.

> Every excellence in any given thing belongs to it according to its being. For man would have no excellence as a result of his wisdom unless through it he were wise. So, too, with the other excellences. Hence, the mode of a thing's excellence is according to the mode of its being. For a thing is said to be more or less excellent according as its being is

27

limited to a certain greater or lesser mode of excellence. Therefore, if there is something to which the whole power of being belongs, it can lack no excellence that is proper to some thing.[16].

And such a being is God, according to Aquinas.

2. The world.

The universe—all that exists except God—was created from nothing *(ex nihilo)*. It is contingent, that is, it came from nothing, and it can go into nothingness. In fact, it would become nothing right now if God were to withdraw His causal power that keeps it in existence. Every finite being is radically contingent or dependent on God for its very existence. Thus, all creatures have the potential not to exist. They do exist, but they may not exist. Indeed, they would not exist if God should so will. In Aquinas' words, "As creatures come forth from nothing so could they go back there, did God permit."[17] But as long as they actually do exist they are composed of actuality and potentiality, whereas God is pure actuality with no potentiality.

The world is not eternal, but God could have created it from eternity, since He is eternal. There was no time before time, only eternity (God). Since the world was created it has passed through, and continues to pass through, successive changes. Time itself is a change that is computed according to a before and an after. Since God undergoes no such changes, He cannot be temporal. Hence, the world can change in its relationship to God, but God does not change. Just as a pillar remains unmoved when a person moves from one side of it to the other, so God remains unchanged as the world changes in relationship to Him.

3. Miracles.

God created the world and has sovereign control over it. Hence,

divine art [i.e., intervention] is not exhausted in the production of creatures, and therefore can operate otherwise than according to the customary course of nature. But it does not follow that by acting against the general run of things divine art contravenes its own principle, for an artist is well able to devise a work of art in a style different from his first production.[18]

According to Aquinas, a true miracle has three characteristics.

First, that it is above the power of natural forces; second, that it is beyond the natural disposition of the subject; third, that it is beside the normal course of events. These three notes are somehow present in every miracle, namely of difficulty for the first, beyond expectation for the second, rareness for the third.[19]

4. Man.

Man is a soul-body unity, a composition of form (soul) and matter (body).[20] Man's immortal soul, however, survives his physical death and will be united with a perfect resurrection body at the end of time.

Although man is lower than angels he is higher than animals. Man is created in the image and likeness of God. Hence, human life should be treated as sacred. Thus, murder is wrong, as are numerous other attacks on man's dignity, such as hatred, cursing, cruelty, rape and suicide. Suicide—self-murder—is wrong because man, as a creature of God, does not own his life; God does. Since only God gives life, only God has the right to take it.

5. Evil.

As in most other points, Aquinas' view on evil is substantially identical to Augustine's. The origin of evil is free choice; the nature of evil is a deprivation or lack of good, as Aquinas wrote,

Evil is a deprivation of good, and a privation is not a nature or real essence, it is a negation in a subject. Evil cannot be caused except by good, and even then indirectly; this is clear both in physical and moral affairs.[21]

God in His providence superintends the course of evil and will finally defeat it. For "however greatly multiplied, evils can never consume the whole of good."[22] For example, "sin cannot destroy man's rationality altogether, for then he would no longer be capable of sin."[23]

In the end, God will triumph over evil by punishing all evil and rewarding all good. And *"God is so powerful that he can make good even out of evil*. Hence, many good things would be missed if God permitted no evil to exist."[24] Thus God has a good purpose for permitting evil.

6. Ethics.

Ethics is based on ethical laws that reflect the very nature of God. There are four kinds of law, as defined by Aquinas. *Eternal* law is God's unchangeable plan by which He sovereignly governs the universe. *Natural* law is the participation of rational creatures in the eternal law—that is, God's absolute law revealed in the nature of man. All men have this natural law. *Divine* law is the revelation of God's law through the Scriptures and the church. Only believers possess this law. *Human* law is a particular application of natural law to the community.[25]

Virtues fall into two classes: natural and supernatural. The first group includes the classical virtues: prudence, justice, courage and temperance. These are part of the natural law revealed in the rational nature of all men. For believers there are also three supernatural virtues: faith, hope and love.[26]

In contrast to some theists (such as William of Ockham) who trace moral laws to the will of God, Aquinas believed that the natural law is rooted in the very nature of God. His view is called ethical essentialism, as opposed to voluntarism (which is Ockham's view). In other words, Aquinas believed that "God wills something because it is right" (in accordance with His unchangeable nature). A thing is not right simply because God wills it (arbitrarily).

7. History and goal.

Like most theists, Aquinas held a linear view of history. Time does not go around in circles. It had a beginning, and it will end. History is moving toward a final goal. In the end the wicked will be punished and the good will see God face-to-face. The direct contemplation of the divine essence is man's final beatitude (blessing), which Aquinas called the Beatific Vision. For "there can be no final happiness for us save in the vision of God."[27] Once the mind of man is directly informed by the infinite good of God's essence, it will be impossible for man to turn away from it. He will rest in its eternal enjoyment and perfection.

C. C.S. Lewis (A.D. 1898-1963).

Perhaps the most influential 20th-century Christian theist was C.S. Lewis, a former atheist and an Oxford professor. His great literary ability to express profound truths in simple language has endeared him to the hearts of millions.

Although Lewis disclaimed being a philosopher or theologian, his insight into the essentials of theism is surpassed by few and better expressed by even fewer.

1. God.

Lewis accepted the traditional Augustine-Anselm-Aquinas view of God as an eternal, necessary, transcendent, morally perfect personal being. He began his famous *Mere Christianity*[28] by arguing that an objective moral law, such as even common disagreements presuppose, entails a Moral Law Giver. That is, there is

> something which is directing the universe, and which appears in me as a law urging me to do right and making me feel responsible and uncomfortable when I do wrong. I think we have to assume it is more like a mind than it is like anything else we know—because after all the only other thing we know is matter and you can hardly imagine a bit of matter giving instructions.[29]

This Moral Law Giver is absolutely perfect, because He is the standard of all right and wrong. For this reason Lewis rejected his former argument that God could not exist because of injustice in the world. He asked:

> Just how had I got this idea of *just* and *unjust*? A man does not call a line crooked unless he has some idea of a straight line. What was I comparing this universe with when I called it unjust?...Of course I could have given up my idea of justice by saying it was nothing but a private idea of my own. But if I did that, then my argument against God collapsed too—for the argument depended on saying that the world was really unjust, not simply that it did not happen to please my private fancies. Thus in the very act of trying to prove that God did not exist—in other words, that the whole of reality was senseless—I found I was forced to assume that one part of reality—namely my idea of justice—was full of sense.[30]

Not only is God absolutely perfect, but He also transcends space and time. According to Lewis, "Almost certainly God is not in Time. His life does not consist of moments following one another....Ten-thirty—and every other moment from the beginning of the world—is always the Present for Him." To put it another way, "He has all eternity in which to listen to the split second of prayer put up by a pilot as his plane crashes in flames."[31]

But despite the fact that God transcends the universe He is, nevertheless, immanent (present and operating) in it. Lewis wrote:

Looking for God—or Heaven—by exploring space is like reading or seeing all Shakespeare's plays in the hope that you will find Shakespeare as one of the characters or Stratford as one of the places. Shakespeare is in one sense present at every moment in every play. But he is never present in the same way as Falstaff or Lady Macbeth. Nor is he diffused through the play like a gas.[32]

2. The world.

Like other theists, Lewis believed in creation out of nothing. For "What God creates is not God; just as what man makes is not man."[33] And matter is not coeternal with God. For,

entropy by its very character assures us that though it may be the universal rule in the Nature we know, it cannot be universal absolutely. If a man says, "Humpty Dumpty is falling," you see at once that this is not a complete story. The bit you have been told implies both a later chapter in which Humpty Dumpty will have reached the ground, and an earlier chapter in which he was still seated on the wall. A Nature which is "running down" cannot be the whole story. A clock can't run down unless it has been wound up.[34]

Not only is matter not eternal, but it is also the product of a Cosmic Mind. "But to admit *that* sort of cosmic mind is to admit a God outside Nature, a transcendent and supernatural God."[35] In brief, the universe is matter, and matter cannot produce mind; only mind can produce matter. The creation of the world was not from some pre-existing matter or stuff. It was created from nothing. God created this world freely.

The freedom of God consists in the fact that no cause other than Himself produces His acts and no external obstacle impedes them—that His own goodness is the root from which they all grow and His own omnipotence the air in which they all flower.[36]

God did not create the world because He had to; He created it because He wanted to. The existence of the universe is entirely contingent on the good will of the Creator.

3. Miracles.

Lewis believed that nature is not the "whole of reality." Miracles can enter into the realm of nature, and once a miracle has done so, then nature will "hasten to accommodate the newcomer." As Lewis wrote:

It is...inaccurate to define a miracle as something that breaks the laws of Nature. It doesn't. If I knock out my pipe, I alter the position of a great many atoms: in the long run, and to an infinitesimal degree, of all the atoms there are. Nature digests and assimilates this event with perfect ease and harmonizes it in a twinkling with all other events.... If God creates a miraculous spermatozoan in the body of a virgin, it does not proceed to break any laws. The laws at once take over. Nature is ready. Pregnancy follows, according to all the normal laws, and nine months later a child is born.[37]

Lewis believed that miracles and nature are interlocked and intricately related because both have their origin in God and are guided according to His purpose and design. Miracles, while changing nature's present course, nevertheless, are consistent with nature's laws. Thus, "miraculous wine will intoxicate, miraculous conception will lead to pregnancy...miraculous bread will be digested." A miracle does not suspend the pattern to which events conform, but merely introduces a *new* event into that pattern.

4. Evil.

According to Lewis, evil is not eternal, as dualism claims.

The metaphysical difficulty is this. The two Powers, the good and the evil, do not explain each other. Neither Ormuzd nor Ahriman can claim to be the Ultimate. More ultimate than either of them is the inexplicable fact of their being there together. Neither of them chose this *tête-à-tête*. Each of them, therefore, is *conditioned*—finds himself willy-nilly in a situation; and either that situation itself, or some unknown force which produced that situation, is the real Ultimate. Dualism has not yet reached the ground of being. You cannot accept two conditioned and mutually independent beings as the self-grounded, self-comprehending Absolute.[38]

Evil arises from the creature's free choice. This does not mean that it is evil to be free. In fact, "Freedom [is] the gift whereby ye most resemble your Maker and are yourselves parts of eternal reality,"[39] wrote Lewis. Christianity agrees with dualism "that this universe is at war. But it does not think this is a war between independent powers. It thinks it is a civil war, a rebellion, and that we are living in a part of the universe occupied by the rebel."[40] This rebellion was not at first a turning to wickedness, for "wickedness, when you examine it, turns out to be the pursuit of some good in the wrong way."[41]

Like Augustine and Aquinas before him, C.S. Lewis believed that evil does not exist in itself but only as a corruption of good. "Goodness is, so to speak, itself: badness is only spoiled goodness. And there must be something good first before it can be spoiled."[42] Even the devil is a fallen angel. So "evil is a parasite, not an original thing."[43]

God does not permit evil without a good purpose. Even physical evil has a moral impact. For "God whispers to us in our pleasures, speaks in our conscience, but shouts in our pain: it is His megaphone to rouse a deaf world."[44]

5. Man.

Man is more than matter. He is a free rational and moral being. He has an immortal soul, but he is in a body that exists in a material world with other bodies. Lewis wrote:

> Again, the freedom of a creature must mean freedom to choose: and choice implies the existence of things to choose between. A creature with no environment would have no choices to make: so that freedom, like self-consciousness (if they are not, indeed, the same thing) again demands the presence to the self of something other than the self.[45]

Man's environment is called nature. But man is more than nature. He is a rational being, and *"no thought is valid if it can be fully explained as the result of irrational causes."* Hence, "every theory of the universe which makes the human mind a result of irrational causes is inadmissible, for it would be a proof that there are no such things as proofs, which is nonsense."[46]

Not only is man a rational being, but he is also a moral being. In fact, without a moral nature man would not be man. Those who would abolish the moral law (*Tao*) would abolish man. "They are not men at all. Stepping outside the *Tao*, they have stepped into the void. Nor are their subjects necessarily unhappy men. They are not men at all: they are artifacts."[47] To destroy the absolute moral law by which man ought to live is to destroy man, for

> either we are rational spirit obliged forever to obey the absolute values of the *Tao*, or else we are mere nature to be kneaded and cut into new shapes for the pleasure of masters who must, by hypothesis, have no motive but their own "natural" impulses. Only the *Tao* provides a common human law of action which can overarch rulers and ruled

alike. A dogmatic belief in objective value is necessary to the very idea of a rule which is not tyranny or an obedience which is not slavery.[48]

6. Ethics.

Man as a moral creature is obligated to live by an absolute moral law. There is a natural moral law which transcends human law. Such was what the framers of the Declaration of Independence had in mind when they wrote of the "Laws of Nature and of Nature's God" and of "certain unalienable rights" with which all men are "endowed by their Creator." Man is a moral creature, created in God's image, and we have certain absolute moral obligations toward all men.

This objective moral law is prescriptive, not descriptive (that is, it lays down the principles by which we ought to live; it does not merely express the way we *do* live). It is not social convention, for it sometimes condemns society. Neither is it herd instinct, for we sometimes act out of a sense of duty that goes against our instinct for self-preservation.[49] We can progress in our understanding of this law, but the moral law itself does not change. There is progress *in* it but no progress *of* it.[50]

7. History and goal.

Life is the proving ground for eternity. During his life, each rational creature makes a lifetime decision. All play the game of life. And "if a game is played, it must be possible to lose it." Of course, adds Lewis,

I would pay any price to be able to say truthfully "All will be saved." But my reason retorts, "Without their will, or with it?" If I say, "Without their will," I at once perceive a contradiction; how can the supreme voluntary act of self-surrender be involuntary? If I say, "With their will," my reason replies "How if they *will not* give in?"[51]

For Lewis, there is an end to life and to history. And, "There are only two kinds of people in the end: those who say to God, 'Thy will be done,' and those to whom God says, in the end, '*Thy* will be done.' All that are in hell, choose it." Lewis believed "without that self-choice there could be no hell. No soul that seriously and constantly desires joy will ever miss it. Those who seek find. To those who knock it is opened."[52]

Thus, Lewis believed, so there is a heaven to gain and a hell to shun. But the doors of hell are locked on the *inside*. I do not mean that the ghosts may not *wish* to come out of hell, in the vague fashion wherein an envious man "wishes" to be happy; but they certainly do not will even the first preliminary stages of that self-abandonment through which alone the soul can reach any good.[53]

IV.   Some basic beliefs of theism.

Most theists hold to a common core of beliefs that comprise their world view. To the degree that they are consistent, all their thoughts and actions are shaped by these common beliefs.

A.   God exists beyond and in the world.

Theism holds to both the transcendence and the immanence of God. God exists beyond and independently of the world, yet He is present in all parts of the world as its sustaining cause. The world was originated by God and it is *conserved* in existence by Him.

B.   The world was created *ex nihilo*.

The world is not eternal. It came into existence by God's fiat (decree). Its existence is totally contingent and dependent upon God. The universe was not created from pre-existing material *(ex-materia)*, as dualism or materialism claims. Nor was it made out of God's essence *(ex Deo)*, as pantheism claims. It was brought into existence by God out of nothing that pre-existed.

C.   Miracles are possible and have occurred.

Although God operates His universe in a regular and orderly way (called the laws of nature), He also transcends the universe. There is a supernatural realm that can invade the natural realm. The sovereign Creator cannot be locked outside His creation. Although God usually works in a regular, "natural" way, on occasion He works in a special, supernatural way. This occasional invasion of nature by the supernatural is called a miracle.

Most theists not only believe that miracles *can* happen but also believe that some actually *have* happened. Jewish theists point to the miracle of the Exodus, Muslims point to God's revelations to Mohammed, and Christian theists point to the resurrection of Christ as chief examples of miracles.

D.   Man is made in God's image.

Theism believes in the creation of man in God's likeness. This means that man has both freedom and dignity that ought to be treated with utmost respect. Man is God's representative on earth; therefore, his life is sacred. Man should be treated as an end, not as a means; he should be loved as a person, not used as a thing.

As a creature of God, man is not sovereign over his own life. He does not have the right to take his life or to murder another person. Only God gives life, and only God has the right to take it.

Since man was created, he has a beginning in time. He is not eternal, even though he is immortal. There is no pre-existence of the soul, as is believed by polytheists and pantheists. Nor is there annihilation of the soul, as the atheists believe.

E. There is a moral law.

Since the theistic God is a moral being and since man is created in God's image, a moral corollary of theism is man's duty to obey God's absolute moral law. This law is absolutely binding since it comes from God, and it is over and above any human laws. It is not merely descriptive (as the laws of nature are); it is prescriptive. It is not an *is*; it is an *ought*.

F. Man is immortal.

Man is immortal, not by his essence, but because God will sustain him as His creature forever. Man's moral actions will ultimately be rewarded or punished. He will not be reincarnated nor given a "second chance at life." Time is the testing ground for eternity.

G. Man will be rewarded or punished.

Each individual life, like all of history, progresses toward an end or goal. As mentioned above, each man will be rewarded or punished in the "afterlife" according to his works in this life. Some modern theists have minimized (or negated) the punishment aspect of human destiny in the hope that all might be saved, but traditional theists see this as wishful thinking. All theists, however, acknowledge a day of reckoning that will bring about justice for all.

V. An evaluation of theism.

A. Some commendations of theism.

There are obviously many appealing features to theism. Some of the more noteworthy ones are included in the following:

1. An exalted view of God.

To many, there is something intuitively appealing about an ultimate being who is absolutely perfect. Many even claim that a God less than morally perfect is not worthy of worship. The God of theism is the apex of moral perfection. No more perfect being can be conceived. As such, the theistic God seems eminently worthy of worship. Add to this the belief that He is personal, and one can understand the great dedication that many martyrs and devotees have expressed for a theistic God.

2. An absolute basis for morality.

In the flux of life theism offers a firm anchor. While cultures and mores change, theists cling to an unchanging God. His absolute moral standard stands above all human societies and even above the human race. As such, it offers a means for measuring all men and all societies which is not subject to change by them. This absolute value standard beyond the world makes ultimate sense out of behavior and moral judgments in the world, a factor that relative value judgments lack. It is difficult to pass objective and ultimate judgment on a system from within the system.

3. The dignity of man.

Most world views hold mankind in high regard. Indeed, many (even atheistic ones) believe that humans should be treated with value and respect. Theism provides a firm basis in this respect for man. By claiming that man is made in God's image and likeness, theism closely associates the dignity of man with that of God. Hence, showing respect for man is, in essence, showing respect for God, who created him.

Theism's belief in the sacredness of human life provides a basis for the preservation of human life and the moral guarantee of individual rights. According to theists, the basis of respect for human beings is anchored in the unchangeable and perfect nature of God. It is difficult to conceive of a more solid basis for respecting other persons.

4. Life has ultimate meaning.

While some adherents of other world views conclude that life is not worth living, theism offers an ultimate purpose for living. It claims that our actions will count not only for time but also for all eternity. In short, theism provides an explanation of where we came from, why we are here and where we are going in a way that many find very satisfying. By offering immortality and eternal rewards, a theistic world view has given hope to untold numbers of world sufferers that a better day is coming. The consolatory power of theism is incredible.

B. Some criticisms of theism.

There are many non-theists who literally believe that theism is too good to be true. Sigmund Freud wrote,

> We say to ourselves: it would indeed be very nice if there were a God, who was both creator of the world and a benevolent providence, if there were a moral world order and a future life, but at the same time it is very odd that this is all just as we should wish it ourselves.[54]

The real question, of course, is not how satisfying a view is, but whether or not it is true.

1. The universe does not need a cause.

Theists contend that there must be a God, since everything needs a cause. Opponents frequently counter this claim with the question: Who made God? It would seem that if everything needs a cause, then so does God. Likewise, if everything does not need a cause, then neither does the world. In either case there would be no need for God.

2. There could be an infinite series of causes.

Many atheists insist that there is no need for a "first cause." Why stop the process? If everything needs a cause, then there could be a cause of a cause of a cause, *ad infinitum*. They claim that it is only the poverty of the theist's imagination that leads him to halt the process and insist on a beginning or first cause. Infinite series are possible, as are infinite numbers in mathematics.

3. A first cause need not be infinite.

Even if there were a "first cause," it need not be infinite. All that is necessary to explain a finite world is another finite cause. So at best, the theistic cosmological argument would only indicate a finite God, not confirm an infinite theistic God.

4. The universe need not be designed.

Theists point to the apparent design in nature as evidence of a Designer. But opponents say that the adaptation of means to an end in nature can be explained by natural processes. Evolution can explain the origin of species; no Creator is needed. Life could have begun by spontaneous generation in a primeval pond. The universe may be a "happy accident." After all, one does not have to throw three dice 216 times to get three 6's. The right combination may come on the first throw. It is possible, therefore, to account for apparent design by chance, time and natural law.

5. Theism is other-worldly in outlook.

Theists believe this world is only temporal. The spiritual world is more real and abiding. According to many critics, this belief leads to an other-worldly attitude and neglect of responsibilities in this life. They point out that some theists are so heavenly minded that they are no earthly good.

6. Theism absolutizes inhumanities.

It has often been pointed out that an absolute ethic, such as theists espouse, leads to great abuse. All sorts of inhumane acts have been sanctioned in the name of divine absolutes. The pretension of getting one's ethic from an absolute God can be used to give divine sanction to subjective, human prejudices. A non-theistic situational or relative ethic does not have this problem.

There are other criticisms of theism and responses to them.[55] Many of these are discussed in the next chapter on the atheistic world view.

NOTES

1. For a summary of the views on each of the theists listed here, see the respective articles on them in *The Encyclopedia of Philosophy*, Paul Edwards, chief ed.
2. St. Augustine, *City of God* 12.2 cited in *What Augustine Says*, Norman L. Geisler, ed. (Grand Rapids, Michigan: Baker Book House, 1982); hereafter referred to as *Augustine* . . . .
3. Augustine. *Confessions* 12.7 (Augustine . . . No. 182).
4. Ibid. 11.13 (Augustine . . . No. 184).
5. Ibid. 11.4 (No. 28).
6. Augustine, *On the Trinity* III, 6, ed. by Philip Schaff in *Nicene and Post-Nicene Fathers* (Grand Rapids: Wm. B. Eerdmans Publishing Co., 1956), Vol. III, p. 60.
7. Ibid. III, 5, p. 59.
8. Augustine, *On Christian Doctrine* 1.24 (Augustine . . . No. 329).
9. Augustine, *Of True Religion* 14 (Augustine . . . No. 484).
10. Augustine, *On Free Will* 2.53 (Augustine . . . No. 496).
11. Augustine, *Against the Epistle of Manichaeus* 38 (Augustine . . . No. 607).
12. Augustine, *On Christian Doctrine* 1.22 (Augustine . . . No. 645).
13. Augustine, *On the Morals of the Catholic Church* 15 (Augustine . . . No. 653).
14. Augustine, *City of God* 14.1 (Augustine . . . No. 638).
15. Thomas Aquinas, *Summa Theologica* I, 104, 3 in *The Basic Writings of St. Thomas Aquinas*, trns. by Anton C. Pegis (New York: Random House, 1944).
16. Aquinas, *Summa Contra Gentiles* 28.1, trans. by Anton C. Pegis in *On the Truth of the Catholic Faith: Book One: God* (New York: Image Books, 1955), p. 135.
17. Aquinas, *Disputations*, V, *de Potentia*, 4, ad 10 as cited in *St. Thomas Aquinas: Philosophical Texts*, Thomas Gilby, ed. (New York: Oxford University Press, 1964), 408, p. 137.
18. Aquinas, *Disputations*, VI, *de Potentia*, I, ad 12 in Gilby, ibid., 363, p. 124.
19. Aquinas, Commentary IV, *Sentences*, XVII, 1, 5, 3 in Gilby, ibid., 366, p. 125.
20. Aquinas, *Summa Contra Gentiles* II, 56, 57 in Gilby, ibid., 533, pp. 197, 198.
21. Aquinas, *Compendium of Theology*, 117 in Gilby, ibid., 468, p. 168.
22. Aquinas, *Summa Contra Gentiles* III, 12 in Gilby, ibid., 491, p. 177.
23. Aquinas, *Summa Theologica* I-II, 85, 2 in Gilby, ibid., 494, p. 179.
24. Ibid. I, 48, 2 and 3 in *The Basic Writings of St. Thomas Aquinas*, p. 467. Aquinas is here quoting Augustine with approval.
25. See ibid. I-II, 91, 1-6, pp. 748-751.
26. See ibid. I, 60-62, pp. 457-480.
27. See Aquinas, *Summa Theologiae* 1a2ae, 2, 8, trans. by Thomas Gilby (New York: McGraw Hill Book Co., 1968), Vol. 16, p. 85.
28. C. S. Lewis, *Mere Christianity* (New York: Macmillan, 1943), chapters 1-5.
29. Ibid., p. 34.
30. Ibid., pp. 45, 46.
31. Ibid., p. 146.

32. C. S. Lewis, *Christian Reflections* (Grand Rapids: Wm. B. Eerdmans Publishing Co., 1967), pp. 167, 168.
33. C. S. Lewis, *Mere Christianity*, p. 138.
34. C. S. Lewis, *Miracles* (New York: Macmillan, 1947), p. 157.
35. Ibid., p. 30.
36. C. S. Lewis, *The Problem of Pain* (New York: Macmillan, 1940), p. 23.
37. C. S. Lewis, *Miracles*, p. 59.
38. C. S. Lewis, *God in the Dock* (Grand Rapids: Wm. B. Eerdmans Publishing Co., 1970), p. 22.
39. Ibid., p. 129.
40. C. S. Lewis, *Mere Christianity*, p. 51.
41. Ibid., p. 49.
42. Ibid., p. 49.
43. Ibid., p. 50.
44. C. S. Lewis, *The Problem of Pain*, p. 81.
45. Ibid., p. 17.
46. C. S. Lewis, *Miracles*, p. 21.
47. C. S. Lewis, *The Abolition of Man* (New York: Macmillan Publishing Co., 1947), p. 77.
48. Ibid., pp. 84, 85.
49. C. S. Lewis, *Mere Christianity*, p. 22.
50. C. S. Lewis, *The Abolition of Man*, pp. 58, 59.
51. C. S. Lewis, *The Problem of Pain*, pp. 106, 107.
52. C. S. Lewis, *God in the Dock*, p. 69.
53. C. S. Lewis, *The Problem of Pain*, p. 127.
54. Sigmund Freud, *The Future of an Illusion* (New York: Doubleday & Company, Inc., 1957), pp. 57, 58.
55. See the end of Chapter 3 for a theistic response to these arguments against theism.

3

Atheism: A World Without God

I. Introduction

"Where is God gone?" he called out. "I mean to tell you! *We have kill-ed him*—you and I! We are all his murderers!...Do we not hear the noise of the grave-diggers who are burying God?...God is dead! God remains dead!"[1]

Not all atheists are as militant as Friedrich Nietzsche, but many are just as emphatic about the non-existence of God. Karl Marx wrote, "Nowadays, in our evolutionary conception of the universe, there is absolutely no room for either a creator or a ruler."[2]

While polytheism dominated much of ancient Greek thought, and theism dominated the medieval Christian view, atheism has had its day in the modern world. Of course, not all who lack faith in a divine being wish to be called atheists. Some prefer the positive ascription of "humanist."[3] Others are perhaps best described as materialists, but all are nontheists and most are antitheistic.

In contrast to a theist, who believes that God exists beyond and in the world, and a pantheist, who believes that God is the world, an atheist believes there is no God either beyond or in the world. There is only a world, or a universe, and nothing more.

Since atheists share much in common with agnostics and skeptics, they are often confused with them.[4] Technically, a skeptic says, "I *doubt* that God exists" and an agnostic declares, "I *don't know* (or can't know) if God exists." But an atheist claims to *know* (or at least believe) that God does not exist. However, since atheists are all nontheists and since most atheists share with skeptics an antitheistic stand, many of their arguments are the same. It is in this sense that much of modern atheism rests heavily upon the skepticism of David Hume and the agnosticism of Immanuel Kant.

II.   A typology of atheism.

Used broadly, the term *atheism* includes many variations. *Traditional* atheism holds that there never was, is, and never will be a God. There are many advocates of this view, including Ludwig Feuerbach, Karl Marx, Jean-Paul Sartre and Antony Flew.

Mythological atheists, such as Friedrich Nietzsche, believe that the God-myth was once a live model by which men lived, but has since died—killed by the advancement of modern man's understanding and culture.

A short-lived form of *dialectical* atheism which was held by Thomas Altizer, and others, proposed that the once alive, transcendent God actually died in the incarnation and crucifixion of Christ. The impact of this was realized in modern times.[5]

Finally, there are *semantical* atheists who claim that God-talk is dead. This view was held by Paul Van Buren[6] and others influenced by the logical positivists[7] who had seriously challenged the meaningfulness of language about God. Those who hold this particular view may not be actual atheists at all, for they can admit to the existence of God and yet believe that it is impossible to talk about Him in meaningful terms. But as Feuerbach once said, those who say that God is alive but claim that we cannot know anything about Him have lost all taste for religion.

There are still other ways to designate the various kinds of atheists. One such way is by the particular philosophy that shapes the expression of their atheism. One could therefore speak of *existential* atheists (Jean-Paul Sartre), *marxistic* atheists (Karl Marx), *psychological* atheists (Sigmund Freud), *capitalistic* atheists (Ayn Rand),[8] *behavioristic* atheists (B. F. Skinner),[9] and so on.

In this chapter we shall discuss atheism in a metaphysical sense. Thus we are speaking about *philosophical* atheists who give reasons for their belief that no God exists in or beyond the world, as opposed to *practical* atheists who simply live as though there were no God.

III.   Some representatives of atheism.

A.   Friedrich Nietzsche.

One of the most colorful advocates of atheism was Friedrich Nietzsche. His rejection of God was instinctive and incisive. With the denial of God, Nietzsche denied all value (hence, nihilism) based on God. Although he was reared in a Lutheran pastor's home, Nietzsche rebelled violently against his religious training. His mother and sisters reared him from a young age after the death of his father.

1.   God.

Nietzsche believed that God never existed, based on several grounds.[10] He believed that it is impossible to have a self-caused being. He also believed that the presence of evil in the world ruled out a benevolent Creator. And he felt that the basis for belief in God was purely psychological. Nietzsche exhorted, "I beseech you, my brothers, remain faithful to the earth, and do not believe those who speak to you of other worldly hopes!" He added, "Once the sin against God was the greatest sin; but God died, and these sinners died with Him. To sin against the earth is now the most dreadful thing...."[11]

Despite Nietzsche's atheism, he did believe that the God-myth was once very much alive. It was the model on which medieval and reformation Europe had based its manner of life. That culture, however, Nietzsche saw in decay. Modernity had caught up to modern man, and he could no longer believe in God. "God is dead!" Nietzsche cried. Thus, modern man must bury God and move on. What he meant was not that an actual being which had once been alive was now dead, but that man no longer needed the psychological "crutch" of belief in God.

2. Ethics.

The shocking realization of God's "death" for Nietzsche brought him to the conclusion that all God-based values and absolutes also had died. Hence, Nietzsche rejected traditional Judeo-Christian values in an almost violent manner. Even general principles such as "injure no man" were questioned by Nietzsche.[12] And the Christian principle of love he ridiculed with these words: "Why, you idiots....'How about praising the one who sacrifices himself?' "[13] Indeed, Christianity "is the greatest of all conceivable corruptions....I call it the one immoral blemish of mankind."[14]

Just what did Nietzsche offer in place of traditional Christian values? He proposed that modern man go "beyond good and evil."[15] He suggested a transvaluation of all values which would reject the "soft" feminine virtues of love and humility for the "hard" man-like virtues of harshness and suspicion.

3. Man.

According to Nietzsche, man is mortal. There is no afterlife. The best that one can do to overcome the limits of his own mortality is to will the eternal recurrence of the same state of affairs.[16] That is, he must will to come back and live the same life over and over and over forever.

Since there is no God and thus no objective values to discover, men must create their own values. Men must not be overcome by the meaninglessness and emptiness of life. Rather, they must become overcomers (supermen).

4. The world.

Since God does not exist, the world is all there is. Matter is in motion, and life moves in cycles. The world is real, and God is an illusion. There is no God to which we must be faithful. Nietzsche viewed "God as the declaration of war against life, against nature...—the deification of nothingness, the will of nothingness pronounced holy."[17] Hence, man is exhorted to "remain faithful to the earth."

5. History and destiny.

Man's history, like his destiny, is cyclical. Neitzsche rejected any Christian goal-oriented end in favor of a more oriental view of cyclical recurrence. History is not going anywhere. There are no ultimate goals to achieve on earth, no paradise to regain. There is simply an individual life to live by courage and creativity. Man creates his own destiny here, and there is no hereafter—except the eternal recurrence of the same state of affairs. The supermen are the geniuses who form destiny. "They say, 'It shall be thus!' They determine the 'whether' and the 'to what end' of mankind....Their knowledge is creating."[18]

B. Ludwig Feuerbach.

Even before Nietzsche, a young Hegelian philosopher named Ludwig Feuerbach was destined to make a permanent atheistic mark upon the world by his unique denial of God. Working from within a Hegalian framework, he was able to stand Hegel's pantheistic system on its head and conclude atheism. Later Karl Marx incorporated Feuerbach's atheism into his own economic theory, where it remains as a part of official marxist ideology.

1. God.

For Feuerbach, God is nothing more than a projection of human imagination. Man is uniquely a self-conscious being. When he reflects upon himself he calls it "God." God is nothing more than the highest and best that man sees in himself. The attributes given to God are really the result of man's self-discovery of what is best in himself.

> ...the object of any subject is nothing else than the subject's own nature taken objectively. Such as are a man's thoughts and dispositions, such is his God; so much worth as a man has, so much and no more has his God. Consciousness of God is self-consciousness, knowledge of God is self-knowledge. By his God thou knowest the man, and by the man his God; the two are identical.[19]

2. Man.

Man is an animal who has reached self-consciousness. This is a qualititative change. Lower animals have consciousness but not self-consciousness, that is, they are aware of their environment, but are unable to ponder their own nature. It is the self-consciousness that enables man to reflect on himself and, by so doing, to come to know his own nature as "God." Without this ability to reflect on and project his own nature outside himself and call it "God" there would be no religion. So man is the religious animal.[20]

3. Ethics.

The main thrust of Feuerbach's ethics was to redirect man's energies from the other world to this one, from heaven to earth. His principle aim was to turn "The friends of God into friends of man, believers into thinkers, worshippers into workers, candidates for the other world into students of this world, Christians, who on their own confession are half-animal and half-angel, into men—whole men."[21]

4. History and goal.

Feuerbach was critical of both the Hegelian and Christian ideas that history is progressing or heading toward some goal. History is not, as Hegel held, the footprints of God in the sands of time. History reveals only man's progressive self-understanding. Religion is the necessary evil by which man comes to this increased understanding of himself in what he first believes to be God. In actuality, however, this self-understanding is only a projection of the best that is in man.[22]

C. Jean-Paul Sartre.

Another popular form of atheism in the 20th century is existential atheism. The writings of Jean-Paul Sartre and Albert Camus have been a significant source of this movement.

1. God.

Like other atheists Sartre believed God's existence was impossible because God must be, by His very nature, a self-caused being. But one would have to exist prior to himself in order to cause himself, which is impossible. In Sartre's terms, the "being-for-itself" can never become the "being-in-itself."[23] That is, the contingent (dependent) being cannot become the necessary (independent) being. Nothing cannot become something. For any being to cause its own existence would necessitate that it exist prior to its existing, which is impossible. Therefore, since a self-caused being cannot exist, God cannot exist.

2. Man

For Sartre, man is a useless passion, an empty bubble on the sea of nothingness. Man's basic project is to become God. But it is impossible for the contingent man to become a necessary being, for the subjective to become objective, or for freedom to become determined. Man is utterly free in his subjective being—in his consciousness and awareness. He is, in fact, condemned to freedom. If one were to attempt to escape his destiny he would still be freely fleeing it. Even suicide is an act of freedom by which one vainly attempts to avoid his freedom. So the "essence" of man is absolute freedom, but absolute freedom has no objective or definable nature. Man is more than an objective essence; he is also a subjective existence.

3. Ethics.

There are no absolute or objective moral presciptions. For "no sooner had you [Zeus] created me than I ceased to be yours," wrote Sartre. "I was like a man who's lost his shadow. And there was nothing left in heaven, no right or wrong, nor anyone to give my orders....For I, Zeus, am a man, and every man must find out his own way."[24]

Not only are there no divine imperatives or moral prescriptions imposed upon man, but there are no objective values. In the last lines of his famous *Being and Nothingness* Sartre wrote, "...it amounts to the same thing whether one gets drunk alone or is a leader of nations."[25] According to Sartre, all human activities are equivalent. We must, in fact, repudiate this "spirit of seriousness" which assumes there are absolute or objective values and accept the basic absurdity and subjectivity of life.

What then should man do? Literally, he should do his own thing. Since there are no ultimate and objective values, man must create his own values. He should act for himself and, if he will, for all mankind. But there is no ethical obligation to do the latter. In the final analysis, each person is responsible for the use of his own unavoidable freedom. What is "good" is whatever he chooses.

4. The world and destiny.

The world for Sartre is real but contingent. It is simply there. It, like man's life, is a given. Philosophically, it is uncaused. It is the field in which man performs his subjective choices. It has no objective meaning, and is therefore absurd. Each man must revolt against this absurdity and create his own subjective meaning. And the fact that several people affirm common subjective projects (Sartre himself had certain marxist leanings) does not constitute objective meaning. Each person is the result of his own choices. For example, Sartre said, "I am my books." Yet each man transcends the world (project) he creates. The author is more than his words. He is more than the "being" he creates. He is the "nothing" (freedom) out of which it was created.

IV. Some basic beliefs of atheism.

A. The arguments for atheism.

The arguments for atheism are largely negative in nature, that is, they are really arguments against theism. The arguments fall roughly into two categories: the arguments against *proofs* for God's existence and the arguments against God's existence. In the former category, most atheists draw heavily on the skepticism of David Hume and the agnosticism of Immanuel Kant.

1. The rejection of theistic arguments.

The traditional theistic arguments fall into four main caregories: cosmological, teleological, ontological and moral. In brief, the cosmological argument says:

(1) Every effect has a cause.

(2) The universe is an effect.

(3) Therefore, the universe has a cause.

One of the most famous proponents of this argument was Thomas Aquinas (1224-1274).[26]

The teleological argument declares in brief:

(1) Every design has a designer.

(2) The universe manifests design.

(3) Therefore, the universe has a designer.

This argument was forcefully presented by William Paley (1743-1805).[27]

The ontological argument can be stated in two ways: First,

(1) God is by definition an absolutely perfect being.

(2) An absolutely perfect being cannot lack anything.

(3) But a being that exists has something that a being that does not exist lacks—existence.

(4) Therefore, an absolutely perfect being must exist.[28]

Second,

(1) God is by definition a necessary being.

(2) But a necessary being cannot *not* exist (otherwise, it would not be a necessary being).

(3) Therefore, a necessary being necessarily exists.

St. Anselm (1033-1109) is credited with developing both forms of this argument.

The moral argument for God's existence has been presented by many since Kant's time. A popular version of it, espoused by C. S. Lewis, is as follows:[29]

(1) There are objective moral laws.

(2) Moral laws come from a Moral Law Giver.

(3) Therefore, a Moral Law Giver exists.

Most of the atheist's objections to these arguments are traceable to the writings of David Hume (1711-1776)[30] and Immanuel Kant (1724-1804).[31] The following is a summary of their objections.

(1) Even if the universe has a cause, it need not be infinite. A finite cause is adequate to explain a finite effect (the universe).

(2) If there is a cause of the universe, then it cannot be perfect, since the world is imperfect. If a cause resembles its effects, then the world must have been caused by an imperfect, finite, male and female group of gods. In our own experience we know that causes of imperfect things are themselves finite and imperfect.

(3) There is no need to assume the existence of an intelligent cause (designer) of the world; chance can explain the apparent design that the world displays. Given enough time, any "lucky" combination will result. The universe may be a "happy accident."

(4) There is no way to prove the principle of causality. We never experience casual connections. We see only one event in nature *followed* by another, but never see it *caused* by another. For example, just because the sun always rises *after* the rooster crows does not mean it rises *because* the rooster crows.

(5) It is possible to have an infinite series of causes. If *every* thing is caused, then we can go backward forever asking "what caused

that?" Hence, there is no need to stop at a first, uncaused cause that necessarily exists.

(6) It is always possible to conceive of anything, including God, as not existing. Hence, nothing exists necessarily. Therefore, even God must not exist necessarily; hence He cannot be a necessary being; hence, God must not exist at all.

(7) The concept of a necessary (or uncaused) being makes no sense. It is not self-explanatory nor can it be explained in terms of some other condition. Hence, as an unconditioned concept, it has no conditions for understanding it.

(8) There cannot be a necessary being because no statements about existence can be logically necessary. The opposite of any state of affairs is logically possible. Therefore, no state of affairs is logically necessary.

(9) The universe as a whole does not need a cause, only the parts do. The parts depend on the whole universe, but the whole does not depend on anything else.

(10) All theistic arguments are based on the ontological argument. But this argument is invalid because it assumes (wrongly) that existence is a predicate or perfection which adds something to the concept of the subject.

(11) What is logically necessary does not necessarily exist. It is logically necessary for a triangle to have three sides, but it is not necessary for any three-sided thing to exist.

(12) We cannot validly infer a real cause from effects that we experience. There is an insurpassable gulf between the thing-to-me (appearances) and the thing-in-itself (reality). We cannot know the latter; we know things only as they appear to us but not as they really are.

(13) Assuming that the principle of causality applies to reality leads to contradictions. For example: 1) there must be a first cause to initiate the causality in a series; yet 2) there cannot be a first cause since it too needs a cause; and so on infinitely.

2. The rejection of theism.

Not only have atheists agreed with skeptics and agnostics that the arguments for theism fail to prove that God does exist, but some atheists have also offered arguments to show that God does *not* exist.

a. An ontological disproof of God.[32]

One atheist argued as follows:

(1) God is by definition a necessary (uncaused) being.

(2) But necessity cannot apply to being.

(3) Therefore, God cannot exist.

In support of the crucial second premise, he noted that necessity is a logical term, not an ontological one. That is, necessity applies to propositions, not to being or reality.

b. A cosmological disproof of God.[33]

This argument against God can be stated in this manner:

(1) God is a self-caused being.

(2) But it is impossible to cause one's own being (for a cause is prior to its effect, and one cannot exist prior to one's existence).

(3) Therefore, God cannot exist.

c. A teleological disproof of God.[34]

A teleological argument against God's existence can be stated as follows:

(1) The universe either was designed or happened by chance.

(2) Chance is an adequate cause of the universe.

(3) Therefore, the universe need not have been designed.

d. A moral disproof of God's existence.

The moral argument against God is by far the most popular. One of the most popular versions of this argument is expressed in this way:[35]

(1) If God were all-good, He would destroy evil.

(2) If God were all-powerful, He could destroy evil.

(3) But evil has not been destroyed.

(4) Therefore, God does not exist.

There are, of course, other arguments against God's existence. But these will suffice to illustrate the kind of reasoning atheists use to justify their cause.

B. The beliefs of atheism.

1. God does not exist.

God does not exist; only the world exists. God is an invention of man. God did not create man; man created God. There are good and sufficient reasons for believing that God does not exist. The fact of evil in this world (discussed below) is one such reason.

2. The world is eternal.

The universe is eternal. If it is not eternal, then it came into existence "out of nothing and by nothing." At any rate, the universe was not created. It is self-sustaining and self-perpetuating. As one nontheist put it, "The COSMOS is all there is, all there was, and all there ever will be."[36] If asked "what caused the world?" most atheists would reply, as did Bertrand Russell, that it was not caused; it is just there. Only the parts of the universe need a cause. The parts all depend on the whole, but the whole needs no cause. If we ask for a cause for the universe, then we must ask for a cause for God. And if we do not need a cause for God, then neither do we need one for the universe.

If one insists that *everything* needs a cause, then the atheist simply insists that one moves backward through an infinite series of causes wherein he never arrives at a first cause (i.e., God). For if *everything* must have a cause, then this "first cause" must have a cause. Thus, it really is not first at all, nor is anything else.[37]

3. Evil exists.

Unlike pantheists, who deny the reality of evil, atheists strongly affirm it. In fact, while pantheists affirm the reality of God and deny the reality of evil, atheists, on the other hand, affirm the reality of evil and deny the reality of God. They believe that theists are inconsistent in trying to hold to the reality of both God and evil.

4. Man is material.

Man is matter in motion. He has no immortal soul. There is no mind apart from man's brain. Nor is there a soul independent of man's body. While not all atheists are strict materialists who identify soul and body, most do believe that if man has a soul, then it is dependent on the body. The soul, in fact, dies when the body dies. The soul (and mind) may be more than the body, the way a shadow is more than the tree. But as the shadow of a tree ceases to exist when the tree does, so too the soul does not survive the body's death.[38]

5. Ethics are relative.

It is generally agreed among atheists that there are no moral absolutes. Certainly there are no divinely authorized absolutes. There may be some widely accepted and long-enduring values. But absolutely binding laws would seem to imply an absolute Law Giver (i.e., God). Hence, such laws are rejected by atheists.

Since values are not *discovered* by man (from some revelation of God), they must be *created* by man. Many atheists believe that values emerge by trial and error. Often the right action is described in terms of what will bring the greatest good in the long run.[39] Some frankly acknowledge that relative and changing situations determine what is right or wrong. Others speak about expedient behavior (what "works"), and some work out their whole ethic in terms of self-interest. But virtually all atheists recognize that man must determine his own values, since there is no God to reveal what is right and wrong. As the *Humanist Manifesto* put it, "Humanism asserts that the nature of the universe depicted by modern science makes unacceptable any supernatural or cosmic guarantee of human values."[40]

6. Man's destiny is death.

Most atheists see no eternal destiny for individual persons, though some speak of a kind of collective immortality of the race. But the denial of individual immortality notwithstanding, many atheists are utopians who believe in an earthly paradise to come. In *Walden II*, B. F. Skinner proposed a behaviorally controlled utopia.[41] Karl Marx believed an economic dialectic of history would inevitably produce a communist paradise. Others, like Ayn Rand, believe that pure capitalism could produce a more perfect society. And still others believe that human reason and science can produce a social utopia. Virtually all recognize the ultimate mortality of the human race but console themselves in the belief that its destruction is millions of years away.

V. An evaluation of atheism.

A. Some contributions of atheism.

There are many insights into the nature of reality that atheists have provided. Several are worthy of note here.

1. The presence of evil.

Unlike pantheists, atheists do not close their eyes to the reality of evil. In fact, most atheists have a keen sensitivity to evil and injustice. They rightly point to the imperfection of this present world and to the need for injustice to be judged and corrected. In this regard they are right that an all-loving, all-powerful God (if He existed) would certainly do something about this situation.

2. Contradictions in some concepts of God.

In contending that God is not caused by another, some theists have spoken of God as though He were a self-caused being *(causa sui)*. This is certainly a contradiction, as atheists have pointed out. No being can cause its own existence, since to do this, the being would have to exist and not exist at the same time. To cause existence is to move from non-existence to existence. But non-existence cannot cause existence. Nothing cannot cause something. Hence, to cause his own existence one would have had to exist prior to his having existed, which is impossible. On this point atheists are right.

3. Positive human values.

Many atheists are humanists. Along with others they affirm the value of man and human culture. They earnestly pursue both the arts and the sciences, as well as express deep concern in ethical issues. Most atheists believe that racism, hatred and bigotry are wrong. Few atheists agree with Hitler, nor do they promote child abuse and rape. Most atheists commend freedom and tolerance. Atheists are not without many other positive human values and moral traits.[42]

4. The loyal opposition.

Atheists serve another role: they are the loyal opposition to theists and others who believe in some kind of God. It is difficult for anyone to see the fallacies in his own thinking. Monologues seldom produce a refined product of thought. Atheists serve as a significant corrective to invalid reasoning by believers. Their arguments against theism should cause dogmatic theists to pause and ponder their beliefs and should help temper the zeal with which many believers glibly dismiss unbelief. Without atheists, those who believe in God would lack a significant opposition with which to have a dialogue and clarify their own concepts of God.

B. Some criticisms of atheism.

Despite the varied contributions of atheism, many believe that the position that God does not exist lacks adequate rational support. First of all, they point out that it is not sufficient to merely attack the arguments for theism. Even if one could disprove the validity of theistic arguments, this would not prove atheism, since there are other views. Furthermore, theists have given answers to the atheists' objections to theism.

1. Critiquing objections to atheists' arguments against theistic proofs.

If the objections against theistic arguments are invalidated, then much of the evidence for atheism fails. Therefore, we will first analyze the alleged invalidity of the atheists' objections to theistic arguments, considering them in the same order presented above.[43]

(1) A finite cause needs an infinite cause.

Contrary to the atheist, the theist holds that one finite or contingent being cannot cause another for the simple reason that everything cannot be contingent (dependent). There must be at least one independent being on which all dependent beings depend. Likewise, all beings cannot be effects; at least one being must be the cause.

The principle of causality states only that "every *finite* (contingent, dependent) being needs a cause." This means that the cause of all finite beings cannot itself be finite. If it were, then it too would need a cause. Therefore, the cause of all finite beings must be an infinite being.[44]

(2) The cause of the universe must be perfect.

One can argue against the atheist that if there were no perfect standard by which we could measure things in the world, we could not judge any of them to be imperfect (not perfect). To say that something is *not* perfect is to imply that we know what *is* perfect.[45]

Further, just because imperfections have appeared in the universe does not mean they were made imperfect initially, any more than the present imperfect state of medieval works of art reflects their original condition.

(3) Chance does not explain the origin of all things; an intelligent cause is needed.

The skeptic would not argue that the very words he uses to express his skepticism are a purely chance product and not an expression of an intelligent being. If he did claim this, then his words would have no meaning and, hence, no truth value to refute theism. Neither would a scientist claim that the presidential faces on Mount Rushmore were the result of chance. Only intelligent intervention adequately explains these results. Yet there is more information in DNA, the simplest form of life, than in either the skeptic's words or Mount Rushmore. Hence, the theist contends that only an intelligent Creator is adequate to account for this vast complexity of information in the code of life.[46]

(4) The principle of causality does not need to be proven.

Countering the atheist's claims, theists often assert that every event has a cause. They note that even the skeptic David Hume never denied the principle of causality; he merely denied that it was either mathematically true or provable by experience. In fact, Hume believed the principle of causality was "certain" and that it would be "absurd" to deny it. He wrote:

> I never asserted so absurd a proposition as *that* anything might arise without a cause: I only maintained, that our certainty of the falsehood of that proceeded neither from intuition nor demonstration; but from another source.[47]

Theists believe that it is absurd to deny causality because it would mean that nothing produced something. But it takes something to produce something. "Nothing comes from nothing. Nothing never could."

(5) It is not possible to have an actually infinite series of causes.

Theists have argued that mathematical (abstract) infinites are possible, but an actual (concrete) infinite series is not. For example, there is an infinite number of mathematical points between the left end and the right end of my book shelf, but I cannot get an infinite number of actual books (or even sheets of paper) on the shelf, no matter how thin they are.[48] Likewise, there cannot be an actual infinite number of causes going back in space and time. No matter how many causes one has, there could always be more. But nothing can be longer than what is actually infinitely long. Hence, an actual infinite number of events or causes is impossible.

(6) It is *logically* possible that nothing ever existed, including a necessary being.

Most theists agree with atheists that it is possible for a necessary being not to exist. If no world ever existed (including myself right now and you as you read this), then it is also logically possible that no necessary being ever existed. That is, it is *logically* possible that nothing ever existed, including God. On this the atheists are right.

However, *if* there is a necessary being, then it is not possible that he not exist, since, by definition, a necessary being cannot *not* exist. In like manner, there need not be any triangular-shaped things in existence, but if there are, then they must have three sides. In short, a *logically* necessary being need not necessarily actually exist. But if an *actually* necessary being exists, then it must necessarily actually exist. It cannot not exist. Hence, the atheists' objection to the concept of a necessary being applies only to a logically necessary being, not to an actually necessary being.

(7) The concept of necessary (or uncaused) being does make sense.

A contingent being is one that *can* not exist. A necessary being is one that *cannot* not exist. Since the latter is logically (and actually) the opposite of the other, then to reject the coherence of a necessary being would involve rejecting the coherence of a contingent being. But those are the only two kinds of being there can be. Hence, as theists point out, to reject the meaningfulness of the concept of a necessary being would be to reject the meaningfulness of all being. But to say that "all being is meaningless" is to make a statement about being which purports to be meaningful. This is self-defeating; it cuts its own throat.

Another way that theists defend the meaningfulness of the concept of an uncaused being is to point to the atheist's concept of an uncaused universe. Most atheists believe that it is meaningful to speak of a universe that had no cause but is simply there.[49] But if the concept of an uncaused universe is meaningful, then so is the concept of an uncaused God. Both are uncaused beings.

(8) Statements about existence can be necessary

Theists argue that if statements about existence cannot be necessarily true, then neither can the atheist's claim be true. That is, the claim that "there are no existentially necessary statements" claims itself to be an existentially necessary statement. If it is not, then it does not succeed in refuting the theists' claim. Unless it really proves that *no* statements about existence are necessarily true, then it follows that one such statement may be true. But the statement that "no statements about existence are necessarily true" is itself a statement about existence. Hence, if this statement is necessarily true, then it defeats itself. And if it is not necessarily true, it does not defeat theism. In either case the theist insists that it fails to disestablish his claim.

(9) The universe as a whole does need a cause.

Theists argue that either the whole universe is *equal* to all its parts or it is *more* than all its parts. If it is equal to them, then it too needs a cause. Adding dependent *parts* will never equal anything more than a dependent *whole,* no matter how big it is. Adding up *effects* never yields a cause; it produces only a big pile of effects. On the other hand, if the universe is *more* than all its effects, then it must be uncaused and necessary. Since the effects (parts) are caused and contingent, then the "whole" must be uncaused and necessary. (If the whole were not uncaused, then it too would be caused and contingent just like all the parts of the universe). But to claim that there is a something more (transcendent), uncaused and necessary on which everything in the universe is dependent is to claim exactly the same thing the theist means by a necessary being on which all contingent beings depend for their existence.

The theist asks the nontheist: if everything in the universe (i.e., every contingent being) suddenly ceased to exist, would there be anything left in existence? If not, then the universe as a whole is contingent too, since the existence of the whole is dependent on the parts. But if something remained after every contingent part of the universe suddenly ceased to exist, then there really is a transcendent, necessary, uncaused something which is not dependent on the universe for its existence. In either case, the theist contends that the atheist's claim fails.

(10) All arguments for God's existence are not based on an invalid ontological argument.

First of all, most theists believe that the ontological argument need not assume that existence is a perfection or predicate that adds to the concept of the subject. Existence does not have to be a predicate; one can simply say that everything that exists must be predicated according to one or more *modes* of existence (for example, contingently, necessarily or impossibly).[50]

Further, all one needs to do is begin with an ontological *definition* of God (namely, God is defined as a necessary being), not an ontological *argument* for God.[51] It is no more illegitimate to define God before one seeks to discover whether He exists than it is to describe a mermaid before one goes deep sea diving in search of one.

The theistic argument for God is parallel to the argument for a three-sided object, which can be stated as follows:

a. If there is a triangular object, then it must have three sides.

b. This three-sided imprint in concrete is evidence for the existence of a triangular object.

c. Therefore, a three-sided object exists.

Likewise,

a. If God exists, then He must necessarily (independently) exist.

b. The existence of contingent (dependent) being(s) is evidence that a necessary being exists.

c. Therefore, a necessary being necessarily exists.

Thus, the argument for God's existence does not depend on the ontological argument. Rather, it depends on the validity of the cosmological inference that every contingent being must have a neccessary being as its cause.

(11) It is true, but irrelevant, that what is logically necessary does not necessarily exist.

Theists do not need to argue (and most don't) that because it is *logically* necessary to define God as a necessary being, then such a being must exist. Rather, most theists insist that the existence of contingent being(s) is evidence that a necessary being exists. But not all theists insist that a logically necessary being demands that it actually exist, any more than the logical necessity that triangles have three sides demands that some triangular object actually exists. In short, this objection of atheism applies only to an ontological argument, not to a cosmological argument.

(12) Causes can be validly inferred from effects.

Theists insist that if this were not true, then we could not validly infer that there was an atheist's mind behind the atheist's thoughts in this very objection he presents. Furthermore, even the atheist assumes that there is a real theist's mind (cause) behind the theist's writings (effects). He does not assume that the cause is only apparent and not real; he assumes that it takes a real mind (cause) to produce real effects (writings).

In fact, the whole distinction between the thing-to-me (appearance) and the thing-in-itself (reality) is self-defeating. The very distinction between appearance and reality presupposes that we can know something about reality. Otherwise, how could one make such a distinction?[52] The only way one can say that the line ends at a particular point is if he can see beyond it. Likewise, one must know where appearance ends and reality begins in order to draw the line. In short, one cannot deny all connection between reality and appearance unless he knows some connection between them.

(13) The principle of causality does not lead to contradictions.

According to theists, the non-theist misunderstands the principle of causality. He assumes (wrongly) that the principle insists that "every thing has a cause." If this were true then it would follow that one should never stop seeking a cause, even for God. However, this is not what most theists mean by the principle of causality. The principle need not be stated as "every *being* has a cause"; rather, it is "every *finite* (contingent) being has a cause." Thus, there is no contradiction between a first cause (which is *infinite*) and the principle of causality which holds that all *finite* beings need a cause. Once one arrives at an infinite and necessary being, there is no need to seek a further cause. A necessary being needs no cause for its own existence. It exists because it must exist. It cannot *not* exist. Only what *can* not exist (namely, a contingent being) needs an explanation of why it exists rather than not exist. Therefore, it is meaningless to ask of a necessary being why it exists rather than not exist. That would be similar to asking why circles must be round. They just *are*.

2. Critiquing the arguments for atheism.

Now that we have discussed the theistic response to the atheists' arguments against theism, let us consider the theistic reply to the arguments *for* atheism. According to theists:

a. The ontological disproof fails.

Theists claim that the "ontological disproof" of God boomerangs. In order for it to be a real disproof, it must be *necessarily* true. But if it is a necessarily true statement about reality that no necessarily true statements about reality can be made, then the proof destroys itself by being an example of what it claims is impossible. On the other hand, if atheists claim that the statement (that no necessarily true statements about reality can be made) is *not* necessarily true, then it is no longer a disproof because it *might* be wrong.

b. The cosmological disproof fails.

Theists contend that the "cosmological disproof" for God fails because it wrongly assumes that God must be defined as a *self-caused* being. However, God is not a self-caused being; God can be an *un*-caused being. This is precisely what classical theism means by

God's aseity (self-existence).[53] God is the uncaused cause of all else that exists. Certainly no atheist who believes that the universe is uncaused can claim that the concept of an uncaused being is meaningless. If it is meaningful to speak of an uncaused universe, then certainly it is meaningful to refer to an uncaused God.

c. The teleological disproof fails.

The problems with the "teleological disproof" is that, at best, it shows only a *possibility* of a chance origin of the universe, not the *necessity* of a chance origin. Simply because it is logically and mathematically *possible* for the universe to have taken its present shape without an intelligent cause, it does not unequivocally follow that it actually did. We could all agree that it is mathematically *possible* for a dictionary to result from an explosion in a printing shop. But if repeated observations in the present are the key to events of the past, then we have grounds for believing that a dictionary was not really formed that way.

Put another way, based on observations in the present, it seems more likely that some intelligent being created the human brain (which contains more genetic information than all the major libraries of the world) that the purely non-intelligent forces caused its development. It is a repeatedly observed fact that it takes intelligence to convey information.[54] For example, if we were to see a simple message, such as "drink Coke," written in the sky, we would immediately assume it was produced by an intelligent source (even if we could not see an airplane). Certainly, we must also conclude that the presence of highly complex information, such as that found in the DNA of living things, indicates an intelligent source that produced it.

d. The moral disproof fails.[55]

Despite their popularity as arguments against God, theists hold that the moral disproofs are also self-defeating. For example, if "destroy" means "annihilate," it becomes obvious that God cannot destroy evil without destroying the *basis* for morality (that is, the free moral agent). In other words, as long as a free agent decides to do evil, then the only way for God to destroy evil is to destroy the free agent's ability to make free moral choices. But once the very basis for morality is destroyed, it is senseless to speak of a *moral* problem of evil. There can be a moral problem only if there are moral beings. But if man is only a robot with no free choice, then there is no moral problem. Hence, there is no basis for asking why God does not destroy the morally bad situation called evil.

On the other hand, if "destroy" merely means "defeat" (without annihilating free choice), then the atheist's argument still fails. In this case the atheist assumes (wrongly) that evil never will be defeated. But he could know this for sure only if he were omniscient. Therefore, he would have to presume to *be* God in order to *disprove* God. This problem can be clarified by making explicit something that is implied in the argument:

(1) If God were all-good, He would defeat evil.

(2) If God were all-powerful, He could defeat evil.

(3) But evil is not *yet* defeated.

(4) Therefore, God does not exist.

Once the time factor is made explicit in premise 3, a possibility of escape from the atheist's conclusion emerges: God may yet defeat evil in the future,[56] therefore, it may be too early to retire God. And as long as there is a possibility that God will put away evil in the future, one need not conclude that God does not exist based on the existence of evil in the present world.

There is, of course, a way to plug up this possibility. The atheist could substitute a new premise for (3) that reads:

(3a) But evil is not yet defeated, and *it never will be*.

This would make the argument valid. However, this new premise raises another problem: How can one know for certain that evil will *never* be defeated in the future unless he is omniscient? That is, how can any finite being know for sure what will happen in the future? The fact that evil has not been defeated up to this point does not establish beyond all doubt that it will not ultimately be destroyed, just as the fact that the world has not yet come to an end does not prove that it *never* will. So the theist insists that the atheist's argument fails to *disprove* God.

Many other forms of the moral argument against God have been offered, but these have similar results. The following is broadly representative of such attempts:

(1) An all-good God must have a good purpose for everything.

(2) But some evil has no good purpose (rape, cruelty, etc.).

(3) Therefore, no all-good God exists.

According to theists, the problem with this form of the argument is that it confuses these two premises:[57]

a. *There is* no good purpose for some evil (an absolute statement of fact based on having *total* knowledge).

b. *I know of* no good purpose for some evil (a statement based on *limited* knowledge).

Since no finite person can claim to have *total* knowledge, we must all concede that there *may be* some good purpose for evil even if no believer in God knows what it is.[58] It is *possible* that there is a God who knows what this purpose is. In fact, if an all-knowing, all-loving God exists, then it is *necessary* that there is a good purpose for all evil. If he did *not* have such a purpose in mind for allowing evil, then He would not be all-knowing and all-loving.

Here again, theists contend that the only way the atheist can succeed at his argument is to assume omniscience and affirm that he knows with all certainty that God could not possibly have a good purpose for all evil. But here too the atheist must assume to be God in order to disprove God.

VI. Summary and conclusion.

According to their opponents, atheists' objections to theistic arguments are not valid. Likewise, their arguments to support atheism seem to lack a solid foundation. This does not mean that there is no truth to anything atheists claim. There are many positive values to what atheists believe, including the reality of the material world and the affirmation of moral principles. However, the basic position of atheism—that no God exists—appears less than *proven*.

This does not mean that no one can *believe* the principles of atheism. They obviously can, and many do. It simply means that atheism has not conclusively established itself as true in relationship to other world views. The door is still open for further exploration as to whether some kind of God exists.

NOTES

1. Friedrich Nietzsche, *Joyful Wisdom*, trans. by Thomas Common (New York: Frederick Ungar Publishing Co., 1960), section 125, pp. 167, 168.
2. See *Marx and Engels on Religion*, ed. by Reinhold Niebuhr (New York: Schocken, 1964), p. 295.
3. For a more complete examination of various kinds of non-theistic humanism see Normal L. Geisler, *Is Man the Measure? An Evaluation of Contemporary Humanism* (Grand Rapids: Baker Book House, 1983), part one.
4. For example, Bertrand Russell's attacks on God (in *Why I Am not a Christian*, New York: Simon and Schuster, 1957) have been misunderstood as a defense of atheism. Actually Russell claimed to be an agnostic (see "What Is an Agnostic?" *Look*, 1953).
5. See Thomas Altizer, *The Gospel of Christian Atheism* (Philadelphia: The Westminster Press, 1966).
6. See Paul Van Buren, *The Secular Meaning of the Gospel* (New York: Macmillan, 1963).
7. See A. J. Ayer, *Language, Truth, and Logic* (New York: Dover Publications, 1946), chapter 1.
8. See Ayn Rand, *For the New Intellectual* (New York: New American Library, 1961).
9. See Sigmund Freud, *The Future of an Illusion*, trans. by W. D. Robson-Scott (New York: Doubleday, 1957); B. F. Skinner, *About Behaviorism* (New York: Alfred A. Knopf, 1974).
10. Friedrich Nietzsche, *Beyond Good and Evil*, Cowan translation (Chicago: Henry Regnery Co., 1966), section 21, p. 23.
11. Nietzsche, *Thus Spoke Zarathustra*, trans. by Walter Kaufmann (New York: Viking Press, 1966), Prologue 3, p. 125.
12. Nietzsche, *Beyond Good and Evil*, section 187, p. 93.
13. Ibid., section 220, pp. 92-94.
14. Nietzsche, *Anti-Christ* (New York: Knopf), p. 230.
15. This whole idea is embodied in a book Nietzsche wrote by the title, *Beyond Good and Evil* (Chicago: Henry Regnery Co., 1966).
16. Nietzsche, *The Will to Power*.
17. Nietzsche, *Anti-Christ*, p. 18.
18. Nietzsche, *The Will to Power*, pp. 18, 19.
19. Ludwig Feuerbach, *The Essence of Christianity* (New York: Harper Torchbook, 1957), p. 12.
20. Ibid., pp. 15.
21. Feuerbach, quoted in "An Introductory Essay" in ibid., p. xi.
22. Ibid., pp. 29-32.
23. Jean-Paul Sartre, *Being and Nothingness*, trans by Hazel Barner (New York: Philosophical Library, Inc., 1956), pp. 755-768.
24. Sartre, *The Flies* in *No Exit and Three Other Plays* (New York: Vintage Books, 1947), pp. 121-123.

25. Sartre, *Being and Nothingness*, p. 767.
26. See Thomas Aquinas, *Summa Theologica* I, 2, 3 in *The Basic Writings of St. Thomas Aquinas.*
27. See William Paley, *Natural Theology* (Indianapolis: The Bobbs-Merrill Co., 1963), chapter 1.
28. This form follows what is sometimes considered Anselm's first statement of the argument. See St. Anselm, *Proslogium*, trans. by S. W. Deane (La Salle, IL: Open Court Publishing Co., 1962), pp. 153-161.
29. See C. S. Lewis, *Mere Christianity* (New York: Macmillan, 1953), Book I, chapters 1-5.
30. Hume's objections are spelled out in his *Dialogues Concerning Natural Religion* (Indianapolis: Bobbs-Merrill, 1962) as well as in his *Enquiry Concerning Human Understanding* (Indianapolis: Bobbs-Merrill, 1955).
31. Kant's objections are found in his *Critique of Pure Reason*, trans. by L. W. Beck (New York: Bobbs-Merrill, 1950).
32. See J. N. Findlay, "Can God's Existence Be Disproved?" in the *Ontological Argument*, Alvin Plantinga, ed. (Garden City, NY: Doubleday, 1965), p. 111f.
33. See Jean-Paul Sartre, *Being and Nothingness* (New York: Washington Square Press, 1966), pp. 758, 762.
34. See David Hume, *Dialogues, part VIII.*
35. See Pierre Bayle, *Selections from Bayle's Dictionary*, trans. by R. H. Popkin (Indianapolis: Bobbs-Merrill, 1965), p. 157f.
36. See Carl Sagan, *Cosmos* (New York: Random House, 1980), p. 4.
37. See Carl Sagan, *Broca's Brain* (New York: Random House, 1979), p. 287.
38. This view is called epiphenominalism.
39. This view is called utilitarianism. It was developed by John Stuart Mill (*Utilitarianism*, New York: Meridian Books, 1962), chapter II.
40. See Paul Kurtz, *Humanist Manifestos I & II* (Buffalo: Promethius Press, 1973).
41. B. F. Skinner, *Walden Two* (New York: Macmillan, 1976), p. 182.
42. For a more detailed description of the values of atheistic forms of humanism, see N. L. Geisler, *Is Man the Measure?* (Grand Rapids: Baker Book House, 1983), chapter 9.
43. For a parallel discussion to these objections see N. L. Geisler, *Philosophy of Religion* (Grand Rapids: Zondervan Publishing Co., 1974), pp. 208-224.
44. See Thomas Aquinas, *Summa Theologica*, I, 7, 1 & 2 in Anton C. Regis, *Basic Writings of St. Thomas Aquinas* (New York: Random House, 1944), pp. 56-58.
45. This point has been made by many theists including Augustine, Anselm, and more recently by C. S. Lewis in *Mere Christianity* (New York: Macmillan, 1953), book I, chapter 2.
46. The information in a single cell organism would fill a whole volume of an encyclopedia. And the genetic information in the human brain would fill all the books in all the major libraries of the world (see Carl Sagan, *Cosmos*, p. 278).
47. David Hume, *The Letters of David Hume*, ed. by J. Y. T. Greig (Oxford: Clarendon Press, 1932), I:187.
48. This argument has a long tradition among Arabian and Christian theists. See William Craig, *The Kalam Cosmological Argument* (London: The Macmillan Press, Ltd., 1979), part I.
49. See Bertrand Russell in "A Debate on the Existence of God," Bertrand Russell and F. C. Copleston in John Hick, ed., *The Existence of God* (New York: The Macmillan Co., 1964), p. 175.
50. See Charles Hartshorne, "The Necessarily Existent" in Alvin Plantinga, ed., *The Ontological Argument* (New York: Doubleday, 1965), pp. 129, 130.

51. This point is developed more fully in N. L. Geisler, *Christian Apologetics* (Grand Rapids: Baker Book House, 1976), pp. 237-240.

52. See Stuart Hackett, *The Resurrection of Theism* (Grand Rapids: Baker Book House, 1982), pp. 54, 60, 62, 65.

53. See Thomas Aquinas, *Summa Theologica,* ibid., I, 9 & 10, pp. 70-82.

54. Herbert Yockey has shown that there is a mathematically identical relation between the information in a written language (which we know comes from intelligent beings) and the information in the DNA of a living cell. See Yockey, "Self Organization, Origin of Life Scenarios and Information Theory" in *The Journal of Theoretical Biology* 91 (1981), 13-31.

55. For a more detailed discussion of the many forms of the arguments for evil, see N. L. Geisler, *The Roots of Evil* (Grand Rapids: Zondervan Publishing Co., 1978).

56. This point is made very effectively by C. S. Lewis in *The Great Divorce* (New York: Macmillan Co., 1946). See especially pp. 69, 124.

57. See George Mavrodes, *Belief in God* (New York: Random House, 1970), chapter 4.

58. Theists claim to know of many good purposes or results for many kinds of evil. For example, warning pains have a good purpose. Tribulation often produces patience. Some evils are necessary by-products of the abuse of good things. For example, indigestion is an inevitable by-product of abusing the freedom to eat; hangovers are by-products of misusing the freedom to drink alcohol. Some consider these to be *good* by-products in that they remind or admonish us to use our freedoms *wisely.* Since there are good results of many evils, then theists concede that there *may be* good results for all evils. If this is so, then the definitive case against God from the presence of evil fails.

4

Pantheism:
A World That Is God

I.   Introduction.

Thus Brahman is all in all. He is action, knowledge, goodness supreme. To know him, hidden in the lotus of the heart, is to untie the knot of ignorance. Self-luminous is Brahman, ever present in the hearts of all. He is the refuge of all, he is the supreme goal. In him exists all that moves and breathes. In him exists all that is. He is both that which is gross and that which is subtle. Adorable is he. Beyond the ken of the senses is he. Supreme is he. Attain thou him![1]

This passage from the Hindu scriptures, the *Upanishads*, briefly summarizes the essence of the pantheistic world view. In pantheism God is all in all. God pervades all things, contains all things, subsumes (includes) all things, and is found within all things. Nothing exists apart from God, and all things are in some way identified with God. In short, pantheism views the world as God and God as the world. Put more precisely, in pantheism all is God and God is all. Nothing exists that is not God.

Pantheism has a long history in both the East and the West. From the Eastern mysticism of Hindu sages and seers to the rationalism of such notable Western philosophers as Parmenides, Benedict de Spinoza, and G. W. F. Hegel, pantheism has always found advocates. But it has been only recently that pantheism has become so popular in the West. In university and college curriculums today, one can find course offerings in Eastern thought and mythology. It is also commonplace to find in bookstores many books written from or influenced by a pantheistic mindset. Even the sciences are turning toward pantheism for some answers. In a recent article, Mary Long refers to the thinking of Victor Ferkiss, who has a pantheistic approach to ecology:

> Religion must be revitalized so as to sustain us during the impending global scarcity of resources. It can best do this, he believes, in the form of *ecotheology*, "an approach to religion that starts with the premise that the universe *is* God." According to this neopantheism, religion's job is to prevent the environmental exploitation of the Universe.[2]

Long believes that the Eastern religions can supply a view of the universe that will unify science and religion. As she says, "In such a [pantheistic] world, scientific discoveries can be in perfect harmony with religious beliefs."[3]

The entertainment industry has also displayed the recent influx of pantheism. For a time the Beatles were greatly influenced by the Transcendental Meditation of the Maharishi Mahesh Yogi and later by the Hare Krishna movement of A. C. Bhaktivedanta (which contains, in part, pantheistic thought). Former Beatle George Harrison had a top-selling record entitled "My Sweet Lord," on which the background singers sang praises to Krishna and other Hindu gods, such as Vishnu.[4] In the 1970s a popular jazz-rock group called The Mahavishnu Orchestra, led by a talented guitarist Mahavishnu John McLaughlin, wrote and performed musical numbers from an Eastern mindset. Indeed, printed on some of their album covers was the pantheistic poetry of McLaughlin's spiritual guide, Sri Chinmoy.[5]

Even movies, such as the *Star Wars* series, have further popularized and facilitated a growing acceptance of pantheism. In *The Empire Strikes Back,* for example, Yoda says concerning "the Force [Tao]":" 'Its energy surrounds us and binds us. Luminous beings we are, not this crude matter...Feel it you must. Feel the flow. Feel the Force around you. Here,' he said, as he pointed, 'between you and me and that tree and that rock.'"[6]

In addition to this is the pantheistic foundation of the New Age movement;[7] the missionary efforts of such groups as Transcendental Meditation, Hare Krishna, the Divine Light Mission, the Vedanta Society of Southern California, and Christian Science; as well as such notable individuals as Alan Watts, D. T. Suzuki, and Radhakrishnan. One can readily see from these examples that the pantheistic world view is widely held.

Let us examine pantheism's tenets to determine whether or not they are true.

II.   A typology of pantheism.

There are many types of pantheism. *Absolute* pantheism is represented by the thinking of the early Greek philosopher Parmenides (in the fifth century before Christ)[8] and the Advainta Vedanta school of Hinduism. This type of pantheism teaches that there is only one being in the world, God. All else that appears to exist does not actually exist.

Emanational pantheism, as set forth by Plotinus (in the third century after Christ), holds that everything flows from God, just as a flower unfolds from a seed.

In *developmental* pantheism, as reflected in the thinking of G. W. F. Hegel (1770-1831), the events of history are viewed as the unfolding manifestations of Absolute Spirit.[9]

Modal pantheism, as espoused by the rationalist Benedict de Spinoza (17th century), argues that there is only one absolute Substance in which all finite things are merely modes or moments.[10]

Multilevel pantheism is found in some forms of Hinduism, especially as expressed by Radhakrishnan.[11] This view proposed that there are various levels or manifestations of God, the highest level manifesting God as the Absolute One and the lower levels successively manifesting God in greater multiplicity.

Finally, there is *permeational* pantheism where the Force [Tao] penetrates all things. This kind is found in Zen Buddhism and was popularized in the *Star Wars* films.

All of these types of pantheism identify God and the world, but they vary in their specific conceptions of this identity. That is, all pantheistic views believe *that* God and the real world are one, but they differ as to *how* God and the world are to be identified.

In the section that follows we shall look at some of these types of pantheism through the writings of various people who held or hold these views. Then we will discuss the main tenets of a pantheistic world view.

III.   Some representatives of pantheism.

   A.   Vedanta's absolute pantheism.

The oldest known form of pantheism may be found in the last section of the Vedas, the Hindu scriptures. This final section is called the Upanishads. Because the Upanishads are at the end of each of the four Vedas, the Upanishads have come to be spoken of as the Vedanta, meaning "end" or "goal" of the Vedas. "Thus it is that when a modern Hindu speaks of the Vedanta he may have both senses more or less in mind, the scriptures referred to being for him that last part of the Vedas and at the same time their ultimate reason for existence, their perfect culmination—in a word, their highest wisdom."[12] No one really knows who wrote the Upanishads or when they were written. They consist of the recorded experiences of Hindu sages.[13] The Upanishads, along with the Bhagavad-Gita, lay the foundation for Vedanta pantheism.[14]

   1.   God.

Vedanta pantheism teaches that only one God (Brahman) exists.[15] This God is infinite in form, immortal, imperishable, impersonal, all-pervading, supreme, changeless, absolute and indivisibly one—and, at the same time, none of these. God is beyond all thought and speech:

> Him [Brahman] the eye does not see, nor the tongue express, nor the mind grasp. Him we neither know nor are able to teach. Different is he from the known, and . . . from the unknown.

He truly knows Brahman who knows him as beyond knowledge; he who thinks that he knows, knows not. The ignorant think that Brahman is known, but the wise know him to be beyond knowledge.[16]

Thus, Brahman is inexpressible and indefinable. Nothing can be truly said or thought of Brahman. This is graphically illustrated by the Hindu philosopher Sankara in his commentary on the Upanishads:

"Sir," said a pupil to his master, "teach me the nature of Brahman." The master did not reply. When a second and a third time he was importuned, he answered: "I teach you indeed, but you do not follow. His name is silence."[17]

2. The world.

Vedanta pantheism also teaches that all is God and God is all. There is only one reality. The world that we see, hear, touch, taste and smell does not actually exist. It appears to exist, but it is in fact an illusion, or *maya*. The universe we perceive is similar to walking through a dense forest at night and seeing what appears to be a snake. But when we return to the same spot in the light of day, we see that the snake is really a rope. Just as the snake *appeared* to exist, so the universe *appears* to exist but it does not actually exist. Rather, the universe is *maya*, an illusion, a superimposition upon the only true reality, Brahman. As the Upanishads state:

Brahman alone is—nothing else is. He who sees the manifold universe, and not the one reality, goes evermore from death to death.[18]

Meditate, and you will realize that mind, matter, and Maya (the power which unites mind and matter) are but three aspects of Brahman, the one reality.[19]

3. Man.

If the universe does not exist—if Brahman is the only reality—then who or what is man? Is man nonexistent or is man Brahman? Vedanta pantheism says that man is Brahman. *Maya*, or the illusory universe, has deceived man into thinking that he is a particular in the universe. But if man would just clear his senses and his mind of *maya* and meditate upon his true Self *(Atman)*, then he would come to realize that Atman is Brahman, the one true reality. That is, the depth of a person's soul is identical to the depth of the universe.

Having attained to Brahman, a sage declared: "I am life....I am established in the purity of Brahman. I have attained the freedom of the Self. I am Brahman, self-luminous, the brightest treasure. I am endowed with wisdom. I am immortal, imperishable.[20]

4. Ethics.

According to Vedanta pantheism, man must transcend the world of illusion before he can discover his true Self.[21] This is accomplished when one goes beyond good and evil. "When the seer beholds the Effulgent One, the Lord, the Supreme Being, then transcending both good and evil, and freed from impurities, he unites himself with him"[22] When a person unites himself with Brahman, he no longer will be plagued by such thoughts as "'I have done an evil thing' or 'I have done a good thing.'" For a person to go beyond good and evil means that he is "troubled no more by what he may or may not have done."[23] He becomes nonattached to his—or anyone else's—past, present, or even future actions. Indeed, even the results of any actions are viewed with indifference: "When your intellect has cleared itself of its delusions, you will become indifferent to the results of all action, present or future."[24]

This drive toward indifference to any action is explained most clearly in the Bhagavad-Gita. In the Gita, a long dialogue occurs between Krishna, a manifestation of Brahman, and his friend and disciple, Arjuna. Arjuna tells Krishna of his reluctance to fight against a people of whom many are his friends. He asks Krishna how killing his friends could possibly be justified. Krishna tells Arjuna that he must detach himself from the fruits of his actions, no matter what they are. Thus, states Krishna:

"...he whose mind dwells
Beyond attachment,
Untainted by ego,
No act shall bind him
With any Bond:
Though he slay these thousands
He is no slayer."[25]

Krishna explains to Arjuna that this state of union with Brahman can be achieved by following one or any combination of the following paths: (1) *raga yoga*—the path of union through meditation and mind control; (2) *karma yoga*—the path of union through work; (3)

jnana yoga—the path of union through knowledge; or (4) *bhakti yoga*—the path of union through love and devotion.[26] But any path one follows must be accompanied by nonattachment or indifference to any action. Only then will good and evil be transcended and thus union with Brahman be attained.

5. Man's destiny.

Realizing one's oneness with Brahman is essential in Vedanta pantheism, for apart from this realization one is doomed forever to the cycle of *samsara*. *Samsara* is the wheel of time and desire, or birth, death and rebirth. It is the wheel to which everything in the world of illusion is shackled. And *samsara* "itself is subject to and conditioned by endless cause, the *dharma* of the universe."[27]

One's life is also determined by the law of *karma*, or action. This is the moral law of the universe. Huston Smith explains that *karma* is "the moral law of cause and effect." It is absolutely binding and allows no exceptions. Karma says that *every* decision made by an individual in the present is caused by all prior decisions in his past lives and will, in turn, affect *every* future decision he makes.[28]

If a person's *karma* is good, then he may follow one of two possible paths. If he has managed to free himself from *samsara*—the cycle of birth and rebirth—then he will attain to higher planes of existence or consciousness until he finally "becomes one with the divine Being in his impersonal aspect and so reaches at last the end of his journey."[29]

If he has been good, but not good enough to free himself from *samsara*, then he will go "to one or another heaven, where he enjoys the fruits of his good deeds which he has done in the body . . . and when these fruits are no more, he is born again, that is, reincarnated" on earth in "a new body appropriate to a new and higher realm of being."[30]

If a person's *karma* is largely evil, then he "goes to the regions of the wicked, there to eat the bitter fruits of his deeds. These fruits once exhausted, he too returns to earth" in a reincarnated state.[31]

At least two observations should be made concerning the law of *karma* and the cycle of *samsara*. First, "it is on this earth that a man determines his spiritual destiny and achieves his final realization."[32] Salvation is solely of man and his efforts. Higher states of existence are rewards of happiness and lower states are punishments that each person earns on his own. "The history of a particular individual, the number of times he experiences rebirth, or reincarnation as it is called, depends entirely upon the quality of his will, upon the moral effort he puts forth."[33] He alone is responsible for his destiny.

Second, ultimately all of mankind will achieve liberation from *samsara* and union with Brahman. Some people may return to earth often, but eventually they will all earn their salvation. As Swami Prabhavananda says, "The Upanishads know no such thing as eternal damnation—and the same is true of every other Hindu scripture."[34]

In summary, Vedanta pantheism is the absolute pantheism of the East that has found popular expression and favor in the West through many religious groups and practices, including Transcendental Meditation and the International Society for Krishna Consciousness. Vedanta pantheism is an absolute monism, declaring that God is all and all is One.

B. Plotinus' emanational pantheism.

Early Greek rationalistic pantheism (e.g., Parmenides' absolute pantheism) finds its zenith in the mystical pantheism of Plotinus. Plotinus was born in Egypt around A.D. 204, and in his late 20s began to study philosophy in Alexandria. Eventually he came under the instruction of Ammonius Saccas, also teacher of Origen, and studied under him for 11 years. Plotinus did not begin writing until after he taught philosophy in Rome for 10 years. His work has been extremely influential in both philosophical and religious thought.[35] As we shall see, Plotinus' teaching provides an excellent example of emanational pantheism.

1. God and the world.

Contrary to Vedanta pantheism, Plotinus held that being or reality is a multiplicity, or many-faceted. Specifically, he believed that there are three levels or planes of being. But prior to and beyond being is the One.

The One is absolutely simple, that is, it has no parts. Also, it is absolutely necessary, in that it must exist. As Plotinus says, the One "has not 'happened' but is by a necessity prior to all necessities it must be."[36] This absolute Unity must exist because multiplicity presupposes a prior unity. We can know what is many only if we know what is One, for "unity must precede Reality and be its author" (VI,

6, 13). The One, therefore, is the absolute source of all being and multiplicity. Hence, the One is beyond and prior to being. In fact, Plotinus argues that the One transcends all of which it is the source, which is everything in reality: "Certainly this Absolute is none of the things of which it is the source—its nature is that nothing can be affirmed of it—not existence, not essence, not life—since it is That which transcends all these." Even its own name, The One, it transcends: "And this name, The One, contains really no more than the negation of plurality.... If we are led to think positively of The One, name and thing, there would be more truth in silence" (III, 8, 101). On this aspect the Hindu sages and Plotinus are agreed.

Now if the One is truly indescribable, then why does Plotinus attempt to describe it? He tells us why: "In our writing and telling we are but urging towards it: out of discussion we call to vision: to those desiring to see, we point the path" (VI, 9, 4). He believes that in some sense his God-talk does apply to God and is therefore helpful. This is so because negative knowledge (not-that, not-this) presupposes some positive awareness. He says, "It is impossible to say 'Not that' if one is utterly without experience or conception of the 'That'" (VI, 7, 29). Thus, we can know something, however little it may be, from the emanations of the One. We approach the One, says Plotinus, "through its offspring, Being" (VI, 9, 5). In short, though we cannot speak or know the One, we can speak or know of the One in terms of what has come from the One (V, 3, 4). What we must keep in mind, however, is that our words and thoughts of the One are not It but only pointers to It. Our words are not true descriptions of the One but give only limited glimpses of the One.

The first level of reality is *Nous*. Nous is the Divine Mind; it is God but not the highest God; it is pure Being. Nous is the first emanant from the One (that is, that which proceeds from the One) (V, 1, 4, 8). When the One flows outward and this emanant looks backward upon its source, there arises the simple duality of Knower and Known (VI, 7, 37). This simple duality is Nous. Nous in turn gives rise to further emanations by bending inward upon itself. Hence, it produces many particular intellects or forms which, turning outward, produce the World Soul, which in turn produces the species of individual souls (VI, 2, 22; VI, 7, 15). The One, Nous and World Soul form Plotinus' emanational Trinity. From this tri-level God, all other things flow both emanationally and necessarily.

The second level of reality has already been briefly mentioned—the World Soul. The World Soul "occupies a middle position between *Nous* and the corporeal world; it is the reflection of the former and the organizer of the latter."[37] The World Soul is even more multiplistic than Nous, for it is further from absolute Unity, the One. The World Soul emanates from Nous when Nous reflects upon itself (VI, 2, 22). And it is the World Soul that animates the whole universe in all of its multiplicity, thus giving it a kind of unity or wholeness (II, 1, 4 & 5).

The last level of reality is the most multiplistic of all—Matter. Since the entire emanational process is a necessary unfolding from unity to greater and greater multiplicity, it is necessary that the last stage it reaches be the most multiplistic. Matter is the last level before complete nonexistence. Indeed, Plotinus describes Matter as Non-Being but adds that this should not be understood to mean "something that simply does not exist, but...rather,, an image of Being or perhaps something still further removed than even an image" (I, 8, 3). In other words, the further removed something is from the source of all Being, the One, the less unity and being it has (VI, 9, 1). Since Matter is the furthest removed from the One, it has the least possible degree of unity and being. To progress further would be to cease to exist at all.

Furthermore, because Matter is the most multiplistic, it "has no residue of good in it" (I, 8, 7). Since the absolute Unity is absolutely good, it follows that each lesser degree of unity is that much less good and that much more capable of evil (I, 8, 5). Since Matter is as far from Unity as anything can get, it has no good in it, but has only the capacity for good. In short, Matter is not pure evil itself; it is rather the absolute privation or lack of any good (I, 8, 3).

Plotinus' emanational pantheism may be summarized this way. That which is beyond and prior to Being, the One, eternally and necessarily unfolds itself just as a seed unfolds into a flower. This unfolding produces Nous, or what Plotinus calls "One-Many." Nous is the One becoming self-conscious, that is, discovering itself. When Nous reflects inward upon itself it produces knowing beings, and when it reflects outward it produces the World Soul, or what Plotinus calls "One-and-Many." From the World Soul all else flows, including Matter or the "Many." Matter is the most multiplistic emanant of all, and it is absolutely "void of all share in Good" (VI, 1, 8; I, 8, 5). Hence, Matter is where evil resides without itself being evil (I, 8, 3).

Up to this point we have seen how the One flows outward, that is, from unity to multiplicity. For Plotinus, however, there is also a return flow from multiplicity to unity. Just as there is a necessity for the Many to unfold from the One, there is a like necessity for the Many to return to the One. The emanational process is like a gigantic elastic band that can be stretched only so far before it snaps back to the source from which it was originally stretched. Of course, one of the aspects of reality to which this occurs is man.

2. Man.

Plotinus believed that man's true self is his soul, which is temporarily coupled with a material body. It is through this attachment to a body that the lower phase of man's individual soul becomes contaminated by Matter (I, 2, 4). If man does not strive toward the ultimate Good and Unity, and instead turns away and concerns himself only with Matter, he will become absolutely evil (I, 8, 13). Thus, for man to be saved and attain ultimate perfection, he must turn from Matter and turn toward the One. Man's salvation consists in overcoming this dualism of body and soul. Man must turn from the outer to the inner, from matter to spirit, by asceticism and meditation.

3. Man's destiny.

The first step of man's deliverance begins in the realm of sense, where some unity has been imposed below by the Absolute above (I, 6, 2, 3). By looking at the "beauties of the realm of sense, images and shadow-pictures, fugitives that have entered into Matter," man comes to realize that "there are earlier and loftier beauties than these" (I, 6, 3, 4). These objects of sense point us to their source (VI, 9, 11). We are not to stop with them but ascend beyond them. Thus, the first step is from the sensible external world (Matter) to the next level of reality, the internal, intellectual world of man's soul.

This second step continues the ascent, beginning from the internal—man's soul—and moving to the eternal—Nous. This movement involves ascending from man's lower soul to his higher soul, and then to Nous, which is above the soul. This step is accomplished when one recognizes the identity of his mind with Mind (Nous); that is, knower and known become one. This merging is achieved through meditation. However, even at this stage ultimate Unity has not yet been attained (III, 8, 10; V, 3, 4). Man must go one step further.

79

The third and last step leads to the highest possible union—oneness with the One. It can be attained only by a mystical union that puts away all multiplicity, even intellect and reason. Says Plotinus, "One wishing to contemplate what transcends the Intellectual attains by putting away all that is of the intellect." He adds, "Our way...takes us beyond knowing...knowing and knowable must all be left aside; every object of thought, even the highest, we must pass by" (V, 5, 6; VI, 9, 4). Thus, one must go beyond the cognitive to the intuitional, beyond the rational to the mystical. In this last stage everything is absolute unity again. What emanated out has returned; all that flowed from It has and must return to It.

In summary, Plotinus' emanational pantheism begins in Unity, which gives rise to increasing multiplicity until the point of non-existence is about to be reached. Then, all returns toward increasing unity, until the greatest unity is reached in the absolute unity of the One. Here a person becomes one with the One and all with the All.

C. The permeational pantheism of D. T. Suzuki.

One of the most influential advocates of pantheism in the West is D. T. Suzuki. C. G. Jung said of him, "Daisetz Teitaro Suzuki's works on Zen Buddhism are among the best contributions to the knowledge of living Buddhism that recent decades have produced."[38] Through Suzuki's "long-term activity as a professor at Columbia University and at various other American universities, as well as [through] his untiring lecture tours throughout the Western world, Suzuki furthered the cause of Zen in its Western interpretation as it became known in the English language."[39] Suzuki has influenced and convinced such Westerners as Christmas Humphreys and Alan Watts.[40] Probably no one else has done more to influence the West toward an Eastern form of pantheism than has D. T. Suzuki.

1. The nature of Zen Buddhism.

The thinking of D. T. Suzuki revolves around Zen Buddhism. Therefore, in order to understand Suzuki's form of pantheism, we must first seek to grasp the nature of Zen. We will first examine what Suzuki believes Zen is *not* and then show what he believes Zen *is*.

According to Suzuki, Zen is not a system or philosophy "founded upon logic and analysis." Zen is opposed to any form of dualistic thinking—that is, making any kind of subject-object distinction.[41] Instead, Suzuki calls us to "hush the dualism of subject and object, forget both, transcend the intellect, sever yourself from the understanding, and directly penetrate deep into the identity of the Buddha-mind; outside of this there are no realities." Nor is Zen a set of teachings. According to Suzuki, "Zen has nothing to teach us in the way of intellectual analysis; nor has it any set doctrines which are imposed on its followers for acceptance." As such, Zen has "no sacred books or dogmatic tenets." Indeed, "Zen teaches nothing." It is we who "teach ourselves; Zen merely points the way."[42]

Zen is not a religion as "popularly understood." As Suzuki explains, "Zen has no God to worship, no ceremonial rites to observe, no future abode to which the dead are destined, and, last of all, Zen has no soul whose welfare is to be looked after by somebody else and whose immortality is a matter of intense concern with some people." When Suzuki says that there is no God in Zen, he does not mean to deny God's existence or to affirm it. As he says, "In Zen, God is neither denied nor insisted upon; only there is in Zen no such God as has been conceived by Jewish and Christian minds."[43]

Further, Suzuki claims that Zen is neither monotheistic nor pantheistic as such. By this he means that Zen denies such religious or metaphysical designations. Unlike the God of Christian theism or Vedanta pantheism, "there is no object in Zen upon which to fix the thought" of the Zen disciple. Furthermore, Zen can have nothing to do with such theoretical constructs of reality, for to do so would be to give up Zen. Rather, "Zen just feels fire warm and ice cold, because when it freezes we shiver and welcome the fire. The feeling is all in all...; all our theorization fails to touch reality."[44]

What, then, may we say is Zen? According to Suzuki, "Zen is the ocean, Zen is the air, Zen is the mountain, Zen is thunder and lightning, the spring flower, summer heat, and winter snow; nay, more than that, Zen is the man." Suzuki recounts that "when a Zen master was once asked what Zen was he replied, 'Your everyday thought.'"[45] Suzuki puts it yet another way:

"Good morning; how are you today?" "Thank you, I am well"—here is Zen. "Please have a cup of tea"—this, again, is full of Zen. When a hungry monk at work heard the dinner-gong he immediately dropped his work and showed himself in the dining room. The master, seeing him, laughed heartily, for the monk had been acting Zen to its fullest extent.[46]

In other words, Zen is life. "I raise my hand; I take a book from the other side of this desk; I hear the boys playing ball outside my window; I see the clouds blown away beyond the neighboring woods:—in all these I am practicing Zen, I am living Zen. No wordy discussion is necessary, nor any explanation."[47]

Hence, Zen is a personal experience of life unencumbered by any abstractions or conceptualizations of life.[48] As Suzuki says: "No amount of reading, no amount of teaching, no amount of contemplation will ever make one a Zen master. Life itself must be grasped in the midst of its flow; to stop it for examination and analysis is to kill it, leaving its cold corpse to be embraced."[49] This, then, is the nature of Zen.

2. God and the world.

In Zen Buddhism, God is man and man is God. Citing the Western mystic Meister Eckhart with approval, Suzuki states: "'Simple people conceive that we are to see God as if He stood on that side and we on this. It is not so; God and I are one in the act of my perceiving Him.' In this absolute oneness of things Zen establishes the foundations of its philosophy."[50]

Not only is man God and God man, but all is God and God is all. Everything and everyone are really One. "Buddhas [i.e., enlightened ones] and sentient beings [i.e., those still ignorant] both grow out of One Mind, and there is no other reality than this Mind."[51] This all-embracing Mind is actually no-mindedness, which is man's spiritual nature. Says Suzuki "This Nature [i.e., man's spiritual nature] is the Mind, and the Mind is the Buddha, and the Buddha is the Way, and the Way is Zen."[52] The Mind may be described as having "been in existence since the beginningless past; it knows neither birth nor death; it is neither blue nor yellow; it has neither shape nor form; it is beyond the category of being and non-being; it is not to be measured by age, old or new; it is neither long nor short; it is neither large nor small; for it transcends all limits, words, traces, and opposites."[53] In short, Mind is all and all is Mind.

Now Suzuki is quick to point out that this form of monism is not a denial of the existence of the world we perceive and feel around us. However, this world we sense outside of us is a "relative world"; it is "the work of ignorance and as such has no final reality." Hence, "it must be considered illusory and empty." Individual beings do exist, but they are not "ultimate and absolutely real." Rather, they are real "only in so far as they are considered a partial realization of Suchness." Indeed, "Suchness . . . lies not hidden *behind* them, but exists immanently *in* them. Things are empty and illusory so long as they are particular things and are not thought of in reference to the All that is Suchness and Reality."[54] Hence, although "our ordinary experience takes this world for something that has its 'self-nature,' i.e., existing by itself," a "higher intuition tells us that this is not so, that it is an illusion, and that what really exists is Mind, which being absolute knows no second."[55]

Buddhists do not like to refer to this Suchness or All as God. The very word "God" is offensive to most followers of Buddhism, "especially when it is intimately associated in vulgar minds with the idea of a creator who produced the world out of nothing, caused the downfall of mankind, and, touched by the pang of remorse, sent down his only son to save the depraved." Instead, a legion of other names has been "invented by the fertile imagination of Buddhists for their object of reverence as called forth by their various spiritual needs."[56]

Furthermore, Absolute Suchness or Reality cannot be grasped "as it truly is," for it goes beyond all categories, even the most basic categories of existence and nonexistence. Suzuki states: "We cannot even say that it is, for everything that is presupposes that which is not: existence and non-existence are relative terms as much as subject and object, mind and matter, this and that, one and other: one cannot be conceived without the other. 'It is not so *(na iti)*,' therefore may be the only way our imperfect human tongue can express it. So the Mahayanists generally designate absolute Suchness as *Cunyata* or void." This indefinable and unthinkable void may be "more fully interpreted" in this way: "'Suchness is neither that which is existence nor that which is non-existence; neither that which is at once existence and non-existence; nor that which is not at once existence and non-existence; it is neither that which is unity nor that which is plurality; neither that which is at once unity and plurality, nor that which is not at once unity and plurality'."[57] This is God, and God is All, and All is Mind, and Mind is Buddha, and Buddha is the Way, and the Way is Zen.

3. Man.

Zen Buddhism maintains that individual human beings "are nothing but a self-manifestation of the Dharmakaya" (i.e., God). Furthermore, "individuals are not isolated existences, as imagined by most people. If isolated, they are nothing, they are so many soap-bubbles which vanish one after another in the vacuity of space. All particular existences acquire their meaning only when they are thought of in their oneness in the Dharmakaya.'[58]

This should not be taken as a denial of man's materiality or immateriality, for man has both and more.[59] However, it is a denial of man's individuality in any ultimate sense. People only appear to be individual beings, but in reality they are all one in the One. It is the ignorance of many people to recognize this fact that constitutes the "veil of *maya*." And it is the goal of Zen to help people go beyond their egoism so that they may realize their oneness in God and as such become immortal.[60]

4. Ethics.

Zen is primarily and fundamentally a "practical discipline of life."[61] Indeed, from "the ethical point of view...Zen may be considered a discipline aiming at the reconstruction of character."[62] This rebuilding of one's character is necessary because of "the most fundamental of all errors and evils"—egoism. Egoism is "the source of all evils and sufferings," and it is Buddhism that "concentrates its entire ethical force upon the destruction of the ego-centric notions and desires."[63]

Basically, Zen's answer to man's egoism is that man should no longer be attached to Ignorance. The ignorance of Ignorance is the clinging "to the dualism of subject and object" as absolute reality and acting in accord with this belief. Man needs to detach himself from Ignorance (i.e., dualism), thus transcending all duality. When this is accomplished, one "is said to be in harmony and even one with Suchness."[64]

This goal can be met only through selfless labor and devotion to others, which requires the prior destruction of all selfish desires. Suzuki believes that the destruction of self-orientation brings enlightenment, hence the ability to love others as ourselves.[65] The realization of this goal is called *Nirvana*.

For a Zen monk, this process toward and within enlightenment involves "a great deal of manual labour, such as sweeping, cleaning, cooking, fuel-gathering, tilling the farm, or going about begging in the villages far and near." The central principle by which the Zen monk is to live his life "is not to waste but to make the best possible use of things as they are given us."[66] The ethical teaching of Zen Buddhism may be succinctly summarized in "The Teaching of the Seven Buddhas":

> Not to commit evils.
> But to do all that is good,
> And to keep one's thought pure—
> This is the teaching of all the Buddhas.[67]

5. History.

Since the world around us is viewed as illusory in Zen, it follows that the history of the world would be considered illusory as well. In the *Lankavatara Sutra* this principle is demonstrated in an answer to Mahamati: "Further, Mahamati, according to the teaching of the Tathagatas of the past, present, and future, all things are unborn. Why? Because they have no reality, being manifestations of Mind itself; and, Mahamati, as they are not born of being and non-being, they are unborn."[68]

This illusory existence of history, however, in no way rules out history's role as part of *maya* or Ignorance. Elsewhere Suzuki states that the "history of mankind in all its manifold aspects of existence is nothing but a grand drama visualizing the Buddhist doctrine of karmic immortality." As is true in many forms of Hindu pantheism, Zen Buddhism holds to the belief in *karma*. Briefly stated, the Buddhist concept of *karma* is: "Any act, good or evil, once committed and conceived, never vanishes like a bubble in water, but lives, potentially or actively as the case may be, in the world of minds and deeds." Suzuki likens the doctrine of *karma* to "the theory of evolution and heredity as working in our moral field."[69]

As everything else in the world of duality must be transcended, so must history. This is done in the following way:

> Events past are already past; therefore have no thoughts of them, and your mind is disconnected from the past. Thus past events are done away with. Present events are already here before you; then have no

attachment to them. Not to have attachment means not to rouse any feeling of hate or love. Your mind is then disconnected from the present, and the events before your eyes are done away with. When the past, present, and future are thus in no way taken in, they are completely done away with.... If you have a thoroughly clear perception as to the mind having no abiding place anywhere, this is known as having a thoroughly clear perception of one's own being. This very Mind...is the Buddha-Mind itself; it is called Emancipation-Mind, Enlightenment-Mind, the Unborn Mind, and Emptiness or Materiality and Ideality.[70]

Hence, the place of history in Zen is no-place.

6. Man's destiny.

The destiny of man, according to Zen, is the achievement of Nirvana—that is, "the annihilation of the notion of ego-substance and of all the desires that arise from this erroneous conception" and the practical expression of "universal love or sympathy (karuna) for all beings."[71] Nirvana is sometimes spoken of as possessing four attributes: Nirvana "is eternal because it is immaterial; it is blissful because it is above all sufferings; it is self-acting because it knows no compulsion; it is pure because it is not defiled by passion and error." In short, Nirvana is Dharmakaya—that is, God.[72] To achieve Nirvana is to realize one's essential oneness with the absolute One.

The achievement of Nirvana is not easy. It does not involve such things as asceticism, the knowledge of certain books or doctrines, or even meditation divorced from life. Instead, the realization of Nirvana begins and ends in life itself. "Salvation [i.e., the attainment of Nirvana] must be sought in the finite itself, there is nothing infinite apart from finite things; if you seek something transcendental, that will cut you off from this world of relativity, which is the same as the annihilation of yourself. You do not want salvation at the cost of your own existence." In other words, "Nirvana is to be sought in the midst of Samsara (birth-and-death)." No one can escape samsara for it is only one's subjective perception of life. If a person will but change his inner awareness, he will see that "the finite is the infinite, and vice versa." Reality is "absolutely one,"[73] and the awareness of this in man's inner life is Nirvana.

The road to Nirvana involves many things. However, the most fundamental aspect is ridding oneself of all dualistic thinking. The root of all such thinking is logic. Suzuki acknowledges that "we generally think that 'A is A' is absolute, and that the proposition 'A is not A' or 'A is B' is unthinkable." But such thinking is too imposing upon us; it has served only to keep us in bondage so that "we cannot attain to a thoroughgoing comprehension of the truth." We must therefore shed ourselves of the shackles of logic and anything else that may keep us from "our spiritual happiness." We must approach life from a new point of view, one in which "the world can be surveyed in its wholeness and life comprehended inwardly." In other words, we need to plunge ourselves "deep into the abyss of the 'Nameless' and take hold directly of the spirit as it is engaged in the business of creating the world." In this experience there "is no logic, no philosophizing; here is no twisting of facts to suit our artificial measures; here is no murdering of human nature in order to submit it to intellectual dissections; the one spirit stands face to face with the other spirit like two mirrors facing each other, and there is nothing to intervene between their mutual reflections."[74]

In order to help the Zen disciple beyond the logical interpretation of reality, the Zen masters created a whole approach to reality that includes cryptic, illogical sayings and questions as well as responses to questions. Each of these is called *koan*.

For example, a very familiar question is "If you have heard the sound of one hand [clapping], can you make me hear it too?"[75] A famous saying from Fudaishi graphically illustrates the irrationality that Zen calls one to embrace:

Empty-handed I go, and behold the spade is in my hands;
I walk on foot, and yet on the back of an ox I am riding;
When I pass over the bridge,
Lo, the water floweth not, but the bridge doth flow.[76]

For the attainment of Nirvana, one must transcend inwardly all those things that keep one from seeing life in its fullness. This step toward Nirvana is called *satori*. Satori is achieved through the *koan*. It is this process from the *koan* to *satori* and then to Nirvana that is the road to spiritual happiness, which is man's ultimate destiny.[77]

The essence of D. T. Suzuki's pantheism is that the world of particulars is both finite and infinite, relative and absolute, illusory and real. What one needs to do in order to see Reality in all its fullness is to free himself from logic, words, concepts, abstractions—in short, anything that keeps him from personally experiencing what is neither being nor non-being. When this occurs Nirvana is attained—one becomes one with the One.

IV. Some basic beliefs of pantheism.

Although there are other types of pantheism that could be discussed, these are sufficient to allow us to see some of the basic beliefs of a pantheistic world view.

A. God is impersonal and one.

A basic belief in any pantheistic system is that God or Reality is ultimately impersonal. Personality, consciousness, intellect and so forth are characteristic of lower-level manifestations of God, but they are not to be identified with God. The One is beyond these things. The One is really It, not He. Further, It is absolutely simple or one. It has no parts. Multiplicity may flow from it, but in and of itself It is simple, not multiple.

B. The world flows out of God.

Those pantheists who grant any kind of reality to the universe all agree that it was created *ex Deo* (out of God), not *ex nihilo* (out of nothing), as theism maintains. There is only one "Being" or Existent; everything else is an emanation or manifestation of It. Of course, absolute pantheists hold that the universe is only an illusion. For them, creation is neither *ex Deo* nor *ex nihilo*; creation does not really exist. Only God exists.

C. God is the world.

In contrast to theists, who view God as beyond the universe and separate from it, pantheists believe that God and the universe are one. For the pantheist, God is all and all is God. The theist grants some reality to the universe of multiplicity, while the pantheist does not. Those who deny the existence of the universe, of course, see no real relationship between God and the universe. But all pantheists agree that whatever reality exists, it is God.

D. Miracles are impossible.

Pantheism implies that miracles are impossible. If all is God and God is all, there is nothing that exists apart from God that could be interrupted or broken into, which is what the nature of a miracle requires. Furthermore, if, as pantheists agree, God is simple (has no parts) and is all there is, then God could not perform any miracles. A miracle implies that God is in some sense "outside" of the world into which He intervenes, but if God *is* identical to the world, then there can be no intervention from the outside. The only sense in which God "intervenes" in a pantheistic world is by a regular penetration of it in accordance with repeated higher spiritual laws, such as the law of *karma*.

There may be *supernormal* activities, but there are no *supernatural* interventions into the universe by a sovereign Creator, as theists claim. Therefore, the pantheistic world view rules out the possibility of miracles.

E. Man needs to unite with God.

Pantheists either believe that man as a distinct being is absolutely unreal (absolute pantheism), or they believe that he is real but far less real than God. Those who believe that man is unreal teach that man needs to overcome his ignorance and realize that he is God. Those who belive that man has some degree of reality teach a dualistic view of man, that is, man *is* a soul and *has* a body. The body holds man down and keeps him from uniting with God. Therefore, man must purge his body of all egoism so that he might release his soul and attain oneness with the absolute One. For all pantheists the goal or end of man is to unite with God.

F. Ethics are not absolute.

Pantheists usually strive to live morally good lives, and they encourage others to do so as well. Often their writings are filled with exhortations to be of good judgment, devoted to the truth, selflessly loving others and so forth. However, these exhortations usually apply to a lower level of spiritual attainment. Once a person has achieved union with God, "he has no further concern with moral laws."[78] In fact, nonattachment to and utter unconcern for one's actions and their results are often taught to be a necessary prerequisite to achieving oneness with God. Since God is beyond good and evil, man must also transcend good and evil in order to reach God. Although morality is often stressed, at best, it is to be only a temporary concern, and at worst, there is no absolute basis for morality at all. Indeed, since ultimate reality is beyond good and evil, good and evil as absolute categories do not really exist. The pantheist thus has no absolute basis for good or bad, right or wrong. Swami

Prabhavananda and Christopher Isherwood admit this when they say:

> ...every action, under certain circumstances and for certain people, may be a stepping-stone to spiritual growth—if it is done in the spirit of nonattachment. All good and all evil is *relative* to the individual point of growth.... *But, in the highest sense, there can be neither good nor evil*" (emphasis ours).[79]

Thus, for the pantheist, "ethical conduct is a means, not an end in itself." It is used only to help one attain to a certain level of "spiritual growth." Ultimately, however, no action is either good or evil, for ultimate reality is neither good nor evil. As Swami Prabhavananda puts it: "If we say 'I am good' or 'I am bad' we are only talking the language of maya [the world of illusion]. 'I am Brahman' is the only true statement regarding ourselves that any of us can make."[80]

Man's good is to become one with God. This is achieved when one overcomes his ignorance by realizing his godhood through union with God. This goal is sought through different techniques by different pantheists.

G.   History is illusory and/or cyclical.

Pantheists seldom talk about history except in modified forms of pantheism that have usually been influenced by Western theism (as with Hegel). They are usually not concerned with it, for either history does not exist or it is regarded as an aspect of the world of appearances or illusion, hence a thing to be transcended. History has no ultimate goal or end. Whenever it is granted a kind of reality, it is always (except in Hegel's pantheism) considered to be cyclical. Like the wheel of *samsara,* history forever repeats itself; there are no unique or final events of history. There is no millennium, utopia, or eschaton.

V.   An evaluation of pantheism.

A.   Some contributions of pantheism.

Like other world views we have discussed, pantheism contains many truths and perspectives from which we can learn. We shall briefly note four of them.

First, pantheists should be commended for their attempt to explain all of reality and not just parts of it. If the world is really a *uni*verse, then any world view must attempt to be all-embracing, not piecemeal. Pantheism does have a holistic view of things.

Second, any comprehensive view of God should include God's immanent (indwelling) presence and activity in the world. A God who will not or cannot relate to man will not receive worship from many, nor will many think He deserves it. Pantheism rightly stresses that God is in the world and is intimately related to it. He is not transcendently remote and totally removed from the universe.

Third, pantheism teaches that only God is absolute and necessary. Anything and everything else must be less than absolute and utterly dependent upon God. Unless God exists, nothing else could exist either. Pantheism is correct in its view that everything else must relate to the ultimate.

Finally, pantheism appropriately stresses that we should not ascribe limitations to God with our limited language about Him. If God is infinite (unlimited) and transcendent, then all limitations must be negated from terms that are applied to Him, otherwise verbal idolatry results. The Infinite cannot be encompassed by finite conceptions.

B. Some criticisms of pantheism.

Pantheism has occasioned numerous criticisms. We have summarized them into a basic list to show how this world view has been evaluated by others.

First, some claim that absolute pantheism is self-defeating, that is, philosophically it cuts its own throat. The absolute pantheist must say, "I am God." By their definition, God is the changeless Absolute. Man, however, must go through a process of change called enlightment, before he reaches this awareness that he is God. Therefore, how can man be God when man changes but God does not?

Some pantheists attempt to escape this criticism by allowing that man has some reality, whether it be emanational, modal, manifestational, or whatever. But if we are really only modes of God, then "why are we not conscious of being so? How did this metaphysical amnesia arise and (yet more seriously) come to pervade and dominate our whole experience?"[81] In fact, if we are being deceived about our consciousness of our own individual existence, how do we know that the pantheist is not also being deceived when he claims to be conscious of reality as ultimately one?

Second, if the world is really an illusion—if what we continually perceive to be real is not real—then how can we distinguish between reality and fantasy? Lao-tse puts the question well: "If, when I was asleep I was a man dreaming I was a butterfly, how do I know when I am awake I am not a butterfly dreaming I am a man?"[82] Other examples illustrate this dilemma: When we cross a busy street and see three lanes of traffic coming toward us, should we not even worry about it because it is merely an illusion? Indeed, should we even bother to look for cars when we cross the street, if we, the traffic and the street do not really exist? If pantheists actually lived out their pantheism consistently, would there by any pantheists left?

Third, many charge that pantheism fails to adequately handle the problem of evil. To pronounce evil as an illusion or as less than real is not only frustrating and hollow to those experiencing evil, but it also seems philosophically inadequate. If evil is not real, then what is the origin of the illusion? Why has man experienced it for so long, and why does it seem so real? Despite the pantheist's claims to the contrary, he, along with the rest of us, experiences pain, suffering, and eventually death. Even pantheists double over in pain when they get appendicitis. They also jump out of the way of an oncoming truck so as not to get hurt. As one put it, if the world is not real, then why is it when I sit upon a pin and it punctures my skin, that I dislike what I fancy I feel?

Fourth, if God is all and all is God, as pantheists maintain, then evil is an illusion and there are no absolute rights and wrongs. There are four possibilities regarding good and evil. (1) If God is all-good, then evil must exist apart from God. But this is impossible since God is all; nothing can exist apart from It. (2) If God is all-evil, then good must exist apart from God. This is not possible since God is all. (3) Perhaps God is both all-good and all-evil. But this is not possible, for it is self-contradictory to affirm that the same being is both all-good and all-evil at the same time. Further, almost all pantheists agree that God is beyond both good and evil, thus, God is neither good nor evil. (4) The last view is that good and evil are illusory, that they are not real categories. This is what most pantheists believe. But if evil were only an illusion, then ultimately there would be no such thing as good and evil thoughts or actions. Hence, what difference would it make whether we praise or curse, counsel or rape, love or murder someone? If there is no final moral difference between these actions, then absolute moral responsibilities do not exist. Cruelty and non-cruelty are ultimately the same. One critic gave this illustration:

> One day I was talking to a group of people in the digs of a young South African in Cambridge. Among others, there was present a young Indian who was of Sikh background but a Hindu by religion. He started to speak strongly against Christianity, but did not really understand the problems of his own beliefs. So I said, 'Am I not correct in saying that on the basis of your system, cruelty and non-cruelty are ultimately equal, that there is no intrinsic difference between them?' He agreed....the student in whose room we met, who had clearly understood the implications of what the Sikh had admitted, picked up his kettle of boiling water with which he was about to make tea, and stood with it steaming over the Indian's head. The man looked up and asked him what he was doing and he said, with a cold yet gentle finality, 'There is no difference between cruelty and non-cruelty.' Thereupon the Hindu walked out into the night.[83]

If pantheists are correct in saying that reality is not moral and that good and evil, right and wrong are inapplicable to what is, then "to be right is just as meaningless as to be wrong."[84] The foundation for morality is destroyed. Anything goes!

A fifth problem with pantheism is that its conception of God seems incoherent. To say that God is infinite and yet somehow shares Its being *(ex Deo)* with creation is to raise the question of how the finite can be infinite. Yet this is what absolute pantheists believe. Other pantheists consider the finite world as less than real, although it does exist. But if God is both infinite and finite and shares part of its being with creatures, then this means that an infinite being must become less than infinite. But how can the Infinite be finite, the Absolute be relative, and the Unchanging change?

A sixth criticism of pantheism has to do with the unknowability of God. The very claim that "God is unknowable in an intellectual way" seems to be either meaningless or self-defeating. For if the claim itself *cannot* be understood in an intellectual way, then it is a meaningless claim. If the claim *can* be understood in an intellectual way, then it is self-defeating, since it affirms that nothing can be understood about God in an intellectual way. In other words, the pantheist expects us to know intellectually that God cannot be understood in an intellectual way. But how can he make a positive affirmation about God that claims only negative affirmations can be made about God? Did not even Plotinus admit that negative knowledge presupposes some positive awareness? Otherwise, one would not know what to negate.

Seventh, and last, critics claim that the pantheist's denial that logic applies to reality is self-defeating. Denying that logic applies to reality involves making a logical statement about reality that no such logical statement about reality can be made. For example, when Suzuki says that to comprehend life we must abandon logic,[85] he uses logic in his affirmation and applies it to reality. Indeed, how can the Law of Noncontradiction (A cannot be both A and not-A) be denied without using it in the very denial? To deny that logic applies to reality, one must make a logical statement about realty. But if no such logical statements about reality can be made, how can the pantheist even explain his view? After all, pantheists do write books.

VI.   Summary and conclusion.

There are many varieties of pantheism, but all teach that God is all and all is God. Everything else that appears to have a distinct existence is only an emanation, manifestation, or mode of the one existent, God. God is viewed as ultimately impersonal; He is beyond consciousness, speech, knowledge, good and evil. Miracles are impossible, and history is either an illusion or cyclical. Man is really God, but he is initially ignorant of this fact. In order for him to be saved from his ignorance he must seek to overcome it by transcending the world of appearances toward union with God. This can be achieved in any number of ways. Asceticism, meditation, moral living and personal life experiences are means to this religious end. However, for many types of pantheism, they eventually will have to be set aside before complete union can be attained.

NOTES

1. "Mundaka," *The Upanishads: Breath of the Eternal,* trans. by Swami Prabhava-nanda and Frederick Manchester (New York: Mentor Books, 1957), p. 45.
2. Mary Long, "Visions of a New Faith," *Science Digest* 89 (Nov. 1981): 39.
3. Ibid., p. 42.
4. "My Sweet Lord," from the album entitled *All Things Must Pass,* by George Har-rison (Apple Records, Inc., New York).
5. For example, see "Revelation," by Sri Chinmoy, from the cover of the album *Birds of Fire,* by the Mahavishnu Orchestra (Columbia Records, New York).
6. See Donald F. Glut, *The Empire Strikes Back* (New York: Ballantine Books, 1980), p. 123.
7. Mark Satin points out that many of the New Age writers are "trying to work out a new, trans-material world view" which is heavily influenced by a pantheistic Eastern philosophy *(New Age Politics,* New York: Dell Publishing Co., 1979, pp. 94-99).
8. For helpful discussions on Parmenides and his philosophy, see John Mansley Robinson, *An Introduction to Early Greek Philosophy* (Boston: Houghton Mifflin Company, 1968), chapter 6; David J. Furley, "Parmenides of Elea," *The Ency-clopedia of Philosophy,* vol. 6, ed. in chief, Paul Edwards (New York: The Mac-millan Company and The Free Press, 1967), pp. 47-51; W. K. C. Guthrie, *The Greek Philosophers from Thales to Aristotle* (New York: Harper & Row, 1975), pp. 48-50; and Gordon H. Clark, *Thales to Dewey: A History of Philosophy* (Grand Rapids: Baker Book House, reprint ed., 1980), pp. 25-28.
9. See G. W. F. Hegel's *The Phenomenology of Mind.* For summaries and evalua-tions of his thinking, see the essay by Winfried Corduan, "Transcendentalism: Hegel" in *Biblical Errancy: An Analysis of Its Philosophical Roots,* ed. by Nor-man L. Geisler (Grand Rapids: Zondervan, 1981), chapter 4; and Gordon H. Clark, *Thales to Dewey,* pp. 440-467.
10. See Benedict de Spinoza, *Ethics.* For summaries and evaluations of his thinking from a theistic point of view, see H. P. Owen, *Concepts of Deity* (London: Mac-millan and Co., Ltd., 1971), pp. 65-75; Robert Flint, *Anti-Theistic Theories,* 3rd ed. (Edinburgh and London: Wm. Blackwood and Sons, 1885), pp. 358-375; and Alasdair MacIntyre, "Spinoza, Benedict (Baruch)," in *The Encyclopedia of Philosophy,* vol. 7, pp. 530-541.
11. See Sarvepail Radhakrishnan, *The Hindu View of Life* (London: Allen & Unwin, 1927) and *The Principle Upanishads* (London: Allen & Unwin, 1958). For summaries and evaluations of his form of pantheism, see Owen, *Concepts of Deity,* pp. 115-124.
12. Swami Prabhavananda, *The Spiritual Heritage of India* (Hollywood: Vedanta Press, 1963), p. 39.
13. Ibid., pp. 39, 40.
14. "Without fear of contradiction it [the Bhagavad-Gita] may be said to be the Holy Bible of India, though, unlike the Upanishads, it is not regarded as Sruti, or revealed scripture, but only as Smrti, or tradition elaborating the doctrines of the Upanishads" (Ibid., p. 95).

15. Alasdair MacIntyre claims that pantheism in both Greek and Indian thought grew out of "a systematic critique of polytheism." See his article "Pantheism" in *The Encyclopedia of Philosophy*, vol. 6, ed. in chief. Paul Edwards (New York: The MacMillan Company & The Free Press, 1967), p. 32.
16. "Kena," *The Upanishads*, pp. 30, 31.
17. Cited in Swami Prabhavananda's *The Spiritual Heritage of India*, p. 45.
18. "Katha," *The Upanishads*, p. 21.
19. "Svetasvatara," ibid., p. 119.
20. "Taittiriya," ibid., p. 54.
21. Swami Prabhavananda, *The Spiritual Heritage of India*, p. 55.
22. "Mundaka," *The Upanishads*, p. 47.
23. "Brihadaranyaka," ibid., p. 111.
24. *Bhagavad-Gita*, trans. by Swami Prabhavananda and Christopher Isherwood (Bergerfield: The New American Library, Inc., 1972), p. 41.
25. Ibid., p. 122.
26. Swami Prabhavananda, *The Spiritual Heritage of India*, pp. 98, 123-129.
27. Charles Corwin, *East to Eden? Religion and the Dynamics of Social Change* (Grand Rapids: Wm. B. Eerdmans, 1972), p. 22.
28. Huston Smith, *The Religions of Man* (New York: Harper & Row, 1958), p. 76.
29. Swami Prabhavananda, *The Spiritual Heritage of India*, p. 70.
30. Ibid., pp. 70, 71.
31. Ibid., p. 71.
32. Ibid.
33. Ibid., p. 27.
34. Ibid., p. 71.

35. For more detail on the life and thinking of Plotinus than can be presented here, see *The Cambridge History of Later Greek and Early Medieval Philosophy*, ed. by A. H. Armstrong (Cambridge: Cambridge Univ. Press, 1967, reprint ed., 1980), pp. 195-268; and Ralph M. McInerny's *A History of Western Philosophy* (Notre Dame: University of Notre Dame Press, 1963), pp. 341-357.
36. Plotinus, *Plotinus: The Six Enneads*, trans. by Stephen MacKenna and B. S. Page, Great Books of the Western World, ed. in chief, Robert Maynard Hutchins (Chicago: Wm. Benton, 1952), VI, 8, 9. All references hereafter from Plotinus are from this work and are cited in the body of the chapter.
37. McInerny, *A History of Western Philosophy*, p. 343.
38. C. G. Jung, "Forward," in *An Introduction to Zen Buddhism*, D. T. Suzuki (New York: Grove Press, Inc., 1964), p. 9.
39. Ernst Benz, "Buddhist Influence Outside Asia," in *Buddhism in the Modern World*, ed. by Heinrich Bumoulin (New York: Macmillan Publishing Co., Inc., London: Collier Macmillan Publishers, 1976), p. 317.
40. Alan Watts is probably the best-known disciple and propagator of Suzuki's brand of pantheism. Some of Watts' works are *Beyond Theology* (New York: Vintage Books, 1964); *The Essence of Alan Watts* (Milbrae, Calif.: Celestial Arts, 1977); *The Spirit of Zen* (New York: Grove Press, Inc., 1958); and *The Way of Zen* (New York: Vintage Books, 1957). For an evaluation of Alan Watts' view, see David K. Clark, *The Pantheism of Alan Watts* (Downers Grove: Inter-Varsity Press, 1978).
41. D. T. Suzuki, *An Introduction to Zen Buddhism*, p. 38.
42. Ibid., pp. 46, 38.
43. Ibid., p. 39.
44. Ibid., p. 41.
45. Ibid., p. 45.

46. Ibid., p. 85.
47. Ibid., p. 75.
48. Ibid., pp. 45, 132.
49. Ibid., p. 132.
50. D. T. Suzuki, *Zen Buddhism*, ed. by William Barrett (Garden City: Doubleday Anchor Books, 1956), p. 113.
51. D. T. Suzuki, *Manual of Zen Buddhism*, (New York: Grove Press, Inc., 1960), p. 112.
52. Suzuki, *Zen Buddhism*, p. 88.
53. Suzuki, *Manual*, p. 112.
54. D. T. Suzuki, *Outlines of Mahayana Buddhism* (New York: Schocken Books, 1963), pp. 140, 141.
55. Suzuki, *Manual*, p. 51.
56. Suzuki, *Outlines*, pp. 219, 220.
57. Ibid., pp. 101-102.
58. Ibid., pp. 46-47.
59. Ibid., p. 149.
60. Ibid., p. 47.
61. Suzuki, *An Introduction*, p. 37.
62. Suzuki, *Zen Buddhism*, p. 16.
63. Suzuki, *Outlines*, p. 124.
64. Ibid., pp. 146, 124, 122.
65. Ibid., pp. 52-55.
66. Suzuki, *An Introduction*, pp. 118, 121.
67. Suzuki, *Manual*, p. 15.
68. Ibid., p. 53.
69. Suzuki, *Outlines*, pp. 207, 183, 200.
70. Suzuki, *Zen Buddhism*, pp. 196, 197.
71. Suzuki, *Outlines*, pp. 50, 51.
72. Ibid., p. 348; cf. p. 399.
73. Suzuki, *Zen Buddhism*, pp. 14, 15.
74. Suzuki, *An Introduction*, pp. 58, 59, 61.
75. Ibid., p. 59.
76. Ibid., p. 58.
77. Ibid., p. 60.
78. Swami Prabhavananda, *The Spiritual Heritage of India*, p. 65.
79. Swami Prabhavananda and Christopher Isherwood, "Appendix II: The Gita and War," in *Bhagavad-Gita*, p. 140.
80. Swami Prabhavananda, *The Spiritual Heritage of India*, ibid., p. 293.
81. H. P. Owen, *Concepts of Deity*, p. 72.
82. Quoted in Os Guiness, *The Dust of Death* (Downers Grove: Inter-Varsity Press, 1973), p. 214.
83. Francis Schaeffer, *The God Who Is There* (Downers Grove: Inter-Varsity Press, 1968), p. 101.
84. Francis Schaeffer, *He Is There and He Is Not Silent* (Wheaton: Tyndale House, 1972), p. 25.
85. Suzuki, *An Introduction to Zen Buddhism*, p. 58.

5

Panentheism: A World In God

I. Introduction.

If you don't look closely at the word "panentheism" it looks like "pantheism," but they are different world views. Pantheism literally means all (pan) is God (theism). But pan-en-theism means all-in-

99

God. Panentheism also has other names, such as process theology (since it views God as a changing being), bipolar or dipolar theism (since it believes that God has two poles), organism (since it views all that actually is as a gigantic organism), and neo-classical theism (because it believes that God is finite and temporal, in contrast to classical theism).

The following chart summarizes the differences between classical theism (see Chapter 2) and panentheism:

THEISM

God is: creator
        (creation *ex nihilo*—from nothing)
        sovereign over world
        independent of world
        unchanging
        absolutely perfect
        monopolar (only actual)
        infinite

PANENTHEISM

God is: director
        (creation *ex materia*—from pre-existing stuff)
        working with world
        dependent on world
        changing
        growing more perfect
        bipolar (actual and potential)
        finite in His actual pole, infinite in His potential pole

Rather than viewing God as the infinite, unchanging, sovereign creator of the world, panentheists think of God as a finite, changing director of world affairs who works in cooperation with the world in order to achieve greater perfection in His nature.

Another distinction will be helpful. Theists think of God's relationship to the world as that of a painter to his painting. The painter exists independently of the painting. Yet his mind is expressed in the painting because he brought it into existence.

By contrast, the panentheist views God's relationship to the world in the same way that a mind is related to a body. Indeed, they believe that God's "body" (the world) is one pole and His "mind" (what is beyond the world) is the other pole. However, like some modern thinkers who believe that the mind is dependent on the brain, they believe that God is dependent on the world. Yet there is also a sense in which the world is dependent on God. There is, in fact, a mutual dependence.

II.   A typology of panentheism.

All panentheists agree that God has two poles, an actual pole (the world) and a potential pole (beyond the world). All agree that God is changing, finite, and temporal in His actual pole. And all agree that His potential pole is unchanging and eternal.

Panentheists differ, however, over whether God in His actual pole is one actual entity (event) or a society of actual entities. Alfred North Whitehead holds the former view, and Charles Hartshorne holds the latter.

Most other differences are primarily methodological. Whitehead's approach is more empirical (based on experience or observation), and Hartshorne's is more rational (based on reason). Hence, Whitehead has a kind of teleological argument for God, whereas Hartshorne is famous for his ontological argument.

Some panentheists, such as John Cobb, reject the disjunction between the two poles in God. He claims that God acts as a unity, not simply in one pole or the other. But all panentheists agree that God has two poles, which are sometimes called His "primordial nature" and His "consequent nature." The characteristics of these natures are shown in this diagram:

Primordial Nature	**Consequent Nature**
potential pole	actual pole
eternal	temporal
absolute	relative
unchanging	changing
imperishable	perishable
unlimited	limited
conceptual	physical
abstract	concrete
necessary	contingent
eternal objects	actual entities
unconscious drive	conscious realization

These characteristics will be discussed more as we continue.

III.   Some representatives of panentheism.

There are many forerunners of a process view of God, the view that God is changing. Among the Greek views was Plato's (c. 400 B.C.) Demiurgos, who eternally struggled with the Chaos to form it into the Cosmos. This provides the dualistic background for what becomes two "poles" in God. Even before this, Heraclitus' (c. 500 B.C.) flux philosophy was similar to the process idea. He asserted that the world is a constantly changing process.

In the modern world, Hegel's (d. 1831) progressive unfolding of God in the world process is another significant step toward panentheism. In addition to this, the cosmic evolutionism of Herbert Spencer (d. 1903) views the whole universe as an unfolding and developing process. Immediately following this view, Henri Bergson proposed a creative evolution (1907) of a Life Force *(elán vital)* that drives evolution forward in "leaps." Later he identified this Force with God (1935). Even before this, Samuel Alexander's *Space, Time and Deity* (1920) pioneered a process view of God's relationship to the temporal universe.

A.   Alfred North Whitehead.

The formal beginning of panentheism is considered to be in the writings of Alfred N. Whitehead, the famous English philosopher and mathematician. His view is presented in his classic *Process and Reality* (1929), followed by *Adventures of Ideas* (1933) and *Modes of Thought* (1938). We will look first at Whitehead's view of God.

1.   God.

God is bipolar. His actual pole is the universe, the cosmos. This pole is in constant change. God's potential pole is beyond the actual world; it is the world of eternal and unchanging potential.

Whitehead's view of God can be clarified by contrasting it with other views. He outlines three main concepts of God:

1. The Eastern Asiatic concept of an impersonal order to which the world conforms. This order is the self-ordering of the world; it is not the world obeying an imposed rule. The concept expresses the extreme doctrine of immanence.

2. The Semitic concept of a definite personal individual entity, whose existence is the one ultimate metaphysical fact, absolute and un-

derivative, and who decreed and ordered the derivative existence which we call the actual world.

3. The Pantheistic concept of an entity to be described in the terms of the Semitic concept, except that the actual world is a phase within the complete fact which is this ultimate individual entity. The actual world, conceived apart from God, is unreal. Its only reality is God's reality. The actual world has the reality of being a partial description of what God is. But in itself it is merely a certain mutuality of "appearance," which is a phase of the being of God. This is the extreme doctrine of monism.[1]

Whitehead rejects all these views. He says, "for most Christian Churches, the simple Semitic doctrine is now a heresy, both by reason of the modification of personal unity and also by the insistence of immanence."[2] It is the radical transcendence (otherness) of the "Semitic" God to which Whitehead objects. Furthermore, "there is no entity, not even God, 'which requires nothing but itself in order to exist.'" That is, God is dependent on the world and the world is dependent on God. "Apart from God, there would be no actual world; and apart from the actual world with its creativity, there would be no rational explanation of the ideal vision which constitutes God."[3]

According to Whitehead, God is actually limited. In fact, "to be an actual thing is to be limited." God cannot be infinite in His actual pole. "If He were, He would be evil as well as good,"[4] because the universe, the all, contains evil in it. Neither is God an independent, self-existing being, for "there is no entity, not even God, 'which requires nothing but itself in order to exist.'"[5] All beings are dependent beings, including God.

Whereas the "Semitic" God is too transcendent, the "pantheistic" God is too immanent. God is not beyond the world nor is He identical with it. God is in the world. To reduce God to an impersonal Force, as the "Asiatic" concept does, is to demean God's religious significance. God is personal. He is intimately related to the world. "God is that function in the world by reason of which our purposes are directed to ends which in our own consciousness are impartial as to our own interests." Further, God is the actual realization (in the world) of the ideal world. "The kingdom of heaven is God."[6]

Why must there be such a God in the world? Because "the order of the world is no accident. There is nothing actual which could be

103

actual without some measure of order. . . . this creativity and these forms are together impotent to achieve actuality apart from the completed ideal harmony, which is God."[7] God functions as the ground for creativity necessary for the attainment of value in the world. "God, as conditioning the creativity with his harmony of apprehension, issues into the mental creature as moral judgment according to a perfection of ideals." Thus, "the purpose of God in the attainment of value is in a sense a creative purpose. Apart from God, the remaining formative elements would fail in their functions."[8]

2. The world.

God and the world are not actually different. God *is* the order (and value) in the actual world. The world is God's consequent nature. It is the sum total of all actual entities (events) as ordered by God. But the world is in process. It is constantly changing. Hence, God in His consequent (actual) nature is also constantly in flux.

The world is pluralistic. It is made up of many "actual entities," which Whitehead defines as "final facts," "drops of experience," or "actual occasions." In other words, the world is an atomistic series of events. "Actuality is incurably atomic."[9]

The world is also in process:

It is fundamental to the metaphysical doctrine of the philosophy of organism, that the notion of an actual entity as the unchanging subject of change is completely abandoned.

The ancient doctrine that "no one crosses the same river twice" is extended. No thinker thinks twice; and, to put the matter more generally, no subject experiences twice. This is what Locke ought to have meant by his doctrine of time as a "perpetual perishing."[10]

Thus, the doctrine "that 'all things flow' is the first vague generalization, which the unsystematized, barely analysed, intuition of men has produced." Hence, "the flux of things is one ultimate generalization around which we must weave our philosophical system."[11] There are no unchanging beings. "The simple notion of an enduring substance, either essentially or accidentally . . . proves itself mistaken."[12] There is no concrete being; all is becoming. "It belongs to the nature of every 'being' that it is a potential for every becoming." "There is a becoming of continuity, but no continuity of becoming."[13]

The world is ordered. Despite the atomic distinctness and continual change in the universe, there is order. This order is given by God. In His primordial (potential) nature God gives order to all eternal objects (forms), and the consequent (actual) nature of "God is the physical prehension by God of the actualities of the evolving universe."[14]

3. Creation.

The universe is eternal. God "does not create eternal objects; for his nature requires them in the same degree that they require him." Thus, God "is not *before* all creation, but *with* all creation."[15] He did not bring the universe into existence; He merely directs its ongoing progress.

As one process theologian put it, creation from nothing is too coercive.

> ...the temptation to interpret God's role in creation by means of coercive power is extremely great. If the entire created order is dependent for its existence upon His will, then it must be subject to His full control...Insofar as God controls the world, He is responsible for evil: directly in terms of the natural order, and indirectly in the case of man.[16]

God is more of a cosmic persuader who lures the actual out of potential.

In one sense, then, the origin or "creation" of the universe is *ex materia* (out of pre-existing stuff). But the eternal "stuff" is the realm of eternal forms or potentials which are there available for God to order and to urge them into the ongoing world process as various aspects of actual entities. But since the realm of eternal objects is God's primordial nature, the movement of creation is also *ex Deo*, that is, out of God's potential pole and into His actual pole (the world). Reality moves from the unconscious to the conscious, from potential to actual, from abstract to concrete, from forms to facts.

What is it that prompts this movement? What actualizes it? The answer is *creativity*. "'Creativity' is the principle of *novelty*." Creativity introduces novelty into the actual world. "The 'creative advance' is the application of this ultimate principle of creativity to each novel situation which it originates." Even God is grounded in creativity. "Every actual entity, including God, is a creature transcended by the creativity which it qualifies." Hence, "all actual entities share with

God this character of self-causation."[17]

In brief, there is a self-caused movement in God from His potential pole to His actual pole. God is a self-caused "being" who is constantly becoming. Thus, the process of creation is an eternal ongoing process of God's self-realization.

4. Evil.

God's self-realization is never perfect nor is it totally incomplete. "There is no reason ... to conceive the actual world as purely orderly, or as purely chaotic." In fact, "the immanence of God gives reason for the belief that pure chaos is intrinsically impossible."[18] God is doing all He can to achieve the most possible out of every moment in world history. "The image under which this operative growth of God's nature is best conceived, is that of a tender care that nothing be lost."[19] Evil is what is incompatible with these divine efforts at any given moment. Since God does not force the world, but only persuades it, He cannot destroy evil. He must simply work with it and do the best He can to overcome it. In short,

> divine persuasion responds to the problem of evil radically, simply denying that God exercises full control over the world. Plato sought to express this by saying that God does the best job He can in trying to persuade a recalcitrant matter to receive the impress of the divine forms....[20]

According to Whitehead, "the nature of evil is that the character of things are mutually obstructive."[21] Thus, whatever a finite God cannot persuade to fit into the overall unity of the actual world is evil. Evil is incompatibility. It is incongruence. Evil is like the leftover pieces of glass that did not fit into the stained glass window. We must remember, however, that the "picture" (order) of the world changes every moment, and what does not fit one moment may fit the next.

5. History and goal.

There is an ongoing evolutionary process in the universe. God is achieving more and more value. It is being stored in His consequent nature, which, as it becomes enriched, is called God's "superjective nature." However, "neither God, nor the world, reaches static completion,"[22] Evil is recalcitrant (cannot be totally controlled), and *no final victory* over it is possible. Hence, Whitehead concludes,

"In our cosmological construction we are, therefore left with the final opposites, joy and sorrow, good and evil, disjunction and conjunction—that is to say, the many in one—flux and permanence, greatness and triviality, freedom and necessity, God and the World."[23]

Since God is neither omniscient nor omnipotent, even God does not know the eventual result of the world process. For "during that process God, as it were, has to wait with baited breath until the decision is made, not simply to find out what the decision was, but perhaps even to have the situation clarified by virtue of the decision of that concrete occasion."[24]

6. Man.

Man is a personal being with his own free choice. Each person has his own "subjective aims." That is, he determines ends; he has final causality. God gives overall aim to the world, and He provides an initial subjective aim or thrust for all things. That is, "God furnishes the initial direction, but the creature is responsible for its own actualization."[25]

The mind-body relation for Whitehead

is very different from the Scholastic view of St. Thomas Aquinas, of the mind as informing the body. The living body is a coordination of high-grade actual occasions; but in a living body of a low type the occasions are much nearer to a democracy.[26]

That is to say, each person in the universe (God included) is a society of actual entities that constantly change. There is no changeless "I" that endures. "The living body is a coordination of high-grade actual occasions." Thus, "the brain is coordinated so that a peculiar richness of inheritance is enjoyed now by this and now by that part; and thus there is produced the presiding personality at that moment in the body."[27]

In short, an individual's unity is not found in any unchanging essence or being. It is self-caused becoming. Whitehead wrote:

I find myself as essentially a unity of emotions, enjoyments, hopes, fears, regrets, valuations of alternatives, decisions—all of them subjective reactions to the environment as active in my nature. My unity—which is Descartes' "I am"—is my process of shaping this welter of material into a consistent pattern of feelings. I shape the activities of the environment into a new creation, which is myself at this moment; and yet, as being myself, it is a continuation of the antecedent world.[28]

As with the broader world, there is no continuity in man's becoming; there is only becoming in man's continuity. The unity of man is in his changing history, not in any unchanging identity. So "both mind and body refer to their life-history of separate concrete occasions."[29]

Personal immortality was not an essential part of Whitehead's view. He saw no scientific evidence for it, but neither did he oppose it. He simply noted that

at present it is generally held that a purely spiritual being is necessarily immortal. The doctrine here developed gives no warrant for such a belief. It is entirely neutral on the question of immortality, or on the existence of purely spiritual beings other than God. There is no reason why such a question should not be decided on more special evidence, religious or otherwise, provided that it is trustworthy.[30]

7. Ethics and values.

There are no absolute values. Value is changing and subjective. "There are many species of subjective forms, such as emotions, valuations, purposes, adversions, aversions, consciousness, etc."[31] God is the measure of all value in the world. But God Himself is undergoing constant change, thus, there is no absolute, unchanging standard of value in the universe. "All value is inherent in actuality itself." But all actuality is changing.

"There is no such thing as bare value." Value is specific and concrete, but only temporarily. "The purpose of God in the attainment of value is in a sense a creative purpose." And "apart from God, the remaining formative elements would fail in their purpose." So "the actual world is the outcome of the aesthetic order [of value], and the aesthetic is derived from the immanence of God."[32]

According to Whitehead, the problem with the theistic Christian ethic is that it looks to an end of the world. "The result was that with passionate earnestness they gave free reign to their absolute ethical intuitions respecting ideal possibilities without a thought of the preservation of society."[33]

For Whitehead, good and evil "solely concern inter-relations within the real world. The real world is good when it is beautiful."[34]

Goodness always comes in degrees of more or less in the real world, just as something can be more or less beautiful than something else. But nothing can be *most* beautiful or *most* perfect. "Morality consists in the aim at the ideal. . . . Thus stagnation is the deadly foe of morality."[35] In brief, there is in reality neither an absolute standard nor a final attainment of total goodness. There is at best, for both God and man, only a relative achievement of more good.

B. Charles Hartshorne.

Close to Whitehead in importance and influence in promoting panentheism is Charles Hartshorne. His persistency in developing and defending a panentheistic world view has led some to give him the title, "father of process theology."[36] As with Whitehead, we will begin with Hartshorne's understanding of God.

1. God.

Hartshorne takes issue with the view of God accepted by Augustine, Anselm and Aquinas. He denies that God is monopolar. Rather he, like Whitehead, understands God to be dipolar or bipolar. As Hartshorne expresses it, God is not

> merely infinite or merely finite, merely absolute or merely relative, merely cause or merely effect, merely agent or merely patient, merely actual or merely potential, *but in all cases both,* each in suitable respects or aspects of his living reality, and in such a manner as to make him unsurpassable by another. He is even both joy and sorrow, both happiness and sympathetic participation in our grief.[37]

God is infinite, eternal, independent and absolute in His abstract or primordial pole, while in His concrete or consequent pole He is finite, temporal, dependent and relative. God is both sets of the metaphysical contraries at the same time but not in the same pole.[38]

The concrete pole is how God is existing at any given moment in His changing experience. The abstract pole is that which is common and constant in God's character given any possible or actual world. For example, when a specific person suffers pain, God also experiences that pain in His own divine life. This is God as *concretely* existing. God considered *abstractly* is the divine being that cannot fail to experience whatever in the world does or does not exist. The abstract pole is God as understood independent of any particular thing. But the abstract pole cannot be understood apart from considering God as concretely experiencing the experiences of others. Put another way, God as concrete is God as He actually is now. God as abstract is God as He must always be. Thus, the divine abstract pole is an abstraction from the divine concrete pole.[39] This is a very important premise, for from it Hartshorne concludes that all of reality is characterized by becoming, not being; by relativity, not absoluteness; by contingency, not necessity. Only reality, even God, considered apart from what it actually is in each moment may be held to be being, absolute and necessary.

In order to better understand this process view of God we will briefly discuss some of the divine attributes. First, we will consider the divine attribute of relative perfection. According to Hartshorne, perfection means that "God cannot conceivably be surpassed or equaled by any other individual, but He can surpass Himself, and thus His actual state is not the greatest possible state."[40] He has no possible rival. However, He is perpetually surpassing Himself at every moment, actualizing more and more potentialities, enriching Himself with more value, forever reaching toward a more complete perfection which can never be fully realized.[42] In Hartshorne's words, "only God can surpass God, but this he perpetually does by ideally absorbing the riches of creation into himself."[43]

Another divine attribute is becoming-being. Hartshorne maintains that "becoming is not a special mode of reality, rather it is its overall character." In fact, "becoming is reality itself." And since the past has already become and the future has not yet become, only the present moment can become (that is, be in the process of being created). Consequently, when one speaks of reality he means "as of now."[44] In "human experiences" these nows "normally" occur "some 10-20 per second."[45] Applied on a cosmic scale, this means that every being that exists, especially God, is in great flux, being created anew each moment. With every new event there are new atoms, new cells, new plants, new animals, new people—even a new God. As Hartshorne says, "new events mean, in a sense, a new God, as a man is a new man every moment."[46] On the other hand, God is also *being* in His abstract pole. "Being" denotes what is common among the succession of events.[47] Of course, one thing that is common among changing entities is change itself. Thus God may be said to be "change-as-such" in his abstract pole while in His concrete pole He is actually changing.

110

The last attribute dealt with here is divine love. This is the attribute that Hartshorne believes comprehensively sums up the idea of God. Love is the "realization in oneself of the desires and experiences of others, so that one who loves can in so far inflict suffering only by undergoing this suffering himself, willingly and fully." Human beings love inadequately, for they cannot fully know or enter into another's experiences and desires. God, however, can adequately love all, for He feels all desires for what they are and experiences all experiences as they are. Only He "unwaveringly understands and tries to help" His creatures; only He "takes unto himself the varying joys and sorrows of all others"; only His happiness is eminently capable of alteration as a consequence.[48] Because God loves all fully and cares about all differences, and because He sympathetically responds to them accordingly, He is the perfect lover.[49]

Hartshorne maintains that God is personal. But, contrary to Whitehead, he does not take God to be an actual entity. Rather, Hartshorne understands God to be "an enduring society of actual entities."[50] But unlike other societies God endures no matter what world exists and regardless of the circumstances in any given world. Further, the divine society includes all nondivine societies.[51] Like other individuals, God is partially new each moment. Hence, God in His present concrete state is not identical to Himself in His previous concrete states. The God one may serve now is not the God one may have served yesterday nor the one he may serve tomorrow.[52]

2. The world.

In their concreteness God and the world are one. It is in this sense that Hartshorne says, "God is the wholeness of the world."[53] However, this does not mean that God is identical to the world, as in pantheism. God literally permeates the world in His concrete pole but without destroying the individuality of His creatures. God accomplishes this by including within Himself the "totality of all ordinary causes and effects" without becoming identical to them. Thus, the world is in God but He is distinguishable though not separable from the world.[54]

An analogy Hartshorne is fond of using to explain God's relationship to the world is the mind-body analogy. He maintains that the human body "is really a 'world' of individuals, and a mind...is to that body something like an indwelling God." Applying this analogy to God, Hartshorne draws the following conclusions concerning God's relationship to the world: God is related to the world as the human mind is related to the human body. As the human mind controls the body, God has direct control over His world-body. In a similar way, God influences the living members of His cosmic body, and they influence Him. The dissimilarity between the human mind-body relationship and the divine mind-body relationship is that God's awareness of what occurs in His world-body is always vivid, distinct and all-encompassing, while a human's awareness of what occurs in his own body is generally indistinct and always partial or fragmentary.[55]

3. Creation.

Hartshorne holds that the proposition "something exists" is a necessary truth and that the proposition "nothing exists" is necessarily false or meaningless. Absolute nothingness could never be experienced; hence, it must be a meaningless idea. Since "nothing exists" is necessarily false, "and since the contradictory of an impossible statement is necessary," it follows that "something exists" is necessarily true.[56] Hence, it is absolutely necessary that something must exist. And what must exist is God and some world or other.[57] Hartshorne believes in an infinity of past actual worlds or world states, thus the present world is not eternal. However, since some world or other must exist, then God must eternally coexist with some world no matter how short or how long it remains in existence.

Hartshorne rejects the traditional theistic view of creation *ex nihilo* (out of nothing). Instead, he maintains that God creates the world *ex materia*. By this he means that God makes "new actualities" from "past events."[58] Indeed, God is not a creator in the sense of bringing the world into existence, but rather the cosmic shaper and orderer of the world "out of an earlier world and its potentialities for transformation." This is how God has created or transformed all worlds from the infinite past and how He will continue to work in the infinite future.[59] But God is not the sole "creator," for the materials from which God creates "are prior acts of self-creation" which were performed by either Himself or His creatures.[60] And since the world is God's body, God may be viewed as the co-creator of Himself in His concrete pole.[61] Therefore, as God transforms the world each moment, He also transforms

Himself into "a new total being, though not a totally new being."[62] In summary, when God transforms the world with its other creatures, He partially creates Himself, and others partially create Him. Hartshorne could not be clearer on this:

> God in His concrete de facto state is in one sense simply self-made, like every creature spontaneously springing into being as something more than any causal antecedents could definitely imply. In another sense, or causally speaking, God, in his latest concrete state, is jointly "made" or produced by God and the world in the prior states of each. We are not simply co-creators, with God, of the world, but in last analysis co-creators, with him, of himself.[63]

4. Man.

Man as a person is a linear society of actual occasions which includes a complex bodily society of actual entities. A person cannot exist bodiless, and no body is without some degree of personality. Actual occasions or experiential events make up bodies, and persons "have *perceptions as well as memories.*" Further, all actual occasions have will and freedom (or self-creativity). Thus, what distinguishes one's personhood or self from one's body are not such things as subjectivity, will, or intellect, but the "persistence of certain defining characteristics" which are "endowed with a *preeminent linear society* or 'soul.'" Consequently, man has no enduring "I" or self to which changes occur. Instead, the only thing about man that does not change is his past series of experiences. Each new moment every human being experiences new experiences; consequently, he becomes a new self or a new whole each moment, with his past experiences serving as mere components of his new ones.[64]

Hartshorne sees little difference between man and his surroundings. He writes, "Apart from the mere test of successful interbreeding, the multiform use of tools, above all, of that kind of tool known as a symbol, is the dividing line between *Homo sapiens* and all surviving animal forms." Elsewhere he says: "Man's very fate depends in part upon his adequate recognition of his lowly status as only a *little* more than an unconscious (although complicated) bit of causal driftwood, but also of the preciousness and glory of that slight surplus."[65]

Man is also free. He is a self-determined being. Even though his freedom is significant, the degree to which he is free is very small.[66]

By his freedom man is to serve God. Indeed, this is the "inclusive aim" of all creatures. The best way to contribute to God is to enrich His happiness by creating value that He can prehend or absorb, then in turn available for creatures to use.[67]

5. Man's destiny.

The end of man is physical death. There is no afterlife in a literal heaven or a literal hell. In fact, "the theory of heaven and hell is in good part a colossal error and one of the most dangerous that ever occurred to the human mind." On the other hand, "death is not destruction of an individual's reality." Death only says to us: "More than you already have been you will not be. For instance, the virtues you have failed to acquire, you will now never acquire. It is too late. You had your chance." True immortality is everlasting fame before God. And this is to "live" forever as value prehended in the cosmic Memory.[68] In short, there is no individual immortality; one survives only in God's memory.

6. Evil.

According to Hartshorne, evil or tragedy is rooted in freedom or creativity. Since creativity is reality itself, evil is "necessarily pervasive." "All free creatures are inevitably more or less dangerous to other creatures, and the most free creatures are the most dangerous."[69] But along with the potential abuse of freedom comes the potential opportunities of freedom. Therefore, "the ideal cannot be to eliminate risk of evil once for all, since this would eliminate novel opportunities for good as well, and would call an arbitrary halt to further realization of the inexhaustible possibilities of good."[70] With universal freedom comes universal risk. God could guarantee no more or no less. Hence:

> Freud was right in saying "the world is not a Kindergarten." But it could not be. Or if it could be or were, the opportunities in such a world must be as trivial as the risks. So we should accept our risk-full world as essentially good and Providential. It is for us to minimize, by our own wisdom, energy, courage, and good will, the most destructive risks, not for us to call upon God to upset death by miracle so that the neglected children of men may have a second and better chance.[71]

It follows that God not only *would* not but also *could* not guarantee the triumph of good over evil. For if "every new phase of the world involves new possibilities of evil inherent in the new cases

114

of creative freedom, each incapable of complete control by any antecedent conditions or any conceivable power other than the actuality in question," then not even God could guarantee that evil will be defeated, stopped, or even destroyed. Besides, evil plays an essential role in the novelty of creation—a role that God can broadly limit but not absolutely control.[72]

7. History and goal.

According to Hartshorne, three basic forces move history onward —God, His creatures and Darwinian evolution. As co-creators, God and his creatures produce new events from past events and in this way create history. The other factor in history is evolution. Everything that exists is subject to the evolutionary "process of ordered chance." Although God has placed some limits on the evolutionary process, He cannot fully control it. The abundance of free entities in the world, which "necessarily involves an aspect of chance or randomness," makes total control impossible, for God could not control them without destroying them. Instead, God sets limits beyond which the randomness cannot go.[73]

As far as the future is concerned, no one knows it. Not even God can know the future in detail, for the details of the future are not there to be known. The future is unsettled and indeterminate since future events "depend partly upon decisions of various persons, decisions not yet made." Hence, God knows "events only when and after they have happened; while future events are, for him, as for us, really future, that is, awaiting their full definition of reality."[74]

Some things can be known in outline about the future. For example, it can be known that God will unfailingly become more perfect. It can also be known that there can be no final end or goal to which all history tends. Hartshorne calls this idea of such an end "petty," a "pseudo concept," an idea with "no very definite meaning, unless an absurd one."[75] In the process view, the end of all history would be the end of God, since He contains the universe in Himself. But, of course, God cannot cease to exist. Hence, an end to all history is impossible.

8. Ethics and aesthetics.

Hartshorne defines ethics as "the *generalization of instinctive concern*, which in turn transcends the immediate state of the self and even the long-run career of the self, and embraces the on-going

115

communal process of life as such." By this he means that "one's present self has duties to one's future self as truly as it has duties to other human beings."[76] Each person, to be truly ethical, should love himself. One must also, as far as is possible, seek to meet his own needs and the needs of others, including those of nature and God.[77]

Aesthetics is important in that it provides the basis of ethics. It does this by informing us what is "good." For "the only good that is intrinsically good, good in itself, is good experience, and the criteria for this are aesthetic. Harmony and intensity come close to summing it up." On this foundation some evils are boredom, a lack of zest and intensity, and discord. What is considred good is the "intensity and beauty of experience, arising not only from visual or auditory stimuli as in painting or music, but in experience of whatever sort." In brief, then, *to be ethical is to seek aesthetic optimization of experience for the community.*"[78]

From this view of ethics it follows that an ethically good act is one that "contributes to harmony and intensity of experience both in agent and in spectators." Thus, because "genuine kindness produces beauty, directly in itself, and indirectly in many ways," to act kindly is to produce good. On the other hand, since "cruelty produces ugliness in the experiences of many," to act cruelly is to produce evil.[79]

C. Schubert M. Ogden.

Both Whitehead and Hartshorne are primarily philosophers. Schubert M. Ogden, however, is a theologian. The philosophy that Ogden has adopted, though not uncritically, is that of Whitehead and Hartshorne.[80] He claims that all he knows about panentheism as a philosophical system he has learned from Hartshorne.[81] Ogden believes that Hartshorne's dipolar doctrine of God coupled with Martin Heidegger's analysis of man provides the "right" philosophy for Christian theology." Ogden also believes that Hartshorne's view of God can be used to supplement Rudloph Bultmann's existentialism.[82] The most comprehensive statement by Ogden of his process world view is his book *The Reality of God and Other Essays* (1963).

1. God.

Ogden rejects the traditional or classical view of God as a "statically complete perfection, utterly independent of anything beyond himself."[83] The arguments he gives against classical theism are similar to those many other panentheists set forth. Ogden gives two antinomies (opposing pricniples) in classical theism that he believes sufficiently show the incoherence of the position.

The first one is the antinomy of creation. Classical theists believe that God created the world freely; thus, God was under no necessity to create. On the other hand, classical theists also maintain that "God's act of creation is one with his own eternal essence, which is in every respect necessary." These two beliefs, Ogden argues, result "in the hopeless contradiction of a wholly necessary creation of a wholly contingent [i.e., freely created] world."[84]

The second antinomy is the antinomy of service. Classical theists understand that "the end of man is to serve or glorify God through obedience to His will and commandments." They also believe that the God man is to serve is a "statically complete perfection incapable in any respect of further self-realization. God can be neither increased nor diminished by what we do." Consequently, Ogden concludes, whatever we do cannot truly be *for* God because our service cannot make any difference *in* God.[85]

Another of Ogden's arguments against classical theism is an outgrowth of the second antinomy and is referred to as an argument from "existential repugnance." As Ogden states it:

> If what we do and suffer as men in the world is from God's perspective wholly indifferent, that perspective is at most irrelevant to our actual existence. It can provide no motive for action, no cause to serve, and no comfort in our distress beyond the motives, causes, and comforts already supplied by our various secular undertakings. But, more than that, to involve ourselves in these undertakings and to affirm their ultimate significance is implicitly to deny the God [of classical theism] who is Himself finally conceived as the denial of our life in the world.[86]

Ogden believes that it will do no good to refer to this wholly indifferent God as "the loving heavenly Father revealed in Jesus, who freely creates the world and guides it toward its fulfillments with tender care." That will only cause one to become entrapped in the antinomies already given. Hence, once one understands that classical theism undercuts modern man's belief in "the importance of the secular"—that is, his affirmation "that man and the world are themselves of ultimate significance"—then he should reject classical theism as existentially repugnant.[87]

Ogden replaces the classical view of God with a neoclassical alternative—panentheism or process theism. In this way God may be understood to be both supremely relative and supremely absolute. God is supremely relative in the sense that He is related to every creature in the world. These relations between God and His creatures are internal, so that the actions of every creature affect the very being of God.[88] As Ogden clearly says, God "as related to *all* things" is the "one individual to whom literally everything makes a difference because it in part determines his own actual being."[89] God is also supremely absolute. By this Ogden means that God cannot fail to be internally related to all. Thus, God is "absolutely relative."[90]

Ogden also views God as both a necessary and a contingent being. To say that God is necessary means that He is "the ultimate source and end of all that either is or could ever be." He is "the necessary ground of any and all beings, whether actual or merely possible."[91] God as contingent, however, is God as all-inclusive. God is contingent because His cosmic body is the whole world and because He is internally related to every nonnecessary creature in the world.[92] In brief, Ogden's neoclassical replacement is basically the dipolar God of Charles Hartshorne.[93]

2. The world and creation.

While affirming that God is more than the world in His abstract pole, Ogden also affirms that God is the world-whole in His concrete pole. This does not suggest that God and the world are identical, as in pantheism. Rather, God is independent "of the actual world (in his abstract identity)" and also inclusive "of the actual world (in his concrete existence)." Ogden believes that this is the kernel of truth in the traditional doctrine of creation by God "out of nothing." Although God has always existed with "*some* actual world of creatures, any such world was itself created 'out of nothing,' in the sense that there once was when it was not." The new world did not actually exist before God co-created it, but it was only potentially "existent" in the "conjoint actuality of God and of the creatures constituting the precedent actual world (or worlds)."[94] However, Ogden denies the traditional theistic concept of creation *ex nihilo*, which holds that there was absolutely nothing other than God before He created the universe.

Since the world is God's body, Ogden believes that God is "necessarily dependent on a world of other beings."[95] God does not need any particular world, only *some* world or other. God and that world—whatever it may be—are interdependent. The world needs God to give it ultimate significance, and God needs the world so that He may prehend (remember) the value actualized by His self-creative creatures and thus reach continually toward a more fulfilled cosmic experience.[96]

It follows from what has been said that the world is pluralistic (although it is unified by God in comprising His body) and self-creative. Although God is omnipotent, He cannot "wholly... determine the decisions of others." However, "by means of His own free decisions" He can "optimize the limits" of the freedom of others. "If God allowed others either more or less freedom than they actually have, there would be more chances of evil than of good resulting from their decisions, rather than the other way around.[97]

Moreover, God partly creates Himself and others, while others partly create themselves and God. The difference between God as creator and creatures as creators is that God's creative activity encompasses all of reality whereas the creatures' creative activity does not. Otherwise, God and creatures are co-creators of each other.[98]

Furthermore, God has been a co-creator with others throughout the infinite pastness of time. Ogden realizes that a literal interpretation of the first two chapters of Genesis conflicts with the idea of an infinite past since it describes a world process that had a "first stage." But he challenges this interpretation of Genesis, pointing out that it misunderstands the nature of myth which is "to illumine the essential structure and meaning of our life in the present." Consequently, the first chapters of Genesis do "not refer to some more or less remote event in the past." When they are demythologized and their existential meaning determined for man today, one sees that "the myth and doctrine of creation affirm primarily that the one essential *cause* of each moment is God's boundless love for it."[99]

3. Man.

Ogden's view of man incorporates process tenets with Heidegger's analysis of man. The result is an existentially oriented process anthropology.

Ogden maintains an evolutionary view of man's origin. He believes that "human existence has emerged from nature and is itself entirely natural." The most distinctive characteristics of man, "such as the capacity for true speech and self-consciousness, realize some of nature's own potentialities, instead of in any way distinguishing it as 'non-natural.'" In fact, "so far from indicating that man and woman in any way stand apart from nature and above it, human culture and history are one way—the distinctively human way—of being natural."[100] Granting man's total naturalness, Ogden states that man is also in some sense created "in God's image." That is, man "is uniquely gifted with the strange power of self-awareness and thus can become the sole recipient of God's universal self-disclosure in and through all of nature and history."[101]

Man is "relational or social." Or, in Heidegger's wording, man is a "being-in-the-world." The "essential structure" of man is "real internal relatedness to others, both human and nonhuman." This relatedness of man to others is not just one of "theoretical knowing"—that is, "the disinterested registration of bare data in consciousness"—but rather "an active participation in others of an essentially practical and emotional kind." The comprehensive term which Heidegger used to sum up this kind of relationship was "care." "And it is just this care, this real affective relation to others, that constitutes the existentiality or essential structure of human existence."[102]

Further, man is born free. He is a self-determined, self-creative being. Indeed, "as Jean-Paul Sartre has said, '[man] is condemned to be free.'" What we must do with our freedom is to responsibly choose "some understanding of our existence and of the ground of confidence it necessarily presupposes."[103] But what is this ground of confidence presupposed in human existence? It is the "basic confidence in the worth of life." Every human being at least presupposes that human life is significant, that it makes a difference, that it is worthwhile. This is the "common faith" of man, "because every attempt to deny it or to controvert it actually presupposes it." As Ogden explains: "I cannot question the worth of life without presupposing the worth of questioning and therefore the worth of the life by which alone such questioning can be done." Even suicide "does not entail so much a denial of life's worth as an affirmation of it. I can hardly choose to end my life unless I assume that doing so is not merely pointless, but somehow is significant or makes a difference."[104]

In short, a proper exercise of our freedom is "to look to God's love alone as providing our ultimate justification," which is His "functional significance in our lives." This functional significance is God's ability to enable our lives to make a genuine difference to other creatures as well as in Himself.[105]

Finally, according to Ogden, man is a temporally ordered series of actual occasions. There is no enduring "I" to which changes occur, only common characteristics of one's history that distinguishes one series of events from another.[106]

4. Evil, redemption and salvation.

Ogden maintains that man's "capacity to form concepts and to use language objectively gives man a tremendous freedom to deliberate and to make decisions, to be his own creator." As far as we know, this ability is uniquely human. It is the misuse of this unique freedom that "gives rise to the problem of moral evil." Moral evil occurs when man's freedom "is used in such a fashion as not to further but to frustrate the general well-being of creation."[107] One way in which this misuse of freedom is exercised is by rejecting "ourselves as the creatures we know ourselves to be." This is what Ogden calls sin, and "at its root is our rejection of God's acceptance of our lives and of all lives."[108]

Ogden affirms that God redeems all by accepting "*all* things into his life," including "unrepentant" sinners—those "who have rejected his [God's] acceptance in rejecting themselves as the creatures they inevitably are." Salvation from sin, however, is another matter. While an unrepentant sinner can be redeemed, he cannot be saved from sin. Only a repentant sinner can be both redeemed and saved. Salvation is the "process that includes not only the redeeming action of God himself but also the faithful response to this action on the part of the individual sinner."[109] Thus, all are redeemed (accepted) into God's all-embracing life, but only those who faithfully accept God's acceptance of them will be saved as well as redeemed.

5. History and man's destiny.

Both man and God are historical beings. Both have a past, present and future, and both are concretely actualized again and again in time. The difference between man's historicity and God's is that God's historicity never began nor can it ever end.[110]

God's literal immanence (indwelling involvement) in the world means that history is real and has ultimate significance. As Ogden says, "Because nature and history are nothing less than the body of

God himself, everything that happens has both a reality and an importance which are in the strictest sense infinite."[111]

As a theologian, Ogden is concerned with showing how a process view coupled with Bultmannian existentialism can give meaning to the principle that "God acts in history." He concludes that this principle may be meaningfully understood in two ways. One is that "every creature is to some extent God's act." In other words, although every creature is partly self-created, every creature is also partly God-created in the sense that "creaturely freedom has definite limits ultimately grounded in God's own free decisions." A second way in which this principle may be affirmed is in the acts of human beings. To the degree that man represents through his speech or action both "his own understanding of God's action" and "the reality of God's action itself,"[112] God may be said to be acting in history.

Ogden denies that history has an ultimate goal. Ogden also denies an actual heaven or hell. Man is destined to "live" on in God's memory as forever loved by Him. For those who have been faithful to God this will be as heaven.[113] For those who denied God's love by rejecting His acceptance of them, this will be to them as hell. They will "be bound to God forever without any possibility of separation from Him, but also without the faith in His love which is the peace that passes understanding."[114]

These concepts of heaven and hell should not be confused with literal individual immortality. Death is the cessation of literal life. Thus, there is no individual life after death. However, there is life in the divine life after death, which consists of the value we contributed to God's experience *before* our deaths. Consequently, the goal of man in history is to "advance the real good" in the world which "is done quite literally to 'the glory of God,' as an imperishable contribution to God's ever-growing perfection, which is, indeed, 'the true life of all.'"[115]

6. Ethics.

Ogden contends that religion, rightly understood, provides the basis for morality. Religion tells us "why we should do anything moral at all." Religion informs us "that because our existence as such is finally meaningful... we are free to pursue the right as we see it and need not succumb to cynicism or despair." In brief, our confidence in the value of life assures us that our moral actions, whatever they might be, "have an unconditional significance" which "no turn of events in the future has the power to annul."[116]

IV.   Some basic beliefs of panentheism.

In spite of the differences among panentheists, there is a good deal upon which they agree. Their agreements make up what may be referred to as the panentheistic world view.

A.   God is bipolar and personal.

All panentheists agree that God has two poles. The consequent or concrete pole is God's reality. It is God as He actually is in His moment-by-moment existence. It is God in the actual particulars of His becoming. In this pole God is finite, relative, dependent, contingent and in process. God's other pole is the primordial or abstract one. It is what is common and constant in God's character no matter what world exists. The divine abstract pole gives a mere outline of God's existence without filling it out with concrete or particular content. In this pole God is infinite, absolute, independent, necessary and immutable.

Panentheists also agree that God's abstract pole is included in His concrete pole. Hence, becoming or being in process characterizes all of reality. But this reality of God is not to be thought of as being, which is viewed as static and uncreative. Creativity pervades all that exists. And God is the supremely creative One. He is eternally *becoming*.

God is also viewed as personal. There is disagreement over whether He is one actual entity (*à la* Whitehead) or an ordered series of actual entities (*à la* Hartshorne). But almost all panentheists believe that God is personal.

B.   The universe is in process.

The universe is characterized by process, change, or becoming. This is so because a multitude of self-creative creatures are constantly introducing change and novelty into it. Also, the universe is eternal. This does not necessarily mean that the *present* universe is eternal. Any number of worlds might have existed in the infinite past, and any number might exist in the future. At any rate, *some* world in *some* form has always existed, and *some* world in *some* form will always exist in the infinite future. Last, all panentheists reject the traditional theistic understanding of creation *ex nihilo* (out of nothing). Instead, they affirm creation *ex materia* (out of pre-existent material), whether the "material" be a former world or God's potential pole or both. In either case, the present universe is considered to be co-created by God and man out of some pre-existing actual "stuff." Hence, God is a transformer or shaper of each world and of each world-state.

C. The universe is God's body.

In a panentheistic world view, God's consequent pole is the world. This does not mean that God and the world are identical, for God is more than the world, and the individuals who make up the world are distinct from God. It does mean, however, that the world is God's cosmic body and that those creatures who make up the world are like cells in His body. Furthermore, God cannot exist without some world or other. He does not need this particular world, but He must co-exist with some world. Similarly, the world cannot exist without God. Hence, the world and God are mutually dependent; they need each other to exist. Moreover, the creatures in the universe contribute value to God's very life. The inclusive aim or goal of all creatures is to enrich God's happiness and thus help Him to fulfill lacks in His perfection.

D. Miracles do not occur.

An implication of panentheism is that supernatural acts are impossible. Since the world is the body of God, there is nothing apart from God that can be broken into or interrupted. Indeed, God is largely a passive recipient of His creatures' activity, rather than an active force in the world. God is a cosmic Sympathizer rather than a cosmic Activist. Consequently, miraculous intervention into the world is out of character with the nature of the panentheistic God. Many panentheists reject miracles because they believe that the contemporary scientific view of the world rules them out. Schubert Ogden takes this stance. This is one reason that he adopts Bultmann's program to demythologize the miracle stories recorded in the Bible.[117]

E. Man is a finite, free moral being.

Panentheists agree that man is personal and free. In fact, man is a co-creator with God and of God. He helps decide not only the course of human and world events but also the course of God. Man's identity is not found in some enduring "I" or self. Rather, like the rest of the world, man's identity is found only in his history. He is a series of events or actual occasions that are becoming, not being. At each moment man is partially creating himself in every decision and act. The goal of man is to serve God by contributing value to His ever-growing experience.

F. Ethical norms are relative.

Many panentheists believe that there are no absolute values. Since God and the world are in great flux, there can be no absolute, unchanging standard of value. On the other hand, panentheists like Hartshorne contend that there is a universal basis for ethics, namely, beauty, harmony and intensity. Anything that promotes or builds upon or acts from this basis is good; anything that does not do so is evil. Even with this universal aesthetic foundation, however, specific ethical commands or rules are not universal. Though in general one should promote beauty and not ugliness, exactly how this should be done is relative.

G. Man has no personal immortality.

The destiny of man is not to be looked for in an actual heaven or hell. Man, like all of God's creatures, will one day die. Most panentheists believe that man will live forevermore only in God's cosmic memory. If a person contributes richly to God's life, then he will have the satisfaction of knowing that God will fondly remember him forever. Those persons who live without contributing much value to God—who, in other words, live unfaithfully—will not be remembered with much fondness by God.

H. History is an endless process of divine achievement.

In panentheism an ongoing evolutionary process helps move events forever forward. At the same time, God and man are seen as co-creators of history. However, unlike theism, panentheism says that history had no beginning and it will have no ultimate end. There will always be the unsurpassable deity who is constantly growing in perfection. And there will always be some world or other filled with self-creative creatures whose inclusive aim is to enrich the experience of God. There is no ultimate destiny, utopia, eschaton, or end.

V.   An evaluation of panentheism.

A. Some contributions of panentheism.

Much can be positively learned from panentheism. The following is a summary of the postive values that many see in this view.

First, panentheists are to be commended for seeking a comprehensive view of reality. They recognize that a piecemeal understanding of things is inadequate. Instead, they have sought to develop a coherent and reasonable view of all that exists. In short, they have developed a complete world view.

Second, many point out that panentheism manages to posit an intimate relationship between God and the world without destroying that relationship as pantheism seems to do. God is *in* the world but not identical to the world. The presence of God in the universe does not destroy the multiplicity that humans experience, but rather preserves it and even bestows upon it purpose and meaning.

Third, granting the existence of a supreme being, panentheists show that the world must depend upon God for its origin and continuation. Unless God exists, the world could not continue to exist. They insist there must be an adequate cause to account for the world.

Fourth, panentheists seriously consider contemporary theories of science and relate their world view to them. Whatever world view one holds, science cannot be ignored. Valid human discoveries in any field or discipline must be incorporated into one's world view. If reality is truly reasonable and noncontradictory, then all of knowledge can be consistently systematized no matter who discovers it or where it is found. Panentheists take this to heart in the development of their world view.

B. Some criticisms of panentheism.

There are several criticisms that have been leveled against panentheism. We will look at some of the more important ones.

First, many critics have charged that the idea of a God who is both infinite and finite, necessary and contingent, absolute and relative is contradictory. A contradiction results when opposites are affirmed of the same thing at the same time and in the same manner or respect. For example, to say that a bucket is both filled with water and not filled with water at the same time and in the same respect is contradictory. Such a thing could never occur for it is logically impossible. Many argue that the bipolar view of deity is contradictory, for no being could be both infinite and finite at the same time.

Hartshorne has responded to the charge of contradiction by pointing out that the metaphysical contraries are not attributed to the same divine pole. Rather, those attributes that belong together, such as infinity and necessity, are applied to one pole while the other attributes that belong together, such as finiteness and contingency, are applied to a different pole. Thus, infinity and finiteness, necessity and contingency, although applied to the same being at the same time, are not applied to God in the same respect.[118]

Christian theist H. P. Owen has replied to Hartshorne by pointing out that there seems to be no real distinction between the two divine poles. Since the abstract pole has no concrete or actual existence, then it must be a mere idea having only mental reality and no extramental existence.[119] Therefore, God must not really be infinite, necessary and so on, but only finite and contingent, or else God must be both sides of the metaphysical contraries at the same time and in the same pole. The first option is contrary to the teaching of panentheism, and the second one is contradictory. In any event there appears to be a serious problem of coherence in the bipolar concept of God.

Second, the idea of God as a self-caused being is problematical. It is difficult to see how any being could cause itself to exist. To believe that this could occur is to believe that potentials can actualize themselves. It would be on par with believing that cups could fill themselves and steel could make itself into a skyscraper. This does seem incredible. How could a being exist prior to itself in order to bring itself into existence? This is what a self-caused being would have to do in order to cause itself to exist. A panentheist might respond to this by saying that God never brought Himself into existence, for He has eternally existed. Thus, a panentheistic concept of a self-caused God means that God creates His *becoming*. That is, God produces changes in Himself but did not cause His own existence. Hence, God did not exist prior to Himself to cause Himself to exist, but rather He actualizes His own potential for growth.

This response, however, leads to a third problem. If God causes His own becoming and not His own being, then what or who sustains God's existence? How can a being change without there existing an unchanging being that grounds the changing being's existence? Everything cannot be in flux. Whatever changes passes from potentiality to actuality, from what is not to what is. Such change could not actualize itself or be self-caused, since potentials are not yet the something they have the potential to be. But nothing cannot produce something. Neither could such changes be uncaused, for every effect or event must have a cause. It seems, therefore, that the universe of change, which is the concrete pole of God, must be caused by something that does not change. Something outside of the changing order must sustain the entire order in existence. Therefore, there must be a being other than what the process philosopher views as "God" that sustains Him in existence. If this is true, then the panentheistic God is not really God, but the Being that sustains Him is really God. Such a God could not be an immutable-mutable being, as is the process deity, but would have to be solely immutable.

Fourth, it is difficult to understand how everything can be relative and constantly changing and one know this to be true. That is, could anyone know that something is changing unless there is some unchanging standard by which to measure the change? But if everything is changing, then there can be no unchanging standard by which to measure the change. In short, one wonders how a panentheist could know that all is in flux without there existing something that does not change. A panentheist might answer that his unchanging standard is the immutable primordial nature of God. But this answer does not seem adequate. If God's primordial pole is only an abstraction, an idea, with no extra-mental reality, then it cannot be an actual measure, only a conceptual one. Besides, when a panentheist says that God is immutable, he means that God is immutably mutable—He cannot fail to always change and always change for the better.[120] Hence, we seem to be right back where we started, with everything changing and no actual unchanging standard by which one can know that anything is changing.

Fifth, the panentheistic concept of personhood appears to conflict with our experiences of ourselves. We can see that we are personal beings who, to some degree at least, endure change. But most of us do not believe that we become new persons each moment we exist. In fact, to even say that "I become a new person each moment I exist" assumes that there is something that endures, namely, the "I" to which the changes occur. Otherwise, what changes? If nothing endures from moment to moment, then can it really be said that anything changes? If there is no sense in which the self is a continuous identity, then it appears that we can only speak of an I-I-I-I series of unrelated actual occasions.[121] And in that series of "I's" the only thing that can be said to change is the series itself, not each individual "I" in the series. This seems to destroy self-identity and to contradict human experience. This problem is particularly acute for Hartshorne, who holds that when one is sleeping or has lapsed into unconsciousness he goes out of existence.[122] This would mean that a parent awakening a child from sleep is actually calling the young one back into existence!

Sixth, some would say that the panentheistic argument that some world or other must have always existed begs the question. Of course, it is impossible that total nothingness could ever be experienced, for no one could be there to experience it; otherwise, it would not be *total* nothingness. But the panentheist presupposes that only what can be experienced can be true. Yet why should this criterion for truth be accepted? Hartshorne implies that there can be no meaning without experience.[123] Thus, a concept that cannot be experienced must be meaningless. And if there can be no meaning without experience, then total nonbeing as incapable of being experienced must be meaningless.

It appears that Hartshorne has established his case purely by definition—he has defined meaning in such a way that it makes total non-being a meaningless concept. That is, he has not *proved* the meaninglessness of "nothing exists" but only assumed it by definition, which is begging the question.

Even if Hartshorne can establish that total nothingness is not possible, the panentheistic view does not logically follow from this premise. This would simply be a way of saying that everything cannot be contingent, which leads naturally to the position that there must be a necessary being beyond the contingent world. This, however, is a theistic position. At any rate, it is not necessary to conclude that panentheism is valid simply because a total state of nothingness is impossible.

Seventh, some have insisted that if "nothing exists" is logically possible, then the very existence of Hartshorne's and Ogden's God is tenuous. According to their view, God cannot exist unless there always exists some world, since they are mutually dependent. The existence of some world is logically necessary; there could never be a time when "some world exists" was false. But if it is logically possible that "some world exists" has not always been true, then it is also logically possible that "God exists" has at some time not been true. However, according to Hartshorne and Ogden, if God is not logically necessary—a being that must always exist no matter what—then the existence of God must be logically impossible. That is, God could never have existed no matter what. Therefore, the failure to demonstrate that "nothing exists" is logically necessary may logically lead to the conclusion that "God exists" is necessarily false.[124]

Eighth, and finally, Ogden's two antinomies and argument from existential repugnance are answerable. His antinomy of creation could be answered by pointing out that all God must will necessarily is His own being. Therefore, for Him to will anything other than His own being must be willed freely, not necessarily.[125] Hence, there is no contradiction in holding that God is a necessary being who freely created a contingent universe.

Ogden's antinomy of service could also be resolved by arguing that God *desires* man to serve Him but does not *need* his service to add to His perfect nature. Man's service for God does contribute to God in the sense that it glorifies or magnifies His character in creation. However, man's service does not add to God's attributes. God is pleased by human service and God cares about it. But man's service does not need to enrich God's wholly perfect being in order to be real service.[126]

Finally, Ogden's argument from existential repugnance is also answerable. One could say to Ogden that his argument assumes a false view of divine independence. Independence need not imply that God is indifferent to the needs and sufferings of His creatures. Rather, all it need mean is that God does not depend on the world to fulfill anything in His nature or character. In fact, if God does not need the world to enrich His being because He is wholly perfect, then God is free to respond to His creatures out of His superabundance.

Ninth, proponents of process theology face a serious dilemma. They believe that God comprehends the whole universe at one time. Yet they also believe that God is limited to space and time. Anything limited to space and time cannot think any faster than the speed of light, which takes billions of years to cross the universe at about 186,000 miles per second. However, it seems quite impossible that a mind which takes this amount of time to think its way around the universe could simultaneously comprehend and direct the whole universe. On the other hand, if God's mind transcends the universe of space and time, and instantly and simultaneously comprehends the whole of it, then this is not a panentheistic view of God but a theistic view.[127]

VI.   Summary and conclusion.

As with the other world views we have discussed thus far, there are some differences among panentheists. However, they do agree that God is bipolar (or dipolar). One divine pole is the world and the other divine pole is other than the world. The world is to God as the human body is to the human mind. God and the world in some form are eternal and mutually dependent. Both the world and God are in great flux, constantly changing, with the world contributing to God's ever-increasing perfection that is unsurpassable by any other. Man, like God, is made up of actual entities or unit-events. There is no enduring "I" or self. Man's goal is to enrich God's life, and his destiny is to be remembered by God forever. Ethics are relative even though they may have a universal basis in aesthetics or religion. And history is moved along by an ongoing evolutionary process and the co-creative activities of God and His creatures. There is no final end to history, for that would mean the end of God, which is impossible.

NOTES

1. Alfred North Whitehead, *Religion in the Making* (New York: Meridian Books, 1967, first published, 1926), pp. 66, 67.
2. Ibid., p. 71.
3. Ibid., pp. 150, 151.
4. Ibid., p. 144.
5. Ibid., p. 104.
6. Ibid., pp. 151, 148.
7. Ibid., p. 115.
8. Ibid., pp. 114, 110
9. Alfred North Whitehead, *Process and Reality* (New York: Harper Torchbooks, 1960, first published, 1929), p. 95.
10. Ibid., p. 43.
11. Ibid., p. 317
12. Ibid., p. 122.
13. Ibid., pp. 71, 53.
14. Ibid., p. 134.
15. Ibid., pp. 392, 521.
16. Lewis Ford, "Biblical Recital and Process Philosophy" in *Interpretation* 26.2 (April, 1972): 201.
17. Whitehead, *Process and Reality*, pp. 31, 32, 135, 339.
18. Ibid., p. 169.
19. Ibid., p. 525.
20. Ford, *op cit.*, p. 202.
21. Whitehead, *Process and Reality*, p. 517.
22. Ibid., pp. 135, 529.
23. Ibid., p. 518.
24. Bernard Loomer, "A Response to David Griffin," *Encounter* 36:4 (Autumn, 1975) :365.
25. Ford, *op cit.*, pp. 202, 203.
26. Whitehead, *Process and Reality*, p. 166.
27. Ibid.
28. Alfred North Whitehead, *Modes of Thought*, p. 228.
29. Whitehead, *Religion in the Making*, p. 112.
30. Ibid., pp. 107, 108.
31. Whitehead, *Process and Reality*, p. 35.
32. Whitehead, *Religion in the Making*, pp. 97, 100, 101.
33. Whitehead, *Adventures of Ideas* (New York: The Free Press, 1967, first published, 1933), p. 16.
34. Ibid., p. 269.
35. Ibid., pp. 269, 270.
36. See F. Duane Lindsey's "An Evangelical Overview of Process Theology," *Bibliotheca Sacra* 134 (January-March 1977):19, and Bruce A. Demarest's essay "Process Theology and the Pauline Doctrine of the Incarnation," in

Pauline Studies: Essays Presented to F.F. Bruce on His 70th Birthday, ed. by Donald A. Hagner and Murray J. Harris (Exeter: The Paternoster Press, Ltd., 1980), p. 122.

37. Charles Hartshorne, *A Natural Theology for Our Time* (LaSalle: The Open Court Publishing Company, 1967), pp. 74, 75; emphasis added.

38. Charles Hartshorne, *Aquinas to Whitehead: Seven Centuries of Metaphysics of Religion,* the Aquinas Lecture, 1976 (Milwaukee: Marquette University Publications, 1976), pp. 22-24; his *The Divine Relativity: A Social Conception of God* (New Haven and London: Yale University Press, 1948), p. ix; and his *Philosophers Speak of God,* co-edited with William L. Reese (Chicago and London: The University of Chicago Press, 1976; first published, 1953), p. 2.

39. Hartshorne, *The Divine Relativity,* pp. 79-81.

40. Charles Hartshorne, *The Logic of Perfection* (LaSalle: The Open Court Publishing Company, 1962), p. 35.

41. Hartshorne, *Creative Synthesis and Philosophic Method,* p. 249.

42. Hartshorne, *A Natural Theology for Our Time,* pp. 126-137.

43. Hartshorne, *Aquinas to Whitehead,* p. 33.

44. Hartshorne, *Creative Synthesis and Philosophic Method,* pp. 13, 118.

45. Charles Hartshorne, "Personal Identity from A to Z," *Process Studies* 2 (Fall 1972): 210.

46. Charles Hartshorne, *Man's Vision of God and the Logic of Theism* (Hamden: Archon Books, 1964; first published, 1941), p. 211.

47. Hartshorne, *Creative Synthesis and Philosophic Method,* p. 15.

48. Hartshorne, *Man's Vision of God,* pp. 31, 111, 165, 166.

49. Charles Hartshorne, "Is God's Existence a State of Affairs?" in *Faith and the Philosophers,* ed. by John Hick (London: Macmillan; New York: St. Martin's Press, 1966), p. 30.

50. Charles Hartshorne, "The Dipolar Conception of Deity," *The Review of Metaphysics* 21 (December 1967): 287.

51. Hartshorne, *A Natural Theology for Our Time,* pp. 76, 77, 136; *The Logic of Perfection,* pp. 10, 93, 262.

52. Hartshorne, *A Natural Theology for Our Time,* p. 104.

53. Hartshorne, *The Logic of Perfection,* p. 126.

54. Hartshorne, *Man's Vision of God,* p. 348. See also his *The Divine Relativity,* pp. 89, 90.

55. Hartshorne, *Man's Vision of God,* pp. 177, 184, 185.

56. Hartshorne, *Creative Synthesis and Philosophic Method,* pp. 159, 161, 162.

57. Hartshorne, *A Natural Theology for Our Time,* pp. 84, 85, and *Man's Vision of God,* p. 108.

58. Hartshorne, *Whitehead's Philosophy,* p. 195.

59. Hartshorne, *Man's Vision of God,* pp. 230-232.

60. Hartshorne, "The Dipolar Conception of Deity," p. 280.

61. Charles Hartshorne, *"Efficient Causality in Aristotle and St. Thomas:* A Review Article," *The Journal of Religion* 25 (January 1945): 29; his *A Natural Theology for Our Time,* pp. 60, 113; and his "Idealism and Our Experience of Nature," in *Philosophy, Religion, and the Coming World Civilization: Essays in Honor of William Ernest Hocking,* ed. by Leroy S. Rouner (The Hague: Martinus Nijhoff, 1966), p. 75.

62. Hartshorne, *"Efficient Causality in Aristotle and St. Thomas:* A Review Article," p. 29.

63. Hartshorne, *A Natural Theology for Our Time,* pp. 113.

64. Hartshorne, "Personal Identity from A to Z," pp. 212, 213.

65. Hartshorne, *The Logic of Perfection,* pp. 139, 233.

66. Ibid., p. 180.
67. Hartshorne, *A Natural Theology for Our Time*, pp. 54, 55. See also his *Aquinas to Whitehead*, pp. 43, 48-49, and his "Two Levels of Faith and Reason," *The Journal of Bible and Religion*, 16 (January 1948): 37.
68. Hartshorne, *The Logic of Perfection*, pp. 254, 259, 262.
69. Ibid., p. 14.
70. Hartshorne, "The Dipolar Conception of Deity," p. 285.
71. Hartshorne, *A Natural Theology for Our Time*, pp. 112, 113.
72. Hartshorne, "The Dipolar Conception of Deity," p. 285.
73. Charles Hartshorne, "Outlines of a Philosophy of Nature: Part II," *The Personalist* 39 (Autumn 1958): 384-85. Cf., his *The Logic of Perfection*, pp. 313-315.
74. Charles Hartshorne, "The Idea of God—Literal or Analogical?" *The Christian Scholar* 34 (June 1956): 133.
75. Hartshorne, *Man's Vision of God*, pp. 265, 266; cf., pp. 195-198.
76. Charles Hartshorne, "Beyond Enlightened Self-Interest: A Metaphysics of Ethics," *Ethics* 84 (April 1974): 213.
77. Ibid., p. 214.
78. Ibid.
79. Ibid.
80. Schubert M. Ogden, "Bultmann's Demythologizing and Hartshorne's Dipolar Theism," in *Process and Divinity: Philosophical Essays Presented to Charles Hartshorne* (LaSalle: Open Court Publishing Company, 1964), pp. 495, 498, 506, 510, 511.
81. Schubert M. Ogden, *Theology in Crisis: A Colloquium on The Credibility of "God"* (New Concord: Muskingum College, March 20-21, 1967), p. 54.
82. Ogden, "Bultmann's Demythologizing and Hartshorne's Dipolar Theism," pp. 511, 498.
83. Schubert M. Ogden, "Toward a New Theism," in *Process Philosophy and Christian Thought*, ed. by Delwin Brown, et al. (Indianapolis: Bobbs-Merrill, 1971), p. 180.
84. Ogden, *The Reality of God and Other Essays* (San Francisco: Harper & Row, 1977, first published, 1963), p. 17.
85. Ibid., pp. 17, 18.
86. Ibid., p. 18.
87. Ibid., pp. 18, 19, 44. See also pp. 48-56.
88. Ogden, *The Reality of God*, p. 47.
89. Ogden, *Faith and Freedom*, p. 80.
90. Ogden, "Toward a New Theism," in *Process Philosophy and Christian Thought*, p. 185. See also his *The Reality of God*, pp. 150, 151.
91. Ogden, *The Reality of God*, pp. 122, 124.
92. Ogden, "Toward a New Theism," in *Process Philosophy and Christian Thought*, p. 186.
93. Ogden, *The Reality of God*, p. 141.
94. Ibid., pp. 62, 63.
95. Ibid., p. 61. cf., p. 176.
96. Ogden, "Toward a New Theism," in *Process Philosophy and Christian Thought*, p. 186.
97. Ogden, *Faith and Freedom*, pp. 76, 77.
98. Ibid., pp. 88, 89.
99. Ogden, *The Reality of God*, p. 214. Cf., "Toward a New Theism," in *Process Philosophy and Christian Thought*, p. 177.
100. Ogden, *Faith and Freedom*, p. 108.

101. Ogden, *The Reality of God,* p. 193.
102. Ibid., pp. 57, 150.
103. Ibid., p. 115.
104. Ogden, *Theology in Crisis,* p. 35. See also his *The Reality of God,* p. 114.
105. Ibid., p. 37.
106. Ibid.
107. Ogden, *Theology in Crisis,* p. 55.
108. Ogden, *Faith and Freedom* p. 86.
109. Ibid., pp. 86-87.
110. Ogden, *The Reality of God,* p. 180.
111. Ogden, "Toward a New Theism," in *Process Philosophy and Christian Thought,* p. 186.
112. Ogden, *The Reality of God,* pp. 180-181.
113. Ibid., pp. 36, 226, 227, 229, 230, and his "The Meaning of Christian Hope,' *Union Seminary Quarterly Review* 30 (Winter-Summer 1975): 160-163.
114. Ogden, *The Reality of God,* p. 228.
115. Ogden, "Toward a New Theism," in *Process Philosophy and Christian Thought,* p. 186.
116. Ogden, *The Reality of God,* pp. 35-36.
117. Ogden, *The Reality of God,* pp. 217, 218, and "Toward a New Theism," in *Process Philosophy and Christian Thought,* pp. 177, 178.
118. Hartshorne, *Aquinas to Whitehead,* pp. 22-24, and his *Man's Vision of God,* p. 322.
119. H.P. Owen, *The Christian Knowledge of God* (University of London: The Athlone Press, 1969), p. 105.
120. For example, see Charles Hartshorne's "Abstract and Concrete Approaches to Deity," *Union Seminary Quarterly Review* 20 (March 1965): 265, and his *Man's Vision of God,* pp. 110, 276.
121. Royce Gordon Gruenler makes and amplifies this criticism in his book *The Inexhaustible God: Biblical Faith and the Challenge of Process Theism* (Grand Rapids: Baker Book House, 1983), esp. chapters 2 and 3.
122. Hartshorne, *The Logic of Perfection,* pp. 220, 221.
123. Hartshorne, *Creative Synthesis and Philosophic Method,* p. 58.
124. Houston Craighead gives this argument and others against Hartshorne's case for the meaninglessness of "nothing exists" in his two articles "Non-Being and Hartshorne's Concept of God," *Process Studies* I (Spring 1971):9-24, and "Response," *The Southwestern Journal of Philosophy* 5 (Spring 1974): 33-37.
125. Thomas Aquinas argues against a similar objection in this way in his *Summa Theologica* I. 19. 3.
126. See Walter E. Stokes, "A Whiteheadian Reflection on God's Relation to the World," in *Process Theology: Basic Writings,* ed. by Ewert H. Cousins (New York: Newman Press, 1971), pp. 137-152, and Norman L. Geisler's "Process Theology," in *Tensions in Contemporary Theology,* ed. by Stanley N. Gundry and Alan F. Johnson (Chicago: Moody Press, 1976), pp. 272, 273, 275, 276.
127. See Gruenler, ibid., pp. 75-79.

6

Deism: A World On Its Own Made by God

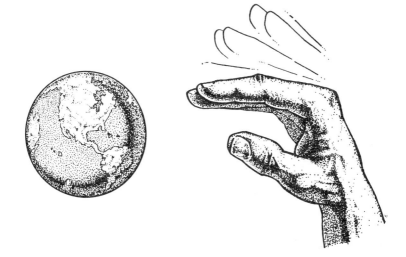

I. Introduction.

Deism flourished in the 16th, 17th and 18th centuries but began to die out in the 19th century. Today its effects live on in the denial of miracles, critical views of the Bible, and in the behavior of many people who act as if a supreme being has little or nothing to do with their lives.[1] The naturalistic spirit of deism also lives on in most forms of finite godism (see chapter 7). The main difference between the two views is that the latter views God as finite, while deists view Him as infinite.

Deism is the belief in a God who made the world but never interrupts it with supernatural events. God does not interfere with His creation. Rather, He has designed it to run by immutable natural laws. He has also provided in nature all that His creatures need to live by.

Deism flourished in Europe—especially in France and in England—and in America before, during and after the Revolutionary War. Some of the more prominent European deists were Herbert of Cherbury (1583-1648), the Father of English Deism, John Toland (1670-1722), Thomas Woolston (1669-1731) and Matthew Tindal (1656-1733).[2] Some of the more notable American deists were Benjamin Franklin (1706-1790), Thomas Paine (1737-1809), Thomas Jefferson (1743-1826) and Stephen Hopkins (1707-1785).[3] An example of a contemporary deistic thinker is Martin Gardner. His book, *The Whys of a Philosophical Scrivener,* is listed in the bibliography.

II. A typology of deism.

All deists agree that there is one God beyond the world who created it. All deists agree that God does not intervene in the world through supernatural acts. However, not all deists agree on God's concern for the world and the existence of an afterlife for man. Based on these differences, four types of deism are discernible.[4]

The first type of deism is largely of French origin. According to this view, God is not concerned with the government of the world. He created the world and set it in motion, but He has no regard for what has happened or will happen to it since then.

In the second form of deism, God is concerned with the ongoing happenings of the world but not with the moral actions of human beings. Man can act rightly or wrongly, righteously or wickedly, morally or immorally. It is of no concern to God.

The third type of deism maintains that God governs the world and that He does care about the moral activities of man. Indeed, God insists that man be obedient to the moral law that He has established in nature. However, man has no future after death. When one dies the final chapter of his life is closed. There is no life for man beyond the grave.

The fourth type of deism contends that God regulates the world and expects man to obey the moral law grounded in nature. This type also holds to a life after death for man, with rewards for the good and punishments for the wicked. This view was common among both English and American deists of earlier centuries.

III.   Some representatives of deism.

The following pages list specific deists of the fourth type. Their form of deism was more influential and widespread than the others. In addition, the effects of their deistic beliefs, especially those of Thomas Paine and Thomas Jefferson, are still evident today through the United States' political foundation and heritage.[5]

A. Matthew Tindal.

One of the best-known and most respected of the deists was the English lawyer Matthew Tindal (1656-1733). His most important deistic work was not published until he was about 74 years of age and is entitled *Christianity As Old As the Creation: or, the Gospel, a Republication of the Religion of Nature* (1730). Because of its influence and completeness, it has been called the "Deistic Bible" and its author "The Great Apostle of Deism." This major work prompted more than 150 replies, including the classic critique of deism, Bishop Butler's *Analogy of Religion* (1872).[6]

1. God.

Tindal's view of God was very similar to that of theists. He believed God to be completely perfect, infinitely loving, eternal, just, merciful, immutable, omnipresent, omniscient, true, omnibenevolent, wise, without parts and invisible.[7] He also held God to be impassible, that is, without passions. As he argued,

> If we dare consult our Reason, it will tell us that Jealousy in point of Honour and Power, Love of Fame and Glory can only belong to limited Creatures; but are as necessarily excluded from an unlimited, absolutely perfect Being, as Anger, Revenge, and such like Passions; which would make the Deity resemble the weak, womanish, and impotent part of our Nature, rather than the manly, noble, and generous.[8]

Likewise God is not moved by man's actions.

Cou'd God strictly speaking, be made angry, provok'd, or griev'd by the Conduct of us wretched Mortals, he wou'd not enjoy a Moment's Quiet; but must be much more miserable than the most unhappy of his Creatures. Or, Had God any Comfort, or Satisfaction to gain from the Thoughts and Actions of his Creatures, he wou'd never have been without an Infinity of them jointly contributing to this End.[9]

2. Creation.

According to Tindal, the universe was created by God *ex nihilo* (out of nothing). Human beings were also brought into existence by a direct creative act of God: "'tis God, who from Nothing brings us into Being, frames us after the Manner that best pleases him, imprints on us what Faculties, Inclinations, Desires and Passions he thinks fit."[10]

As to why God created all things, Tindal states that it was not because of any lack or need in God, since He is absolutely perfect. Rather, God's motive for creating was solely for the good of His creatures.[11]

3. God and the world.

According to Tindal, God not only created all things but He also constantly preserves or sustains all things. Hence, everything is dependent on God for its existence and preservation, whereas God is dependent on nothing for His existence or character. Indeed, God needs nothing from His creatures since He is perfect and all-sufficient in Himself.[12]

God is also the cosmic Governor of the world. His divine laws are those of nature, which govern the activities of His creatures. These natural laws are perfect, immutable and eternal, for they are the same ones "by which God governs his own Actions." Consequently, these laws are the same ones by which God "expects all the rational world shoul'd govern" their actions. To ensure this, God "continues daily to implant" His law "in the Minds of all Men, Christians as well as Others."[13]

The extent of this natural law is explained by Tindal:

it not only commands that Evil Doers should be punish'd, but that Men, according to the different Circumstances they are under, shoul'd take the most proper Methods for doing it, and vary as Exigencies re-

140

quire; so it not only requires that Justice shoul'd be done Men as to their several Claims, but that the readiest, and most effectual Way of doing it shoul'd be taken; and the same may be said of all other Instances of this Nature.[14]

In short, God has established the end or goal of all actions—the honor of God and the good of man—but not the means. Natural law reveals *what* man should work toward, but it does not reveal exactly *how* man should attain that end.[15] According to Tindal, this is only proper, for "if God interposes further, and prescribes a particular Way of doing these Things, from which Men at no Time, or upon no Account ought to vary; he not only interposes unnecessarily, but to the Prejudice of the End for which he thus interposes."[16] Therefore, God does not need to intercede in the affairs of His creation, nor should He. The natural laws that He has established are sufficient for the continued governing of the world.

4. Man.

Man is personal, rational and free, but it is man's reason "which makes us the Image of God himself, and is the common Bond which unites Heaven and Earth." By his reason man can prove the existence of God, demonstrate God's attributes, and discover and work out the whole of natural religion. Tindal wrote:

> By *Natural Religion*, I understand the Belief of the Existence of a God, and the Sense and Practice of those Duties, which result from the Knowledge, we, by our Reason, have of him, and his Perfections; and of ourselves, and our own Imperfections; and of the Relation we stand in to him, and to our Fellow-Creatures.[17]

Every person is capable of arriving at the basic articles of natural religion: believing in God, worshiping God, doing what contributes to one's personal good or happiness, and promoting the common happiness.[18]

Tindal readily acknowledged that not all people accept the natural religion revealed in nature. The reason for this, he thought, was because of an "innate weakness" in man to believe in superstition. Most of the problems of mankind come from this weakness.[19]

Although many people have strayed from natural religion, God has made man to act in conformity with nature. Those who do not act this way are contradicting their own rational nature, thus acting irrationally.[20]

5. Evil.

Tindal believed that evil comes about by people succumbing to superstition and thus acting against the natural order of things. He did believe that some people are in need of a savior for their wicked ways, and for these people Jesus Christ came to "teach" them "to repent of the Breach of known Duties." As Tindal pointed out, Jesus said, "I am not come to call the righteous, but sinners to repentance" (Matthew 9:13). By this statement of purpose, Jesus "is dividing Mankind into two Parts, the 'whole' or 'righteous,' and the 'sick' or 'Sinners'; and that his business was entirely with the latter." Hence, as even Jesus Christ proclaimed, "there is but one universal Remedy for all sick Persons, *Repentance* and *Amendment,*" and this has been revealed in Nature since the Creation of the world.[21] Furthermore,

> if 'God, who is no Respecter of Persons, will judge the World in Righteousness'; and 'they that in every Nation fear him, and work Righteousness shall be accepted of him'; they, certainly, are whole, and need no Physician, who do of themselves what will make them acceptable to him; living as, those whom Christ came to reform were taught to live....[22]

6. Ethics.

Tindal wrote that "the Principle from which all human Actions flow is the Desire of Happiness." This central principle is the "only innate Principle in Mankind" and it is "implanted" by God. Since human beings are rational creatures, their happiness is found when they govern all their "Actions by the Rules of right Reason." These rules are grounded in the "moral Perfections of God," which are discoverable in nature. When people live "according to the Rules of right Reason, we more and more implant in us the moral Perfections of God, from which his Happiness [and ours] is inseparable.[23]

From these premises, said Tindal,

> we may conclude, that Men, according as they do, or do not partake of the nature of God, must unavoidably be either happy, or miserable: And herein appears the great Wisdom of God, in making Men's Misery and Happiness the necessary and inseparable Consequence of their

Actions; and that rational Actions carry with them their own Reward, and irrational their own Punishment . . . ; and that there's no Virtue, but what has some Good inseparably annex'd to it; and no Vice, but what as necessarily carries with it some Evil . . . .[24]

Tindal rejected the idea that God could have used any book or books to a better degree than He uses nature to reveal what is right and wrong to man. For "'tis impossible in any Book, or Books, that a particular Rule cou'd be giv'n for every Case." Consequently, we have to refer "to the Light of Nature to teach us our Duty in most Cases; especially considering the numberless Circumstances which attend us, and which, perpetually varying, may make the same Actions, according as Men are differently affected by them, either good or bad."[25]

7. History and goal.

Tindal had little to say about history. He believed that history shows how people have been duped by greedy, dishonest religious leaders who have taken advantage of man's proneness to believe in superstition.[26]

Tindal also attempted to discredit the historicity of the Bible. He ridiculed many Bible stories, such as the accounts of the Garden of Eden, the fall of man, Jacob's wrestling with an angel, and Balaam's talking donkey. He also argued that many of the miracles recorded in the Bible had parallels in pagan mythical stories and thus were mythical as well.[27]

Tindal did believe in an afterlife for man. He held that man's rational nature will survive death and pass on to another life where there are no "sensual things to divert his Thoughts." There will also be a "Last Day" wherein God will judge every human being, not for "what you have said, or what you have believ'd; but what you have done more than others." God's judgment will be impartial and fair since "God, at all Times, has given Mankind sufficient Means of knowing whatever he requires of them; and what those Means are."[28]

B. Thomas Paine.

Among the most militant deists in early America was Thomas Paine (1737-1809). His political writings, such as *Common Sense* (1776) and *The Rights of Man* (1791-1792), were greatly influenced by his deistic beliefs.[29] Paine's thinking was influential in both the American and French revolutions. But his importance did not end there. In his work *The Age of Reason* (1794-1795), Paine set forth his defense of deism in such a way as to make it readable to all people. Believing that republicianism and equality were being severely threatened by church leaders, Paine wrote *The Age of Reason* to destroy all claims to supernatural revelation and, by so doing, discredit the clergy.[30]

1. God.

"I believe in one God, and no more," wrote Paine. Like theists, Paine believed that the one God is all-powerful, all-knowing, all-good, infinite, merciful, just and incomprehensible.[31]

· But unlike theists, Paine maintained that the only way to discover that such a God exists is "by the exercise of reason." He rejected all forms of supernatural revelation, believing them to be unknowable. He claimed that "revelation when applied to religion, means something communicated *immediately* from God to man." Consequently, even if something were revealed by God "to a certain person, and not revealed to any other person," it could be "revelation to that person only."[32]

> When he tells it to a second person, a second to a third, a third to a fourth, and so on, it ceases to be a revelation to all those persons. It is revelation to the first person only, and *hearsay* to every other, and, consequently, they are not obliged to believe it.[33]

Hence, although "no man will deny or dispute the power of the Almighty to make such a communication, if he pleases," such a revelation could be knowable only to the person who received it directly from God.[34]

Paine also argued that supernatural revelation is impossible given the inadequacy of human language to convey it. God's revelation must be absolutely "unchangeable and universal."[35] Given this, human language could not be the means for its communication:

> The continually progressive change to which the meaning of words is subject, the want of a universal language which renders translation necessary, the errors to which translations are again subject, the mistakes of copyists and printers, together with the possibility of willful

alteration, are of themselves evidences that the human language, whether in speech or in print, cannot be the vehicle of the word of God.[36]

Thus, Paine rejected all claims by any religious group to have received a verbal or written revelation from God. Instead, he held that all such beliefs were "no other than human inventions, set up to terrify and enslave mankind, and monopolize power and profit."[37] The "revealed religion" he had the most contempt for was Christianity. He summarized his feelings well when he said:

Of all the systems of religion that ever were invented, there is none more derogatory to the Almighty, more unedifying to man, more repugnant to reason, and more contradictory in itself, than this thing called Christianity. Too absurd for belief, too impossible to convince, and too inconsistent for practice, it renders the heart torpid, or produces only atheists and fanatics. As an engine of power, it serves the purpose of despotism; and as a means of wealth, the avarice of priests; but so far as respects the good of man in general, it leads to nothing here or hereafter.[38]

"The only religion," added Paine, "that has not been invented, and that has in it every evidence of divine originality, is pure and simple Deism." In fact, deism "must have been the first, and will probably be the last that man believes."[39]

2. Creation.

Paine believed that the universe had a beginning. It was brought into existence by God and is sustained in existence by Him. He also believed that God created "millions of worlds," which are all inhabited by intelligent creatures who "enjoy the same opportunities of knowledge as we do." God created all these worlds, in part, so that the "devotional gratitude" and "admiration" of His creatures would be called forth in their contemplation of these worlds.[40]

3. God and the world.

Paine wrote, "THE WORD OF GOD IS THE CREATION WE BEHOLD: And it is in this word, which no human invention can counterfeit or alter, that God speaketh universally to man." The universe "reveals to man all that is necessary for man to know of God." Through it man can know that God exists, what God is like.

and what God expects from man.[41]

Paine held that the universe reveals the existence of God in a number of ways. One is through the very existence of material things. He argued that it is evident to everyone that the things which constitute the universe could not have made themselves. Thus, there must be "a first cause eternally existing, of a nature totally different to any material existence we know of, and by the power of which all things exist; and this first cause, man calls God."[42]

Paine also argued that motion reveals the existence of God. Since the universe consists of matter that cannot move itself, the rotation of the planets would be impossible without the existence of an external first cause that set them in motion. This first cause must be God.[43]

A third argument he offered for God's existence was from design. Since the "work of man's hands is a proof of the existence of man," and since a watch is "positive evidence of the existence of a watch-maker," then "in like manner the creation is evidence to our reason and our senses of the existence of a Creator."[44]

The world also reveals to man what God is like:

Do we want to contemplate His power? We see it in the immensity of His creation.

Do we want to contemplate His wisdom? We see it in the unchangeable order by which the incomprehensible whole is governed.

Do we want to contemplate His munificence? We see it in the abundance with which he fills the earth.

Do we want to contemplate His mercy? We see it in His not withholding that abundance, even from the unthankful.

Do we want to contemplate His will, so far as it respects man? The goodness He shows to all, is a lesson for our conduct to each other.[45]

In short, from the world man gains all his knowledge. Whatever man needs to know, all he must do is to consult "the scripture called the Creation."[46]

4. Man.

According to Paine, man is a rational, personal and free being. He also believed all men were created equal and that every human being's "religious duties consist in doing justice, loving mercy, and endeavoring to make our fellow creatures happy."[47]

146

Paine adamantly denied the Christian belief that the human race is in rebellion against God and thus in need of salvation. As he stated, "In truth, there is no such thing as redemption . . . .man stands in the same relative condition with his Maker [that] he ever did stand, since man existed, and . . . it is his greatest consolation to think so."[48]

5. Evil.

Nowhere did Paine attempt to reconcile the presence of evil with the deistic concept of God. Indeed, the only evil he even seemed to notice was the evil caused by social injustice or brought about by "revealed religion." The former, he claimed, can be dealt with largely on a political level. The latter, which makes up the greatest class of evils, is best prevented by not admitting "of any other revelation than that which is manifested in the book of creation," and by considering every other so-called "word of God" as a "fable and imposition" upon mankind.[49]

6. Ethics.

Paine succinctly summarized the heart of his ethical beliefs when he wrote:

> . . . That the moral duty of man consists in imitating the moral goodness and beneficence of God manifested in the creation towards all His creatures; that, seeing, as we daily do, the goodness of God to all men, it is an example calling upon all men to practice the same towards each other; and, consequently, that everything of persecution and revenge between man and man, and everything of cruelty to animals, is a violation of moral duty.[50]

Further, if man were "impressed as fully and as strongly as he ought to be with the belief of a God, his moral life would be regulated by the force of that belief." In other words, man "would stand in awe of God, and of himself, and would not do the thing that would not be concealed from either." On the other hand, "it is by forgetting God in his works, and running after the books of pretended revelation that man has wandered from the straight path of duty and happiness, and become by turns the victim of doubt and the dupe of delusion."[51]

7. History and goal.

Like Tindal, Paine did not set forth a view on history. Also like Tindal, yet more radically, Paine claimed that the Bible was historically unreliable. He ridiculed and considered mythical such biblical stories as the creation narrative, the fall of Satan and man, the heroic acts of Samson, Jonah and the great fish, Satan's temptation of Jesus, and the virgin birth, resurrection, and the ascension of Jesus Christ. Paine also contended that the traditional ascriptions of authorship to practically every book in the Bible were wrong and that most of the books were written quite later than traditionally believed. For example, he argued that the entire New Testament was written "more than three hundred years after the time that Christ is said to have lived."[52]

Paine did not believe that supernatural acts of God had ever occurred in history. Accepting the laws of nature as prescriptions for how nature "is supposed to act," he defined a miracle as "something contrary to the operation and effect of those laws." But, he added, "unless we know the whole extent of those laws, and...the powers of nature, we are not able to judge whether anything that may appear to us wonderful or miraculous, be within, or be beyond, or be contrary to, her natural power of acting." Hence, our limited knowledge of nature leaves us with "no criterion to determine what a miracle is; and mankind, in giving credit to appearance, under the idea of there being miracles, are subject to be continually imposed upon." As a consequence of these considerations, "nothing can be more inconsistent than to suppose that the Almighty would make use of means, such as are called miracles." Besides, the chances are "at least millions to one that the reporter of a miracle tells a lie" compared with the likelihood that nature would change to allow for a miracle. "We have never seen, in our time, nature go out of her course; but we have good reason to believe that millions of lies have been told in the same time."[53]

8. Man's destiny.

Paine did express hope in a life after death for man. He believed that morally good people would be happy in the afterlife and morally wicked people would be punished. Those who were neither particularly good nor particularly bad, but rather indifferent, would be "dropped entirely."[54]

C. Thomas Jefferson.

The author of the Declaration of Independence (1776) and the third president of the United States, Thomas Jefferson (1743-1826) was a deist. Some of his earliest writings made him "the major penman of the American Revolution."[55] He fought hard for religious freedom and the abolition of slavery in the United States. His philosophical and religious views undergird his writings, but are not generally made explicit except in his personal correspondence to others. It is chiefly from these letters that his deism may be clearly discovered.

1. God and the world.

Jefferson believed that there is one God and that He is the Creator, Sustainer and Manager of the universe. He held that this God is infinitely wise, good, righteous and powerful. The truth of these characteristics, thought Jefferson, is clear from the design of the universe:

> I hold (without revelation) that when we take a view of the universe, in its parts, general or particular, it is impossible for the human mind not to perceive and feel a conviction of design, consummate skill, and indefinite power in every atom of its composition. The movements of the heavenly bodies, so exactly held in their course by the balance of centrifugal and centripetal forces; the structure of the earth itself, with its distribution of lands, waters and atmosphere; animal and vegetable bodies, examined in all their minutest particular; insects, mere atoms of life, yet as perfectly organized as man or mammoth; the mineral substances, their generation and uses; it is impossible, I say, for the human mind not to believe that there is in all this design, cause and effect up to an ultimate cause, a Fabricator of all things from matter and motion, their Preserver and Regulator.[56]

Influenced by the scientist Isaac Newton, Jefferson understood the world to be in harmony, under the rule of natural law and open to human investigation. The world is like this because God created it that way.

2. Man.

As stated in the Declaration of Independence, Jefferson considered it "to be self-evident, that all men are created equal; that they are endowed by their Creator with certain unalienable rights; that among these are life, liberty, and the pursuit of happiness." These "unalienable rights" are grounded in nature, which is itself unchangeable. And since these rights are natural ones, they are universal. Other rights that Jefferson took to be natural are the right of association, the right to self-government, and the right to be free in regard to religion.[57]

For Jefferson, God's creation of all people as equal had logical consequences. One was that slavery had to be abolished as an accepted practice in the United States. Jefferson attempted to accomplish this end by seeking to pass a plan he drafted, the "Report of Government for the Western Territory" (1784), which provided in part for the abolition of slavery in all the states after the year 1800.[58] His legislation was defeated by one vote. Two years later he wrote of this decision:

> The voice of a single individual...would have prevented this abominable crime from spreading itself over the country. Thus we see the fate of millions unborn hanging on the tongue of one man, and Heaven was silent in that awful moment! But it is to be hoped it will not always be silent, and that the friends of the rights of human nature will in the end prevail.[59]

Man is a "rational animal" who has been "endowed by nature ...with an innate sense of justice." Both man's reason and his sense of morality could go wrong, for neither "wisdom" nor "virtue" are hereditary in man. However, truth will eventually prevail over error and man can "be restrained from wrong and protected in right, by moderate powers, confided to persons of his own choice."[60]

3. Government and religion.

Jefferson wrote, "We consider society as one of the natural wants with which man has been created; and that he has been endowed with faculties and qualities to effect its satisfaction by concurrence of others having the same want." He believed that there are three forms of societies: (1) those which have no government; (2) those under "governments wherein the will of everyone has a just influence"; and (3) those which are under "governments of force." Jefferson believed that the first form of government is generally the best, but impractical "with any degree of population." The third form of government is "a government of wolves over sheep" and thus denies the natural rights of man. The second form is best represented in the United States and "has a great deal of good in it." For example, it allows the "mass of mankind" to enjoy "a precious degree of liberty and happiness." But its major evil is that it is subject to various degrees and manifestations of "turbulence." However, "even this evil is productive of good."[61]

It prevents the degeneracy of government, and nourishes a general attention to the public affairs. I hold it that a little rebellion now and then is a good thing, and as necessary in the political world as storms in the physical.... It is a medicine necessary for the sound health of government.[62]

Man can "be governed by reason and truth." And as man's mind progresses, the laws and institutions he establishes must also change. "Institutions must...keep pace with the times." Therefore, "let us provide in our constitution for its revision at stated periods."[63]

The function of government leaders, Jefferson said, "is to declare and enforce only our natural rights and duties, and to take none of them from us." Furthermore, the "legitimate powers of government extend to such acts only as are injurious to others." For example, "it does me no injury for my neighbor to say there are twenty gods, or no God. It neither picks my pocket nor breaks my leg." Hence, government should both uphold the natural right of religious freedom and not meddle in religious affairs.[64]

Jefferson was convinced that no religious view or group should be given legal sanction over and against any other view or group. As he said, "I am for freedom of religion, and against all maneuvers to bring about a legal ascendancy of one sect over another."[65] Besides maintaining that such an action would be a violation of one's natural right of freedom of religion, Jefferson also believed that it would be disadvantageous for religion and in the past was the cause of numerous evils:

Difference of opinion is advantageous in religion. The several sects perform the office of a censor morum [moral sense] over each other. Is uniformity attainable? Millions of innocent men, women, and children, since the introduction of Christianity, have been burnt, tortured, fined, imprisoned; yet we have not advanced one inch towards uniformity. What has been the effect of coercion? To make one-half the world fools, and the other half hypocrites. To support roguery and error all over the earth.[66]

Jefferson's personal religious views were not as radical as Thomas Paine's but were closer to those of Tindal and a Unitarian thinker named Joseph Priestley. Jefferson rejected the major traditional teachings of Christianity, such as the deity, virgin birth, resurrection and ascension of Christ, original sin, salvation by faith alone, the substitutionary death of Christ and the infallibility of the Bible. He believed that Jesus Christ was the greatest reformer and moralist who ever lived. Unfortunately, Jesus' teachings "have come to us mutilated, misstated, and often [are] unintelligible."[67] Among the "band of dupes and imposters" who corrupted Jesus' moral teachings was the apostle Paul who "was the great Coryphaeus, and first corruptor of the Doctrines of Jesus." As a consequence, Jefferson sought to purify Jesus' moral instruction from the errors that had been imposed upon it and put together his own version of the Bible, "The Life and Morals of Jesus of Nazareth." The contents were derived from various portions of the four Gospels, arranged in the order that seemed most natural to Jefferson. It included much of Jesus' teaching, but omitted everything miraculous.[68]

It should be said that Jefferson considered himself a Christian. But as even he admitted, he was not a "Christian" who accepted the deity of Christ in the historic sense of the term. He said, "I am a Christian in the only sense in which I believe Jesus wished anyone to be, sincerely attached to his doctrines in preference to all others; ascribing to himself every human excellence, and believing that he never claimed any other."[69]

4. Evil.

Jefferson believed that man has both good and evil qualities. Indeed, "experience proves, that the moral and physical qualities of man, whether good or evil, are transmissable in a certain degree." He further believed that it is a primary function of government to protect people from injuring each other and to be attentive to the needs and desires of the masses. However, when a government fails to perform this function then its officers "become wolves." This is not an unusual occurrence. The proneness of people to wield abusive power over others "seems to be the law of our general nature, in spite of individual exceptions; and experience declares that man is the only animal which devours his own kind." The kind of government that tends to promote this evil is that run by kings, nobles, or priests. He felt that governments of this kind abound in Europe and "there is scarcely an evil known in these countries which may not be traced to their king as its source."[70] When governments become tyrannical, it is the obligation of the governed to overthrow them.

5. Ethics.

The moral law grounded in nature applies to both nations and individuals: "I have but one system of ethics for men as for nations ...moral duties are obligatory on nations as on individuals....It is strangely absurd to suppose that a million human beings, collected together, are not under the same moral laws which bind each of them separately."[71]

The source of man's morality is his "love for others" which has been "implanted" in man by nature. It is this "moral instinct... which prompts us irresistably to feel and to succor" the distress of others. Jefferson believed that moral actions are relative in that "the same actions are deemed virtuous in one country and vicious in another." But this occurs because "nature has constituted *utility* to man [as] the standard...of virtue."[72]

Jefferson considered the greatest moral teachers to have been Epicurus and Jesus. He considered himself a follower of both but identified himself most closely with Epicurus. Concerning this he wrote: "I...am an Epicurian. I consider the genuine (not the imputed) doctrines of Epicurus as containing everything rational in moral philosophy which Greece and Rome have left us."[73]

6. History.

Like the other deists who have been covered, Jefferson said little about history. He did think that the study of history was important for the safeguarding of the people's freedom. As he wrote:

> History, by apprising them of the past, will enable them to judge of the future; it will avail them of the experience of other times and other nations; it will qualify them as judges of the actions and designs of men; it will enable them to know ambition under every disguise it may assume; and knowing it, to defeat its views.[74]

Jefferson also maintained that God had never broken into history to perform miracles or to give supernatural revelation. Such accounts to the contrary, he claimed, were the result of human fabrication, superstition, or fanaticism.[75] For example, of the virgin birth of Christ he said, "The day will come when the account of the birth of Christ as accepted in the Trinitarian churches will be classed with the fable of Minerva springing from the brain of Jupiter."[76]

7. Man's destiny.

Jefferson believed that man survives death. While on his death-bed Jefferson penned these words as a farewell to his surviving daughter:

Life's visions are vanished, its dreams are no more;
Dear friends of my bosom, why bathed in tears?
I go to my fathers, I welcome the shore
Which crowns all my hopes and which buries my cares.
Then farewell, my dear, my lov'd daughter, adieu!
The last pang of life is in parting from you.
Two seraphs await me long shrouded in death;
I will bear them your love on my last parting breath.[77]

In his abbreviated (desupernaturalized) version of the Bible, Jefferson did not omit Jesus' references to rewards in heaven for the righteous and punishment in hell for the wicked. Just how literally he took them is another question.

IV.   Some basic beliefs of deism.

Although there are points upon which deists differ, by and large what they hold in common provides a comprehensive picture of the deistic world view.

A.   God is one in nature and person.

All deists agree that there is only one God. This God is eternal, unchangeable, impassible, all-knowing, all-powerful, all-good, true, just, invisible, infinite—in short, completely perfect, lacking in nothing.

Furthermore, God is an absolute unity, not a triunity. God is only one person, not three persons. Deists hold the Christian theistic concept of the Trinity to be false if not meaningless. God does not exist as three co-equal persons. Thomas Jefferson wrote that "the Trinitarian arithmetic that three are one and one is three" is "incomparable jargon." Thomas Paine believed that the Trinitarian concept resulted in three different gods, and thus was polytheistic.[78] In contrast, deists contend that God is one in nature and one in person. Unitarians have carried on this deistic concept of God for many generations.

154

B. The world is finite and operates by natural laws.

The universe is the creation of God. Before the universe existed there was nothing except God. He brought everything into being. Hence, unlike God, the world is finite. It had a beginning while He has no beginning and no end.

The universe operates by natural laws. These laws flow from the very nature of God. Like Him they are eternal, perfect and immutable, representing the orderliness and constancy of His nature. They are the rules by which God measures His own activity and the standards by which He expects His creation to live.

C. The world is man's sole revelation of God.

God is as different from the universe as a painter is from a painting, a watchmaker from a watch, and a sculptor from a sculpture. On the other hand, like a painting, watch and sculpture, the universe reveals many things about God. Through its design it proclaims the existence of a cosmic Designer and reveals what this Designer is like and what He expects from man. The regularity and preservation of the universe show that there is a God who created, regulates and sustains the world. This world is dependent on God; God is not dependent on the world.

God does not reveal Himself in any other way but through creation. The universe is the deist's Bible. It alone reveals God. All other alleged revelations, whether oral or written, are human inventions.

D. Miracles do not occur.

Deists believe that God either cannot or will not intervene in nature. Those deists who believe that God cannot perform miracles often base their arguments on the immutability of the laws of nature. A miracle would be a violation of the natural laws. But natural laws are unchangeable and therefore cannot be violated, for a violation would involve a change in the unchangeable laws. Therefore, miracles are impossible.

Those deists who believe that God can perform a miracle but will not often support their argument by pointing out man's proneness toward superstition and deception, the lack of sufficient evidence in support of miracles, and man's unbroken experience of the uniformity of nature. They insist that the nature of the perfect Mechanic is magnified in that He made the machine of nature to run without constant need of repair. For deists, all miracle accounts are the result of human invention or superstition. In reality, miracles do not happen.

E.   Man is endowed with reason and should live by reason.

Deists agree that man has been created by God and is adequately suited to live happily in the world. They also contend that man is personal, rational and free. He has been endowed with various natural rights that should not be violated by any individual, group, or government agency. He has the rational ability to discover in nature all he needs to know in order to live a happy and full life. Reason is the guide to life.

Furthermore, like all other animals, man was created with strengths and weaknesses. Among his strengths are his reason and freedom. Among his weaknesses are his proneness toward superstition and the desire to dominate those of his own race. Both of these innate weaknesses have led to all forms of supernatural religions and oppressive governments.

F.   Ethics are grounded in nature.

The basis of human morality is grounded in nature. It is there that each person discovers how he should govern his own life, his association with other creatures and his relationship to God. For many deists the only innate principle in man is his desire for happiness. The way that man satisfies this innate desire is by governing all his actions according to reason. When man fails to do this he becomes miserable and acts immorally.

Deists differ on the universality of moral laws. They agree that the basis of all value is universal because it is grounded in nature. But they disagree as to which specific moral laws are absolute and which are relative. The fact that there is a right and a wrong is not in dispute. The problem is in determining exactly what is right and wrong in each case and circumstance. Some deists, like Jefferson, simply conclude that specific moral rules are relative: what is considered right in one culture is wrong in another culture. Other deists disagree, arguing that a correct use of reason will always lead one to an absolute right and an absolute wrong, although the application of these absolutes may vary with culture and circumstance.

G. Man's destiny includes an afterlife.

Although some deists deny that man survives death in any respect, many deists believe that man does live on after death. For most of these deists, man's afterlife is of an immaterial nature, where the morally good people are rewarded by God and the morally bad ones are punished by Him.

H. History is linear and purposeful.

In general, deists have little to say about history. They commonly hold that history is linear and purposeful. They also hold that God does not intervene in history through supernatural acts of revelation or miracles. They differ on whether God concerns Himself with what occurs in history. Many of the French deists in the 17th and 18th centuries believed that God was unconcerned with the ongoings of history. Most English deists, however, considered God to exercise a certain degree of providential care over the affairs of human history, yet without miraculous intervention.

According to many deists, the study of history has great value. If nothing else, history demonstrates the tendency of man toward superstition, deception and domination, and the terrible consequences that follow when this tendency goes unchecked and unchallenged.

V. An evaluation of deism.

A. Some contributions of deism.

As with the other world views covered thus far, there are a number of positive things that one may learn from deism. Some of these are summarized below.

First, many have agreed with the deists' insistence on the importance and use of reason in religious matters. The many claims made about miracles and supernatural revelation must be tested to verify their truth or falsity. No reasonable person would step into an elevator if he had good reason to believe that it was unsafe. Neither should anyone place his trust in a religious claim if he has good reason to believe that it is false. Man must use his reason to judge whether a religious claim is true or false, then respond accordingly.

Second, the deists have been commended for their belief that the world reflects the existence of God. The regularity and orderliness of the world suggest a cosmic Designer. The inadequacy of the world to account for its own operations and existence seems to imply an ultimate explanation beyond the world—God. Furthermore, the limited perfections discoverable in nature may imply that there is an unlimited perfect being beyond nature, a being who created and sustains all things. This natural evidence is available to all mankind to view and respond to in a reasonable way.

Third, many have credited deists for their exposure of much religious deception and superstition. Their relentless attacks on many religious beliefs and practices have helped numerous people to better evaluate their religious faith and to purge it of various corruptions.

B. Some criticisms of deism.

Although deism has made some positive contributions, many have found reason to criticize the deistic world view. The following are some of the more imporant criticisms that have been made. As a result of these and other criticisms, deism largely died out. Many of its characteristics, however, live on in Unitarianism, finite godism and religious humanism.

First, a number of critics have charged that the deists' understanding of God is incompatible with their rejection of miracles. A being who could bring the universe into existence from nothing could certainly perform "lesser" miracles if He so chose. A God who created water could part the sea or make it possible for a person to walk on it. The immediate multiplication of loaves of bread and fish would be no problem to a God who created all matter and life in the first place. A virgin birth or even a physical resurrection from the dead would be "minor" miracles in comparison to the miracle of creating the universe from nothing. In short, it seems self-defeating to admit a miracle like creation and then to deny the possibility of other miracles.

Second, some have pointed out that the deists' understanding of natural law is no longer valid. Scientists today consider the laws of nature to be general, not necessarily universal or absolute. Natural laws describe how nature generally behaves. They do not dictate how nature must always behave. Therefore, it is not valid to rule out miracles because they would violate *unchangeable* natural laws. Furthermore, many theists reject the concept of God as a great

Mechanic because it is too mechanistic and impersonal. They favor a model of God as a loving Father who is concerned enough to intervene in a world in which His children cry out for help.

Third, if God created the universe for the good of His creatures, then it seems reasonable to assume that He would miraculously intervene in their lives if their good depended on it. Surely an all-good Creator would not abandon His creation if He could help them. Instead, it seems that such a God would continue to exercise the love and concern for His creatures that originally prompted Him to create them, even if it meant providing that care through miraculous means.

Fourth, the deists' attack on supernatural revelation has often been challenged. If miracles are possible then one cannot reject out of hand every claim to supernatural revelation without first examining the evidence for its support. Only if it lacks supporting evidence should it be rejected. But if the evidence does substantiate the claim, then the alleged revelation should be considered authentic. In either case, it should not simply be ruled out categorically without further investigation.

Further, the fact that many individuals and groups have invented and abused religious beliefs is not sufficient grounds for rejecting *all* alleged supernatural religions. After all, government has been abused, but few would care to live where there is no government. Also, knowledge has often been misused for evil purposes, but who would do away with all education on this account?

Also, the mutability of human language and the fact of human error do not appear to be valid arguments against supernatural revelation. An all-powerful, all-knowing God could conceivably overcome these problems. At least such problems should not rule out the possibility of God's revealing Himself to man and having that revelation transmitted in either oral or written form. Again the evidence should first be consulted.

Fifth, and finally, the deists' case against Christianity and the Bible have been tested by many and found wanting. For example, the belief that many of the miracle stories in the Bible are mythical and have human origins has been challenged by such Christian theists as J. Gersham Machen, C. S. Lewis and others.[79] Referring to the miracle-focused Gospel of John, C. S. Lewis said, "I have been reading poems, romances, vision-literature, legends, myths all my life. I know what they are like. I know that not one of them is like this."[80] Moreover, Paine's position that most of the books of the Bible were written by people other than the ones who claimed to have written them and were written much later than traditionally claimed has been rejected by many archaelogists and biblical scholars of different religious persuasions.[81] Likewise, many suggest that the deistic attack on traditional trinitarian beliefs are shallow and unfounded.[82]

NOTES

1. These and other effects are brought out by Lee Hudson in his article "Deism: The Minimal Religion of Social Utility" in *Dialog* 16 (Summer 1977): 205-210.
2. See John Orr, *English Deism: Its Roots and Its Fruits* (Grand Rapids: Wm. B. Eerdmans Publishing Company, 1934), chapters 3 and 4; and Norman L. Geisler, *Christian Apologetics* (Grand Rapids: Baker Book House, 1976), chapter 9.
3. Herbert M. Morais, *Deism in Eighteenth Century America* (New York: Russell & Russell, 1960; first published, 1934), pp. 17, 85-126.
4. J. O'Higgins, "Hume and the Deists: A Contrast in Religious Approaches" in *The Journal of Theological Studies* 23 (October 1971): 479, 480.
5. Morais, *Deism in Eighteenth Century America,* chapters 4 and 5; Hudson, "Deism: The Minimal Religion of Social Utility," pp. 205-210; and The Declaration of Independence (1776).
6. Orr, *English Deism,* p. 140.
7. Matthew Tindal, *Christianity As Old As the Creation:* or *The Gospel, A Republication of the Religion of Nature* (New York & London: Garland Publishing, Inc., 1978, first published, 1730), pp. 39, 41, 42, 44, 45, 65, 66, 87.
8. Ibid., p. 39.
9. Ibid.
10. Ibid., pp. 29, 30.
11. Ibid., p. 30.
12. Ibid., pp. 30, 44-46.
13. Ibid., pp. 59, 114.
14. Ibid., p. 115.
15. Ibid., pp. 70, 107.
16. Ibid., p. 115.
17. Ibid., p. 13.
18. Ibid., pp. 11-18.
19. Ibid., pp. 169, 165.
20. Ibid., p. 26.
21. Ibid., pp. 48, 49.
22. Ibid., p. 49.
23. Ibid., pp. 23, 24, 30.
24. Ibid., p. 25.
25. Ibid., p. 27.
26. Ibid., p. 169.
27. Ibid., pp. 229, 340, 349, 170, 192.
28. Ibid., pp. 25, 26, 51, 1.
29. Thomas Paine, *Complete Works of Thomas Paine,* ed. by Calvin Blanchard (Chicago and New York: Belford, Clarke & Co., 1885), p. 39; and Alfred Owen Aldridge, "Paine, Thomas" in *The Encyclopedia of Philosophy,* 8 vols., reprint ed., ed. in chief, Paul Edwards (New York: Macmillan Publishing Co., Inc., &

The Free Press; London: Collier Macmillan Publishers, 1972; first published, 1967), 6:17.

30. Morais, *Deism in Eighteenth Century America*, pp. 120-122.
31. Paine, *Complete Works of Thomas Paine*, pp. 5, 26, 27, 201.
32. Ibid., pp. 26, 7.
33. Ibid., p. 7.
34. Ibid.
35. Ibid., p. 25.
36. Ibid., p. 19; cf., pp. 55, 56.
37. Ibid., p. 6.
38. Ibid., p. 150.
39. Ibid.
40. Ibid., pp. 47, 46.
41. Ibid., pp. 24, 26, 309.
42. Ibid., p. 26; cf., p. 28.
43. Aldridge, "Paine, Thomas" in *The Encyclopedia of Philosophy*, 6:17; and Morais, *Deism in Eighteenth Century America*, p. 124.
44. Paine, *Complete Works of Thomas Paine*, p. 310.
45. Ibid., p. 201.
46. Ibid.
47. Ibid., pp. 309, 41, 5.
48. Ibid., p. 24.
49. Ibid., p. 37; see also Aldridge, "Paine, Thomas" in *The Encyclopedia of Philosophy*, 6:18.
50. Paine, *Complete Works of Thomas Paine*, p. 56.
51. Ibid., pp. 150, 309.
52. Ibid., pp. 9-12, 15, 19, 20, 21, 53, 61-131, 133.
53. Ibid., pp. 51-53.
54. Ibid., pp. 5, 56; and Aldridge, "Paine, Thomas" in *The Encyclopedia of Philosophy*, 6:18.
55. Ralph Ketcham, "Jefferson, Thomas" in *The Encyclopedia of Philosophy*, 4:259.
56. Henry Wilder Foote, *Thomas Jefferson: Champion of Religious Freedom, Advocate of Christian Morals* (Boston: The Beacon Press, 1947), p. 10.
57. Saul K. Padover, *Thomas Jefferson and the Foundations of American Freedom* (New York: Van Nostrand Reinhold Company, 1965), pp. 89-91, 143, 148, 155, 156.
58. Ibid., pp. 92, 93.
59. Foote, *Thomas Jefferson*, p. 18.
60. Padover, *Thomas Jefferson and the Foundations of American Freedom*, pp. 143, 131-135, 178, 91.
61. Ibid., pp. 148, 97, 98.
62. Ibid., p. 98.
63. Ibid., pp. 135, 160.
64. Ibid., pp. 161, 178, 181.
65. Ibid., p. 119.
66. Ibid., pp. 178, 179.
67. Foote, *Thomas Jefferson*, pp. 49, 47. See also Francis I. Fesperman, "Jefferson's Bible" in *Ohio Journal of Religious Studies* 4:2 (October 1976): 78-88.
68. Fesperman, "Jefferson's Bible," pp. 81, 83, 84.
69. Foote, *Thomas Jefferson*, p. 4.
70. Padover, *Thomas Jefferson and the Foundations of American Freedom*, pp.

164, 97, 103. Cf., Foote, *Thomas Jefferson*, p. 31.

71. Foote, *Thomas Jefferson*, p. 42.
72. Padover, *Thomas Jefferson and the Foundations of American Freedom*, pp. 150, 151.
73. Ibid., p. 175.
74. Ibid., p. 184.
75. Fesperman, "Jefferson's Bible," p. 81.
76. Foote, *Thomas Jefferson*, p. 49.
77. Ibid., p. 68. The two seraphs Jefferson mentioned were his deceased wife and daughter Mary.
78. Padover, *Thomas Jefferson and the Foundations of American Freedom*, p. 49; Paine, *Complete Works of Thomas Paine*, p. 41.
79. J. Gersham Machen, *The Virgin Birth of Christ*, reprint ed. (Grand Rapids: Baker Book House 1977, first published, 1930); C. S. Lewis, *Miracles: A Preliminary Study* (New York: Macmillan Publishing Co., Inc., 1947); and Ronald Nash, *Christian Faith and Historical Understanding* (Grand Rapids: Zondervan/Probe, 1984).
80. C. S. Lewis, *Christian Reflections*, ed. by Walter Hooper (Grand Rapids: Wm. B. Eerdmans Publishing Company, 1967), p. 155.
81. Clifford A. Wilson, *Rocks, Relics and Biblical Reliability* (Grand Rapids: Zondervan Publishing House; Dallas: Probe Ministries International, 1977); K. A. Kitchen, *Ancient Orient and Old Testament* (Downers Grove: Inter-Varsity Press, 1966); F. F. Bruce, *The New Testament Documents: Are They Reliable?* 5th ed. (Grand Rapids: William B. Eerdmans Publishing Co., 1960); John A. T. Robinson, *Redating the New Testament* (Philadelphia: The Westminster Press, 1976); and Norman L. Geisler and William E. Nix, *A General Introduction to the Bible* (Chicago: Moody Press, 1968).
82. Orr, *English Deism*, pp. 267-74; Joseph Butler, *The Analogy of Religion Natural and Revealed to the Constitution and Course of Nature* (1872).

7

Finite Godism: A World With a Finite God

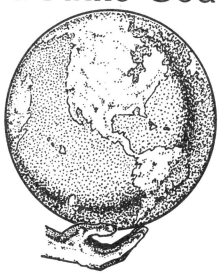

I. Introduction.

Are you capable of forgiving and loving God even when you have found out that He is not perfect, even when He has let you down and disappointed you by permitting bad luck and sickness and cruelty in

His world, and permitting some of those things to happen to you? Can you learn to love and forgive Him despite His limitations...?[1]

This is the question asked by Rabbi Kushner in his best-selling book defending a finite God. Many finite godists come to the conclusion that God is limited when they attempt to reconcile their theistic tradition with the pervasive presence of evil. The reasoning goes like this:

1. If God were all-powerful, He could destroy evil.
2. If God were all-good, He would destroy evil.
3. But evil has not been destroyed.
4. Therefore, either God does not exist or He is limited.
5. But there is evidence that God exists.
6. Therefore, God must be limited.

II. A typology of finite godism.

There are many different possibilities for a finite God position, not all of which have well-known representatives. The finite God could be personal (as most hold) or impersonal (as Henry Wieman[2] held). God's limitations could be internal (inherent in His nature, as J. S. Mill held) or external (imposed by the world, as Plato held). God could be limited in His goodness but not in his power (as held by very few), or in His power but not in His goodness (as believed by Brightman[3] and Bertocci). Or God could be limited in both power and goodness (Mill's view). Finally, this God could be one pole (as most hold) or bipolar (as Whitehead held).

Since bipolar finite godism was treated in chapter 5 under the name "panentheism," we will examine only monopolar examples here. Although most finite godists believe that God is transcendent (beyond the universe), some have a finite God who is immanent (within the universe). Henri Bergson[4] is an example of the latter view holding that God is the vital force that drives the process of evolution onward.

III. Some representatives of finite godism.

   A. John Stuart Mill (1806-1873).

John Stuart Mill was a pioneer in modern scientific thinking. He is credited with laying down the rules for inductive scientific reasoning. His work on probability formed the basis for much later thought on the topic. It is from this vantage point that Mill approaches the question of God.

1. God.

Mill succinctly stated the net results of his scientific approach to the question of the existence and nature of God:

> A Being of great but limited power, how or by what limited we cannot even conjecture; of great, and perhaps unlimited intelligence, but perhaps, also, more narrowly limited than his power: who desires, and pays some regard to, the happiness of his creatures, but who seems to have other motives of action which he cares more for, and who can hardly be supposed to have created the universe for that purpose alone.[5]

In brief, according to Mill, God is limited in both power and goodness. We can infer from nature that God has benevolent feelings toward His creatures, "but to jump from this to the inference that his sole or chief purposes are those of benevolence, and that the single end and aim of Creation was the happiness of his creatures, is not only not justified by any evidence but is a conclusion in opposition to such evidence as we have" (p. 192).[6] Probably the only legitimate inference about God that we can draw from nature "is that He does not wish His work to perish as soon as created" (p. 190).

Mill did not see "how we can even satisfy ourselves on grounds of natural theology, that the Creator foresees all the future; that he foreknows all the effects that will issue from his own contrivances" (p. 182). Therefore, according to Mill, all the evidence shows is an intelligence that is superior to human intelligence, but God is neither omnipotent nor omniscient. In fact, the very fact that the Creator used contrivances—the adaptation of means to achieve ends—indicates His limits. "Who would have recourse to means if to attain his end his mere word was sufficient? The very idea of means implies that the means have an efficacy [power to produce an effect] which the direct action of the being who employs them has not" (p. 177).

Despite Mill's belief that there could be other finite creators, he favored monotheism.

> Every other theory of the government of the universe by supernatural beings, is inconsistent either with the carrying on of that government

167

through a continual series of natural antecedents according to fixed laws, or with the interdependence of each of these series upon all the rest, which are the two most general results of science (p. 133).

Other than the general principles of design in nature, Mill could see little indication of the Creator's benevolence because "the end to which it is directed, and its adaptation to which end is the evidence of its being directed to an end at all, is not a moral end" (p. 189).

The limitations of God are not external. That is, they are not due to the resistance or restraints of the material with which He works. Rather,

the limitation of His power more probably results either from the qualities of the material—the substances and forces of which the universe is composed not admitting of any arrangements by which His purposes could be more completely fulfilled; or else, the purposes might have been more fully attained, but the Creator did not know how to do it (p. 186).

In short, God is limited within Himself, not simply by the exterior world or by other beings.

2. Creation.

The universe was not created out of nothing, according to Mill. "The indication given by such evidence as there is, points to the creation, not indeed of the universe, but of the present order of it by an Intelligent Mind, whose power over the materials was not absolute" (p. 243). In fact,

there is in Nature no reason whatever to suppose that either Matter or Force, or any of their properties, were made by the Being who was the author of the collocations by which the world is adapted to what we consider as its purposes; or that he has power to alter any of those properties (p. 178).

Thus, matter and energy are eternal, and "out of these materials He had to construct a world in which His designs should be carried into effect through given properties of Matter and Force, working together and fitting into one another" (p. 178).

Like Plato, Mill posited a finite God and eternal matter—a theistic dualism. Creation is not *ex nihilo* (out of nothing), nor is it *ex Deo* (out of God). Rather, it is *ex materia* (out of pre-existing matter.).

3. The world.

Mill believed in a material universe which he called "Nature." This "denotes the entire system of things with the aggregate of all their properties..." (p. 64). Nature is "a collective name for all facts, actual and possible" or "the mode...in which all things take place." Since all things take place in a regular and uniform way, we can speak of the "Laws of Nature" (p. 6), such as Newton's law of gravity. This is so because "all phenomena which have been sufficiently examined are found to take place with regularity, each having certain fixed conditions, positive and negative, on the occurrence of which it invariably happens" (pp. 5, 6). Because the operations of nature are uniform, "the progress of science mainly consists of ascertaining those conditions" (p. 6).

4. Miracles.

Although God is the author of nature's laws and could by His will intervene, there is no evidence that He does. Mill agreed that David Hume's argument against miracles leaves the impression "that the testimony of experience against miracles is undeviating and indubitable" (p. 221). Mill came to the same antisupernatural conclusion as Hume, only by another route. Mill believed that "a new physical discovery, even if it consists in the defeating of a well established law of nature, is but the discovery of another law previously unkown" (p. 221).

Thus, whatever new phenomenon is discovered "is found still to depend on law; it is always exactly reproduced when the same circumstances are repeated" (p. 222). But a miracle claims to supersede all natural laws, not just one natural law by another. However,

in the progress of science, all phenomena have been shown, by indisputable evidence, to be amenable to law, and even in the cases in which those laws have not yet been exactly ascertained, delay in ascertaining them is fully accounted for by the special difficulties of the subject (p. 223).

What is the basis for Mill's confidence that there is a natural explanation for all events? It is the absence of all experience of a supernatural cause and the frequent experience of natural causes.

The commonest principles of sound judgment forbid us to suppose for any effect a cause of which we have absolutely no experience, unless

169

all those of which we have experienced are ascertained to be absent. Now there are few things of which we have more frequent experience than of physical facts which our knowledge does not enable us to account for... (pp. 229, 230).

"There is, in short, nothing to exclude the supposition that every alleged miracle was due to natural causes" (p. 231). And as long as that supposition is possible, "no man of ordinary practical judgment, would assume by conjecture a cause which no reason existed for supposing to be real, save the necessity of accounting for something which is sufficiently accounted for without it" (p. 231).

Miracles were not categorically ruled impossible by Mill. He admitted that the existence of God makes them possible. Mill believed that "if we had the direct testimony of our senses to a supernatural fact, it might be as completely authenticated and made certain as any natural one. But we never have." Thus, there is "a vast preponderance of probability against a miracle...." From this Mill concluded "that miracles have no claim whatever to the character of historical facts and are wholly invalid as evidences of any revelation" (p. 239).

5. Evil.

To Mill, one of the most convincing evidences of God's finiteness is the presence of evil in the world. He concluded that "if the maker of the world can [do] all that He will, He wills misery, and there is no escape from the conclusion" (p. 37).

Mill also stated, "In sober truth, nearly all the things which men are hanged or imprisoned for doing to one another, are nature's every day performances" (p. 28). In addition, "killing, the most criminal act recognized by human laws, Nature does once to every being that lives; and in a large proportion of cases, after protracted tortures such as only the greatest monsters whom we read of ever purposely inflicted on their living fellow-creatures" (pp. 28, 29).

Mill continues with a list of the horrible evils of nature.

Nature impales men, breaks them as if on the wheel, casts them to be devoured by wild beasts, burns them to death, crushes them with stones like the first Christian martyr, starves them with hunger, freezes them with cold, poisons them by the quick or slow venom of her exhalations, and has hundreds of other hideous deaths in reserve, such

170

as the ingenious cruelty of a Nabis or a Domitian never surpassed. All this, Nature does with the most supercilious disregard both of mercy and of justice, emptying her shafts upon the best and noblest indifferently with the meanest and worst (p. 30).

Mill considered all of these evils to be absolutely contradictory to an all-powerful, all-good being. At best there is only a partially good deity with limited power.

6. Ethics.

In view of nature's gross evil, "the doctrine that man ought to follow nature, or in other words, ought to make the spontaneous course of things the model of his voluntary actions, is equally irrational and immoral" (p. 64). How can we use nature as our norm when its actions are so evil? Our duty, then, is not to imitate nature but to strive to amend it. And even though some aspects of nature are good, "it has never been settled by any accredited doctrine, what particular departments of the order of nature shall be reputed to be designed for our moral instruction and guidance" (p. 42). Thus, "it is impossible to decide that certain of the Creator's works are more truly expressions of His character than the rest" (p. 43).

Since Mill rejected the supernatural, he could not turn to revelation as a source of ethics. In fact, he believed that "there is a very real evil consequence on ascribing a supernatural origin to the received maxims of morality" (p. 99). It has the effect of consecrating imperfect rules and protecting them from all criticism.

Mill had great respect for Jesus and felt that His moral example was exemplary (pp. 253, 254). However, when it came to spelling out what the Christian "Golden Rule" meant, Mill favored utilitarianism. That is, we should act in such a way as to bring "the greatest good (pleasure, happiness) to the greatest number of persons."[7] There are no absolute ethical norms. Even telling the truth is not an absolute. "That even this rule, sacred as it is, admits of possible exceptions is acknowledged by all moralists."[8] The best we can do is to build up from experience general rules that can guide us in determining the course most likely to lead to the end of the greatest good. But "the beliefs which have thus come down are the rules of morality for the multitude, and for the philosopher until he has succeeded in finding better."[9]

171

7. Man and his destiny.

For Mill, man is not simply material. He has a mind or soul. In fact, "there is, therefore, in science, no evidence against the immortality of the soul but that negative evidence, which consists in the absence of evidence in its favour." Even the negative evidence is not as strong as negative evidence often is (p. 201). Nonetheless, Mill held that the belief that disembodied souls go about visibly or interfere in the events of life is disproved by the same weight of evidence that disproves witchcraft. "But that it does not exist elsewhere, there is absolutely no proof" (p. 201).

However, Mill also noted that there is no real evidence, either in the natural world (including scientific evidence) or in the nature of God, that warrants the inference that souls are immortal (pp. 208-210). Belief in immortality, therefore, is based merely on hope.

Mill, however, was confident that *if* there is life after death,

nothing can be more opposed to every estimate we can form of probability, than the common idea of the future life as a state of rewards and punishments in any other sense than that the consequences of our actions upon our own character and susceptibilities will follow us in the future as they have done in the past and present (pp. 210, 211).

If there is a future life, said Mill, it will simply be a continuation of the life we have on earth. To assume a radical break at death in the mode of our existence is contrary to all analogies drawn from this life. If life continues, we must assume that the same laws of nature will continue as well.

Despite the lack of evidence for immortality, Mill believed that life here and now is worth living. Thus, "the gain obtained in the increased inducement to cultivate the improvement of character up to the end of life, obvious without being specified" (p. 250).

Mill also found grounds for optimism about the future of the human race.

The conditions of human existence are highly favourable to the growth of such a feeling inasmuch as a battle is constantly going on, in which the humblest human creature is not incapable of taking some part, between the powers of good and those of evil, and in which every even the smallest help to the right side has its value in promoting the very slow and often almost insensible progress by which good is gradually

172

gaining ground from evil, yet gaining it so visibly at considerable intervals as to promise the very distant but not uncertain final victory of Good (p. 256).

Not only did Mill express optimism about the final victory of mankind over evil, but he also believed that humanistic efforts in this direction were sure to become the new religion of mankind.

To do something during life, on even the humblest scale if nothing more is within reach, towards bringing this consummation ever so little nearer, is the most animating and invigorating thought which can inspire a human creature; and that it is destined, with or without supernatural sanctions, to be the religion of the Future I cannot entertain a doubt (p. 257).

B. William James (1842-1910).

James was a pragmatist who approached the world and God from an experiential point of view. His test for the truth or falsity of a world view was simply "Does it work?" In James' own words, "What concrete difference will its being true make in one's actual life?" Truth is not inherent in an idea. "Truth *happens* to an idea. It becomes true, is *made* true by events."[10] Thus, for James, the world view that works best is true.

1. God.

According to James, the world view that worked best was a form of finite godism. Such a God avoids "the hallowed unreal God of scholastic theology [theism], or the unintelligible pantheistic monster...."[11] James felt that the pantheistic God swallows all individuals in absolute unity of its consciousness, while the theistic God is so transcendently distinct from His creatures, that "they have absolutely *nothing* in common."[12]

In view of these extremes James believed,

the line of least resistance, then, as it seems to me, both in theology and in philosophy, is to accept, along with the superhuman consciousness, the notion that it is not all-embracing, the noting, in other words, that there is a God, but that He is finite, either in power or in knowledge, or in both at once.[13]

James concluded, "All the evidence we have seems to me to sweep us very strongly towards the belief in some form of superhuman life with which we may, unknown to ourselves, be conscious."[14] However, such a God "need not be infinite, it need not be solitary." He admitted that "thus would a sort of polytheism return upon us . . . ,"[15] but did not view these consequences as bad. He admitted that polytheism is a possible world view for a pragmatist. What is true is that "the practical needs and experiences of religion seem to me sufficiently met by the belief that beyond each man and in a fashion continuous with him there exists a larger power which is friendly to him and to his ideals." However, "all that the facts require is that the power should be both other and larger than our conscious selves."[16]

Even to claim this much about God was for James a matter of "over-belief." All James knew for sure was that "whatever it may be on its *farther* side, the 'more' with which in religious experience we feel ourselves connected is on its *hither* side the subconscious continuation of our conscious life."[17] Therefore,

disregarding the over-beliefs, and confining ourselves to what is common and generic, we have in *the fact that the conscious person is continuous with a wider self through which saving experiences come,* a positive content of religious experience which, it seems to me, *is literally and objectively true as far as it goes.*

James speculated very little about his "over-beliefs" in a finite God. But he concluded his classic book on religious experience with this venture: "Who knows whether the faithfulness of individuals here below to their own poor over-beliefs may not actually help God in turn to be more effectively faithful to his own greater tasks?"[19]

Despite the particular differences various world views express about God, James felt assured that all religious experiences have one thing in common:

They all agree that the "more" really exists; though some of them hold it to exist in the shape of a personal god or gods, while others are satisfied to conceive it as a stream of ideal tendency embedded in the eternal structure of the world. They all agree, moreover, that it acts as well as exists, and that something really is effected for the better when you throw your life into its hands. It is when they treat of the experience of "union" with it that their speculative differences appear most clearly.[20]

174

Beyond this there is only speculative overbelief. Christian theism, for example, would "define the 'more' as Jehovah, and the 'union' as his imputation to us of the righteousness of Christ."[21] But that would be unfair to other religions, and, according to James, "would be an over-belief." But this is only one of many possible ways God can be conceptualized, and James believed that it was not the most practical way.

2. The world.

James was opposed to both pantheistic and materialistic (atheistic) conceptions of the world. The world is not reducible to matter, he said, nor is it pure mind or spirit. James took a pluralistic view of the universe, that is, that there are many different things. However, he strongly opposed the idea of creation being distinct from God, saying,

> The theistic conception, picturing God and His creation as entities distinct from each other, still leaves the human subject outside of the deepest reality in the universe. God is from eternity complete, it says, and sufficient unto Himself; He throws off the world by a free act and as an extraneous substance, and He throws off man as a third substance, extraneous to both the world and Himself. Between them, God says "one," the world says "two," and man says "three"—that is the orthodox theistic view.[22]

3. Miracles.

James' view of the relationship of God and the world became clearer when he wrote, "The books of natural theology which satisfied the intellects of our grandfathers seem to us quite grotesque, representing as they did, a God who conformed the largest things of nature to the paltriest of our private wants." He also said, "The God whom science recognizes must be a God of universal laws exclusively, a God who does a wholesale, not a retail business."[23]

For James, God is more organically connected with the world.

> The divine can mean no single quality, it must mean a group of qualities, by being champions of which in alternation, different men may all find worthy missions. Each attitude being a syllable in human nature's total message, it takes the whole of us to spell the meaning out completely.[24]

175

Despite the naturalistic tone of these statements, James thought of himself as a supernaturalist of sort. His sort was not theistic, to be sure, for James spoke of his "own inability to accept either popular Christianity or scholastic theism ..."[25] because he believed they surrendered too easily to naturalism. "It takes the facts of physical science at their face-value, and leaves the laws of life just as naturalism finds them, with no hope of remedy, in case their fruits are bad."[26] Like Immanuel Kant, James felt that theistic belief in the supernatural

confines itself to sentiments about life as a whole, sentiments which may be admiring and adoring, but which need not be so, as the existence of systematic pessimism proves. In this universalistic way of taking the ideal world, the essence of practical religion seems to me to evaporate.[27]

Such a theistic view James called "crasser" supernaturalism. This he rejected for a more "refined" supernaturalism that admits "providential leadings, and finds no intellectual difficulty in mixing the ideal and the real world together by interpolating influences from the ideal region among the forces that causally determine the real world's details."[28]

Although James disavowed the term, his belief is similar to certain forms of pantheism wherein God animates the world the way a soul animates a body. He saw this kind of supernaturalism in stark contrast to the rank naturalism which he described as

the curdling cold and gloom and absence of all permanent meaning which for pure naturalism and the popular science evolutionism of our time are all that is visible ultimately, and the thrill stops short, or turns rather to an anxious trembling.

This kind of naturalism, "fed on recent cosmological speculations, mankind is in a position similar to that of a set of people living on a frozen lake, surrounded by cliffs over which there is no escape."[29]

Whatever one labels it, James' view of reality went beyond physical reality and included a broader "scientific" understanding of supernormal and parapsychological events generally denied by the scientific community of his day. Of these James wrote: "Miraculous healings have always been part of the supernaturalist stock in trade, and have always been dismissed by the scientist as figments of the imagination." He added, "No one can foresee just how far this legitimation of occulist phenomena under newly found scientist titles may proceed—even 'prophecy,' even 'levitation,' might creep into the pale."[30]

However, if one insisted on claiming that any of these events were supernatural interruptions of a natural process, James objected strongly. He argued that the "supernatural" is, in a real sense, only a part of our wider (subconscious) self.

> If, then, there be a wider world of being than that of our everyday consciousness, if in it there be forces whose effects on us are intermittent, if one facilitating condition of the effects be the openness of the "subliminal" door, we have the elements of a theory to which the phenomena of religious life lend plausibility. I am so impressed by the importance of these phenomena that I adopt the hypothesis which they so naturally suggest. At these places at least, I say, it would seem as though transmundane energies, God, if you will, produced immediate effects within the natural world to which the rest of our experience belongs.[31]

James gave a naturalistic interpretation even to the so-called supernatural conversions claimed by Jonathan Edwards and Charles Wesley. He claimed that "converted men as a class are indistinguishable from natural men; some natural men even excel some converted men in their fruits...." Hence, the believers in the non-natural character of sudden conversion have had practically to admit that there is no unmistakable class-mark distinctive of all true converts."[32]

4. Evil and morals.

According to James, evil is real. He flatly rejected the strict pantheistic belief that situations, such as evil, are not really true of the finite world. He said:

> With this radical discrepancy between the absolute and the relative points of view, it seems to me that almost as great a bar to intimacy between the divine and the human breaks out in pantheism as that which we found in monarchical theism....[33]

As for what is right and wrong for one to do in this world, James believed that "there is no such thing possible as an ethical philosophy dogmatically made up in advance.... We all help to determine the content of ethical philosophy so far as we contribute to the race's moral life. In other words, there can be no final truth in ethics any more than in physics...."[34]

At this point James' pragmatism shows through clearly. He candidly stated, "'The true,' to put it very briefly, is only the expedient in the way of our thinking, just as 'the right' is only the expedient in the way of our behaving."[35]

James believed that "saintliness" flowed from religious experience. In fact, he rejected Nietzsche's view that the saint is a weak individual, pointing to strong figures like Joan of Arc and Oliver Cromwell as counter examples. James lauded the saintly (holy) life, saying, "In a general way, then, and 'on the whole,' our abandonment of theological criteria, and our testing of religion by practical common sense and the empirical method, leave it in possession of its towering place in history...." He concluded, saying, "Let us be saints, then, if we can, whether or not we succeed visibly and temporally."[36]

There is, however, no absolute standard for the saintly life of good. Each must find what works best for him. James offered only the general guideline that we should avoid "pure naturalism" on the one hand because of its ineptness, and "pure salvationism" on the other hand because of its other-worldliness.[37] Between these we must find the expedient path of what works best for us.

5. Man.

Human beings are more than material. Although mankind evolved from lower forms of life, he has arrived at a higher form of life. In fact, humans are immortal. Even if "thought is a function of the brain,"[38] this relationship does not compel us to deny immortality. Dependence on the brain for this natural life would in no wise "make immortal life impossible—it might be quite compatible with supernatural life behind the veil hereafter."[39] Scientifically we can prove only the *concomitance* (co-occurrence) of the functioning of the mind with the brain, not the *dependence* of the mind on the brain for its continued existence.[40]

6. History and man's destiny.

James was opposed to both optimistic and pessimistic views of human destiny. As for unhappy men who think the salvation of the world impossible, theirs is the doctrine known as pessimism. Optimism in turn would be the doctrine that thinks the world's salvation inevitable. Midway between the two there stands what may be called the doctrine of meliorism . . . . [41]

Meliorism treats salvation as neither necessary nor impossible." As a pragmatist James felt compelled to accept improvement in the world as probable but not inevitable, because "pragmatism has to postpone a dogmatic answer, for we do not yet know certainly which type of religion is going to work best in the long run."[42]

James' realism led him to reject the belief that "all must be saved"[43] or that "total reconciliation" will occur. He said, "I am willing that there should be real losses and real losers, and no total preservation of all that is." For "when the cup is poured off, the dregs are left behind forever, but the possibility of what is poured off is sweet enough to accept."[44]

In justification of this conclusion, James offered this scenario:

Suppose that the world's author put the case to you before creation, saying: "I am going to make a world not certain to be saved, a world the perfection of which shall be conditional merely, the condition being that each several agent does its own 'level best.' I offer you the chance of taking part in such a world. Its safety, you see, is unwarranted. It is a real adventure, with real danger, yet it may win through. It is a social scheme of co-operative work genuinely to be done. Will you join the procession? Will you trust yourself and trust the other agents enough to face the risk?"[45]

Given such a proposal most persons, James believed, would prefer the risk of such an adventure over the alternative of non-existence. Such, he believes, is the world we have.

C. Peter Bertocci (1910-   ).

One strong finite god tradition in America has been that of personal idealism, represented by Edgar S. Brightman (1884-1953). He was succeeded at Boston University by his former student, Peter Bertocci, whom we will use as our example here.

1. God.

God is a cosmic mind who guides the development of all things. This "God is all-good but not all-powerful."[46] Bertocci poses the question:

179

If God is omnipotent, and therefore the creator of so much evil, how can He be good? Or if He is good, and did not intend evil, can He be omnipotent in the sense defined? Must there not be something beyond the control of His good will which is the source of evil in the world?[47]

Bertocci opts for the latter alternative, basing his conclusion on the presence of actual evil in the world. He pointedly asks: "The toll taken by mental and physical disease, the horrible pain and torture which can be man's lot, and the suffering beyond the point where it can seem to anyone's good—are these *necessarily* the best an omnipotent God can do?" (p. 415). Bertocci concludes that "there results a world in which evil frustrates the creative realization of values. We have accordingly suggested that God is all-good but not all-powerful" (p. 420).

In answer to the question "Why can't the cosmic mind be evil?" Bertocci says, "He *might* be, but he *will* not" (p. 421). The reason, he adds, is that "a person *can* destroy what his intelligence knows to be good, but he will be all the less likely to do this if he knows the consequences of evil" (p. 421) It is true "that God too is free to do good or evil. For his moral goodness, like ours, cannot be automatic" (p. 423). God is not necessarily good. However, God is wise and

the religious conviction that God is good—the conviction that love, binding all persons and things together in creative union, is central to the universe—is thus reasonably justified. To suppose that the highest Intelligence we know would find some sort of delight or self-fulfillment in allowing unnecessary human suffering, or animal pain, *if he could do something about it,* is to reject everything we know about the nature of wisdom (p. 423).   ·

Although God is the highest intelligence, He is not omniscient. For example, God does not know the future of individual free beings. If He did, then their acts would not be free, since what an omniscient mind knows *must* come to pass. God does know the future of groups in general, but only to the degree that insurance companies can make predictions or that scientists can prescribe statistical probabilities of subatomic particles (p. 449). But "insofar as our natures and environments depend on our own free action or the free activities of others, He cannot predict our destinies" (p. 450).

God is not only intelligent, but also personal. "A person is a unity of consciousness capable of reason, of moral obligation and ideals, and of free will" (p. 442). But like all other persons, God endures throughout change. That is,

we find ourselves acting and changing and yet knowing that we are changing and acting and, at the same time, knowing that the moment we just lived through is *our* past and that what we envisaged a moment ago is now *our* present. When we say that God is a person we mean this kind of being (p. 443).

As a personal being, God loves the world. That is, His purposes for it and interaction with it are always good. Thus,

The moral power of God consists of His absolute goodness. When we *think of God as the cosmic Lover, sensitive to the responsiveness of His creatures, affected by their love and hate, willing within limits to alter His activities as this is demanded by His relationship to all sensitive creatures, we are thinking of an ideal Person.* To put it almost too crisply: God is God because He can suffer for goodness more than any other person (p. 461).

2. The world.

God is the ultimate cause of the universe. He is the "why" of all that exists. "How" things came to be is another question. Here Bertocci agrees with the theory of evolution. However, he rejects both the pantheistic and the atheistic views of origins, reasoning, "But if God did not create the world 'out of' himself, and if he did not create it 'out of something not himself,' how did he create it? Many theologians and philosophers reply: Out of nothing!" (p. 450). Despite the admitted difficulties in conceptualizing this view, Bertocci believes it is the best conclusion. But creation from nothing does not necessitate a temporal creation.

So far as we can judge from the portion of the world we know, there never has been a time when God was not wanting, thinking, oughting, and willing some world and possibly some change in it. God, then, can be eternal and infinite in some respects and changing in other respects (p. 446).

As far as the *nature* of this eternal creation is concerned, the personal idealists claim that "the physical universe is not some nonmental stuff or electrical energy which God created, as many dualistic theists have held." Rather, "the physical or spatial world is a part of God's nature, and as such it is mental in structure" (p. 430). For example, "a chair, crowbar, or mountain *is* the energizing of God's will." This is not to identify God and the physical world as one. It is only to point out that "the spatial world is an expression of God's nature, but God is more than the physical universe..." (p. 430).

3. Evil.

Despite the fact that an all-good God created the world, the world contains real evil in it. Ultimately this is traceable to a Given in God's nature. This Given is a nonrational element, an unreasoned raw content, which God must take into account in all His activity. "In basic structure God's experience does not differ from ours. There is form and content in God's mind, and there is challenge, enjoyment, and struggle in his life" (pp. 432, 433). Bertocci hastens to add that "God's finiteness thus does not mean that he began or will end; nor does it mean he is limited by anything external to Himself" (p. 434). Thus, "the evil in the world which has no conceivable good purpose is due not to the fact that God wills evil, but to the fact that he finds *in* his nature a non-rational content which he no more can rid himself of than of the laws of his thinking" (p. 434). Both rational and nonrational elements are aspects of his unified nature.

Not all evil is without purpose. Some evil is due to human carelessness; much turns out for good in the long run, and some heightens our appreciation for the good. Furthermore, this life is not the whole story (p. 299). However, the real problem of suffering is that some evil blocks the reasonable good necessary for a happy life. But "certainly, if God is all-powerful and all-knowing, he could have framed a universe in which the unnecessary afflictions of evil were absent" (p. 398). This world is neither the best of all possible worlds conceivable nor even the best achievable by an omnipotent being (pp. 406, 407). How do we know? Because there is evil in the world "whose destructive effect, so far as we know, is greater than any good which may come from it" (p. 398).

4. Man and his destiny.

Man is the result of an evolutionary process. "Among the mutations, a new line of creation (but similar in many respects to other lines) produced man" (p. 161). This does not mean that the laws of physics and chemistry alone produced man. Man is a conscious rational being and "conscious thinking itself... is not controlled by the laws of physics and chemistry as are the brain cells" (p. 198). Man is more than a complicated physical machine. His craving for friendship, love, creativity, beauty and holiness are aspects of man that are more than physical (p. 192).

Man is a free, purposing, thinking being. When man evolved, "human beings forged ahead, constituting an independent development, representing a new thrust on the part of Nature (or God), and being a law unto themselves" (p. 162). As a free being man can choose to enact one alternative rather than another. Furthermore, man's "free will is not acquired" (p. 228). It is part of his very nature.

Man also has a mind. *"The human mind is an irreducible kind of being, not identical with its body and not dependent upon the body for its existence, though affected by the body"* (p. 202). Thus, I can be aware of myself. "What we mean by *I* refers both to this fact of self-conscious existence and of conscious existence..." (p. 203). This personal, self-conscious identity is also immortal. Bertocci agrees with G. H. Palmer, who commented about his diseased wife: "...who can contemplate the fact of it and not call the world irrational if out of deference to a few particles of disordered matter, it excludes so fair a spirit?" (p. 528).

This afterlife, however, "is not the reward for goodness in this life." Nonetheless, only "those persons are immortal whom God judges to be capable of developing worthily at any time in their future existence" (p. 546). Only God knows whether some persons may sink so low that even He despairs of arousing any higher aspirations in them. But there will be no punishment for sin. God is a loving Father, and "to suppose that God would eternally damn any creature...is morally hideous" (p. 545).

5. Ethics.

Man is not only free and rational, but also moral; thus, there is a moral law by which men ought to live. That is, "the universe has a moral order which man cannot break with impunity" (p. 367). This law is "a fundamental moral law for all men, a law which is consistent with their nature as creative, rational beings" (p. 361). This moral law is not merely descriptive; it is prescriptive. Furthermore, the moral law cannot be reduced to the voice of society, entirely manmade and dependent on the whims, interests and needs of human minds. Nor is the moral law solely the voice of God. Values are "universal but not independent of man" (p. 256).

The alternative is not *either* relative *or* absolute (that is, independent of the human mind). The alternative is *either* relative *or* universal *or* absolute. True, if values are absolute they are independent of human minds and also universal. But values can be universal (applicable to all human beings) without being independent of human experience (p. 256).

An example of such a true "universal" value is love or goodwill toward others. That is, "all persons ought to respect the needs and abilities of others and try to help them find *growing* satisfaction" (p. 266). Such a value ought to be pursued by all men."The final test is the ability of that value to knit other values together more harmoniously and lastingly" (p. 264). Such enduring values are not known intuitively. "It takes time, courage, and criticism to discover the universal value of love" (p. 265).

6. History and goal.

There is no ultimate or finally assured goal to human history. God is finite and, as such, He cannot achieve all that He plans. "Yet God is unwavering in His struggle to make the best of every situation" (p. 435). However, "can we give assurance that it is absolutely impossible in theory for such a reversal to take place? The answer is no" (p. 432).

In fact, God's efforts have not always been successful in the past,"as the disappearance of whole species in the course of evolution suggest" (p. 454). Even for God "there must be disappointment consistent with the realization that incomplete control forces unmerited suffering by man" (p. 467). Nevertheless, Bertocci takes consolation in the fact that "although He [God] cannot achieve all that He plans, He has managed to control the nonrational content of His nature rather than be controlled by it" (p. 435). The Given is not running wild. Despite obstacles, God's will finds ways to avoid ultimate blind alleys and final defeat. Based on God's past record of achievement, we have hope that it will probably continue.

IV.   Some basic beliefs of finite godism.

Not all finitists agree on all points of their views on God and the world. The following summary emphasizes the points they have in common and notes some differences.

A. God is finite in power and/or love.

The most fundamental characteristic of the finite God view is that God is limited in His very nature. Some say that He is limited in power but not in goodness, while few (if any) claim the reverse. Some claim that God is limited in both power and goodness. All agree that God is not infinite in power.

Although some (such as Plato) seem to hold that God is not intrinsically limited in His nature, they believe that the world (which God did not create) places *external* limits on His ability to do all that He wants. If God did not create the world and does not sustain its existence, then He is not able to do just anything He chooses with it; He cannot destroy it.

B. Creation is out of nothing or out of pre-existing matter.

Finite godism has no uniform view on creation. Some who come out of the dualistic Greek tradition (following Plato) hold to creation *ex materia* (out of pre-existing, eternal matter). According to this view, God did not bring the world into existence; He merely *shaped* the matter that was already there. Thus, there is something about the extent and nature of matter over which even God has no ultimate control. He simply has to work *with* the world and do the best He can under the limitations it places on His creative powers.

Some believe that God brought the universe into existence *ex nihilo* (out of nothing). This view is influenced by theism. In this case, God's limitations are internal. He is limited by His own nature, not by something "out there" with which He has to cope and over which He has no final word.

In either case, all finite godists agree on two basic aspects about creation: 1) It was not *ex Deo* (out of God), as pantheists believe; and 2) God is limited either in or by creation.

C. The world operates by natural law.

There are few things about the world on which all finite godists agree. All agree that the world is there and that it runs by natural law. But there is no unanimity on whether it always existed and/or always will exist. Specific views on the nature of the world range from one end of the spectrum of Mind-Matter to the other. Probably the only other widely held view today is that the physical universe is not eternal or unlimited in energy, but is subject to the law of entropy and is running down.

D. Miracles.

Most finite godists reject miracles. Some admit that supernatural interventions are possible in principle but deny that they happen in practice. In this respect, finite godism is similar to deism, which claims a supernatural Creator but disclaims any supernatural acts in the creation. However, deism is distinguished from finite godism in that the deistic God has no intrinsic limits on His power. But both views see miracles as a violation of natural law. Since they place a high emphasis on the regularity and uniformity of the world, they do not wish to concede that miracles interrupt it.

E. Man is created and may survive death.

Ultimately man was created by God. Since Darwin's time, however, finite godists have been convinced that God used a natural evolutionary process to produce man. Some finite godists (such as Henri Bergson) even equate God with the evolutionary force in nature.

Most finite godists admit that humans have a soul, and some believe that persons are immortal. All reject a purely materialistic view of man.

F. Evil limits God.

Evil is real. In fact, the presence and power of evil places limits even on God. Evil is both physical and moral. The former quality is not always possible to avoid, but man can do something about the latter. Cooperating with God's efforts for good (or even going beyond them if necessary) is part of our moral duty in the world.

There are various explanations for the origin of evil. Some say that it has always existed in some form (dualism). Others attribute much of it to man's free choices. But all agree that there is no guarantee that evil will ever be totally destroyed.

G. Ethics are enduring and helpful for human life.

Few finite godists believe in ethical absolutes. Since God is not unchangeable, it follows that no value based in Him would be immutable either. Many, however, believe that values are objective and enduring. Some even hold that certain values are unconditional. For the most part, however, since they do not believe that God has revealed any unequivocal ethical norms, individuals are left to decide for themselves the right course of action in each situation. Often the right action is thought to be the one that brings the greatest good.

H. Human destiny is uncertain.

Here too there are divergent views. Some finite godists are more optimistic than others. Some point to a steady evolutionary progress of the universe as the hope for final victory. Most are less certain that good will vanquish all evil. All admit that it is possible that no final victory will be achieved; it is even conceivable that evil may overcome good. Most finite godists find this latter view intuitively repugnant. However, since God is limited and is Himself struggling with evil, there is no assurance of a final solution. The struggle may simply go on endlessly.

V.   An evaluation of finite godism.

A.   Some contributions of finite godism.

There are many positive values of the finite God view. Some of the more significant ones will be briefly noted here. For a more detailed exposition consult the primary sources listed at the end of the chapter.

1.   A realistic approach to evil.

Unlike some world views, finite godism cannot be blamed for avoiding the problem of evil. It has not, like the proverbial ostrich, stuck its head in the sand and ignored the real presence of evil. In fact, it is in facing the problem squarely that most finite godists have come to their position.

2.   Limitations on the use of divine power.

Whatever else can be said about the meaning of the word "omnipotent," it cannot mean that God can literally do anything. Finite godists correctly point to a limitation of the use of God's power. For example, God cannot use His power (limited or unlimited) to create and destroy at the same time. God cannot will to give creatures free choice and yet at the same time force them to act contrary to their choices.

Likewise, finite godism points to a real problem in many views of evil, namely, that "the best possible world" may not actually be achievable. Or, more properly put, just because we can *conceive* of our universe with less (or no) evil does not mean that God can *achieve* such a universe. In this sense, as long as there is a world of free creatures (who at times do what is evil), the use of God's power will be limited to some degree.

3. The need for man to struggle against evil.

Another value that emerges from most forms of finite godism is an antidote for fatalism. The outcome of the struggle of good and evil does, to some extent, depend on man. Our efforts can make a difference. Complete determinism is fatal to the needed motivation to fight evil. Finite godists cannot be charged with a passive resignation to the inevitable. Their view calls for real human involvement to overcome evil.

There are other positive features of various finite-God views. But many of these are held in common with theism or other views, so they need not be commended here. The above are essential and characteristic of finite-God views.

B. Some criticisms of finite godism.

Finite godism is not without its critics. The criticisms fall into several basic categories.

1. A finite God would need a cause.

Some argue that a finite God is only a superior creature and all creatures need a Creator. This criticism can be stated from different perspectives. For example, the principle of causality says that every finite being has a cause. If this is so, then a finite God needs a cause. But if God is caused, then He is not really God. The one who created or caused Him is God.

Another way to state the problem is to note that a finite being is a contingent (dependent) being, not a necessary (independent) being. A necessary being is one which *cannot* not exist. A contingent being is one which *can* not exist. But if God could not exist, then it is possible for nothing to exist. However, something does exist. Hence, how is it possible for God to be contingent, as a finite God would seem to be? On the other hand, if a finite God were a necessary being, and therefore independent, then He would have to be unlimited in His being. A necessary being could not be limited to anything—including the threat of nothingness, since a necessary being could not possibly *not* exist. Otherwise, it would not be a *necessary* being. In short, it can be argued that a finite, contingent being could not be the Creator; rather, it would need a Creator.

2. A finite God is not worthy of worship.

Another criticism leveled at a God limited in goodness is that anything only partly good is not worthy of wholehearted worship. To worship means to attribute ultimate worth to something or someone. Why should one attribute absolute worth to what is not absolutely worthy? Every finite being is a creature, and worship of the creature, rather than the Creator, is idolatry. Or, to borrow Paul Tillich's terms, an ultimate commitment should not be given to anything less than an Ultimate. But a partially good being is not an ultimate Good. Why, then, should anyone worship a finite God?

3. Evil does not eliminate an infinite God.

The argument for a finite God has an apparent loophole concerning evil. The argument goes like this:

(1) If God were all-powerful, He could destroy evil.
(2) If God were all-good He would destroy evil.
(3) But evil has not been destroyed.
(4) Therefore, there cannot be an all-powerful God.

However, the third premise should read:

(3a) But evil has not *yet* been destroyed.

Adding the word "yet" immediately opens up the possibility that evil will yet be defeated in the future. If the finite godist insists that this will never happen, then he is presuming to know more than he as a *finite* creature is able to know.

When we examine the wording of Bertocci's argument carefully, we discover that he admits this very point. He acknowledged that there is evil "whose destructive effect, *so far as we know,* is greater than any good which may come from it." But that is precisely the problem: how can a finite man see far enough into the future to claim for certain that nothing will ever be done to ultimately defeat evil and bring in a greater good? However *improbable* it may seem to us, it is still *possible* that the future may bring good news.

Furthermore, if there is an all-powerful and all-good God, His existence automatically guarantees that evil will be defeated in the future. This can be seen as follows:

(1) An all-good God has the desire to defeat evil.

189

(2) An all-powerful God has the ability to defeat evil.

(3) But evil has not yet been defeated.

(4) Therefore, evil will be defeated in the future.

Stated this way, the question of whether evil is compatible with an infinite God is resolved. If an infinite God exists, then it is guaranteed that He will defeat evil, since such a God would have both the desire and the power to do so. Thus, it appears that finite godism has not successfully eliminated an infinite God by way of evil.

4. By what standard can we measure God?

There is another problem for modern forms of finite godism. If God is not completely good, then by what standard are we measuring Him? We cannot measure Him by the standard of His own nature, for He measures up to that perfectly. But if we measure God by some absolute moral law beyond God, then the Legislator of this absolute law would be God. Laws come from law givers, and moral prescriptions come from moral prescribers. Thus, would not absolutely perfect moral laws have to come from an absolutely perfect Moral Law Giver? In short, if a finite God falls short of an absolute standard of goodness, then He is not really God. The absolute moral being beyond Him would be God.

Perhaps this dilemma is what causes most finite godists to limit only God's power and not His goodness. To an outsider, however, this view appears to be both an arbitrary judgment and wishful thinking. Furthermore, how can God be an infintely good being when He is only a finite being? How can one be more of anything than he has the capacity to be? How can the attributes of God be extended further than His actual nature allows? Can one's knowledge, for example, be extended further than his brain allows?

5. The concept of a limited God poses a dilemma.

Finite godism claims that God cannot destroy all evil. Some say that this is because of intrinsic limitations in His nature. Others claim that extrinsic limits have been placed on Him. But the only extrinsic limitation that the Creator could not destroy would be an eternal, uncreated and necessary being. But if there is an eternal, uncreated and necessary being beyond God, then that being is the Creator, and our "finite God" turns out to be only a limited creation. If, on the other hand, the being outside God is created and contingent, while God is uncreated and necessary, then God could destroy that being. Thus,

190

He would not be limited by it. Therefore, if God can create and destroy anything, then why not admit that He is all-powerful?

In brief, the dilemma is this: if God can destroy all else in the universe besides Himself, then He is all-powerful. If there is some other indestructible being outside God, then He is not God; this other being is God. But in either case, the finite-God view would seem to be wrong, for there would be an all-powerful being who could destroy the finite God.

6. Uncertainty over the outcome of evil limits moral motivation.

Finite godists claim that there is no guarantee that good will ultimately triumph over evil. If this is true, then those who work for good may work for naught. Of course, it often happens in the everyday course of events that our efforts are frustrated. However, a religious commitment is not based on day-to-day occurrences; it is an ultimate commitment. Can a finite God who cannot guarantee the ultimate victory of good over evil really inspire an ultimate commitment? How many people will really make an ultimate commitment to work for something they have no assurance will ultimately win? One can be inspired to say courageously, "I would rather lose in a battle that will ultimately win than win in a battle that will ultimately lose." Thousands upon thousands have died with a belief like this. But how many will be motivated to proclaim, "I would rather lose in a battle that may ultimately lose than in one that will ultimately win"? Yet this seems to be the claim of a devotee of a finite God. It is doubtful that such a futile commitment would be made by the masses of persons needed to give even a faint prospect of victory for finite godism, which depends so much on human efforts for good.

NOTES

1. Rabbi Harold Kushner, *When Bad Things Happen to Good People* (New York: Avon Books, 1981), p. 148.
2. See Henry N. Wieman, *The Source of Human Good* (Chicago: University of Chicago Press, 1946), especially pp. 6-8, 54-62.
3. For Edgar S. Brightman's view see his *A Philosophy of Religion* (New York: Prentice-Hall, Inc., 1940).
4. See Henri Bergson, *Creative Evolution*, trans. by Arthur Mitchell (Westport, Conn.: Greenwood Press, Inc., 1911), and *Two Sources of Morality and Religion*, trans. by R. Ashley Audra and Cloudesley Brereton (New York: Doubleday, 1935), especially chapter 3.
5. See John Stuart Mill, *Three Essays on Religion: Nature, Utility of Religion, and Theism* (London: Longmans, Green & Co., 1885), p. 194.
6. All page numbers to J. S. Mill quotes are from *Three Essays*...unless otherwise noted.
7. John Stuart Mill, *Utilitarianism* (New York: Meridian Books, 1962, first published, 1863), chapter 2.
8. Ibid.
9. Ibid.
10. William James, *Essays in Pragmatism* (New York: Hafner Publishing Co., 1968), pp. 160, 161.
11. William James, *A Pluralistic Universe* (London: Longmans, Green, and Co., 1909), p. 316.
12. Ibid., p. 26.
13. Ibid., p. 311.
14. Ibid., p. 309.
15. William James, *Varieties of Religious Experience* (New York: A Mentor Book, 1958, first published, 1902), p. 396.
16. Ibid.
17. Ibid., p. 386.
18. Ibid., p. 388.
19. Ibid., p. 391.
20. Ibid., p. 385.
21. Ibid.
22. James, *Pluralistic Universe*, p. 25.
23. James, *Varieties*, pp. 372-374.
24. Ibid., p. 368.
25. Ibid., p. 393.
26. Ibid.
27. Ibid.
28. Ibid., p. 392.
29. Ibid., p. 122.
30. Ibid., p. 378.
31. Ibid., p. 394.
32. Ibid., p. 192.

33. James, *Pluralistic Universe*, p. 40.
34. James, *Essays in Pragmatism*, p. 65.
35. Ibid., p. 170.
36. James, *Varieties*, p. 290.
37. Ibid., p. 140.
38. William James, *Human Immortality: Two Supposed Objections to the Doctrine* (London: Archibald Constable & Co., Ltd., 1906), p. 24.
39. Ibid., pp. 38, 39.
40. Ibid., pp. 42, 43.
41. William James, *Pragmatism and Other Essays* (New York: Washington Square Press, Inc., 1963, first published, 1907), p. 125.
42. Ibid., p. 132.
43. Ibid., pp. 129, 130.
44. Ibid., p. 130.
45. Ibid., p. 127.
46. Peter Bertocci, *Introduction to the Philosophy of Religion* (New York: Prentice-Hall, Inc., 1953).
47. Ibid., p. 415. All page numbers cited from here on in this chapter are from Bertocci, *op. cit.*

8

Polytheism: A World With Many Gods

I.   Introduction.

Polytheism is the belief that there are two or more personal gods that have distinct spheres of influence in the universe. Unlike theism and deism, these gods are not viewed as beyond the space-time world. Rather, they are in the world. Also unlike theism and deism, these gods are not creators of the universe but are its shapers and transformers. However, polytheism is not necessarily incompatible with pantheism, which believes in an ultimate impersonal life force or mind which pervades the whole universe. In fact, some religions (e.g., Hinduism) have both pantheistic and polytheistic aspects.

II. A typology of polytheism.

There are a number of ways to distinguish among the various forms of polytheism. One is through the number of gods believed to exist. Dualism is the view that there are only two ultimate realities. The Greek and Roman forms of polytheism held that there were many gods, but they were not innumerable. On the other hand, Mormonism maintains that there are countless numbers of gods.

Another means to distinguish among the several forms of polytheism is by the way they view the origin of the gods. Generally, polytheists agree that the gods had a beginning but have no end. Some believe, however, that nature gave birth to the gods, while others contend that, although the beginning of the gods is unknowable, no god became a god without first becoming a man.

III. Some representatives of polytheism.

Polytheism has a long history in both the West and the East. Many Eastern religions and philosophies have been and still are polytheistic. Among these are some forms of Hinduism, Confucianism, Shinto, Taoism and Jainism.[1] In the West, the belief in many gods appears in several of the ancient Greek writers, like Hesiod and Homer (eight century B.C.), and throughout the ancient culture of the Roman Empire. There are several distinct manifestations of polytheism in contemporary Western society, including Mormonism and the views of David L. Miller. In addition, there are the occult forms of polytheism, including the UFO religions and the extraterrestrial types.

A. Hesiod.

Hesiod was a Greek farmer and poet who lived around the eighth century B.C. His poetry days began, he claimed, when the daughters of Zeus, called muses, met him while he was tending sheep and taught him a "glorious song." It was they, claimed Hesiod, who inspired his two main writings, *Works and Days* and the *Theogony*.[2] *Works and Days* is both a how-to book on agriculture and a handbook of morality. The *Theogony* primarily deals with the origin of the world and the gods, and the rise of Zeus' power over the other gods. According to a very ancient tradition, Hesiod was murdered by his hosts at Oenoe in Locris, because they suspected him of seducing their sister.[3]

1. Creation.

The present world-order arose out of chaos. In Hesiod's words:

Verily at the first Chaos came to be, but next wide-bosomed Earth, the ever-sure foundation of all the deathless ones who hold the peaks of snowy Olympus, and [then came] dim Tartarus in the depth of the wide-pathed Earth, and Eros (Love), fairest among the deathless gods, who unnerves the limbs and overcomes the mind and wise counsels of all gods and all men within them. From Chaos came forth Erebus and black Night; but of Night were born Aether [the upper atmosphere of the earth] and Day, whom she conceived and bare from union in love with Erebus. And Earth first bare starry Heaven, equal to herself, to cover her on every side, and to be an ever-sure abiding-place for the blessed gods. And she brought forth long Hills, graceful haunts of the goddess-Nymphs who dwell among the glens of the hills. She bare also the fruitless deep with his raging swell, Pontus, without sweet union of love. But afterwards she lay with Heaven and bare deep-swirling Oceanus.....[4]

Although chaos had a beginning, it did not come into existence from nothing. For Hesiod, "chaos" is not formless disorder. Rather, it is the huge gap "we now see, with its lower part filled with air and mist and cloud, between earth and the dome of heaven."[5] The claim that the opening of this gap had a beginning presupposes that there was a pre-existent state of affairs where heaven and earth were one. Although Hesiod does not explicitly state this, he does tell how this primordial unity became separated. It began when Heaven hid his children in their mother Earth because he hated them from their birth. Earth thought this was evil, she plotted against Heaven with their son, Cronos. Earth took Cronos "and hid him in an ambush, and put in his hands a jagged sickle, and revealed to him the whole plot."

And Heaven came, bringing on night and longing for love, and he lay about Earth spreading himself full upon her [which designates their primordial unity]. Then the son from his ambush stretched forth his left hand and in his right took the great long sickle with jagged teeth, and swiftly lopped off his own father's members and cast them away to

197

fall behind him. And not vainly did they fall from his hand; for all the bloody drops that gushed forth Earth received, and as the seasons moved round she bare the strong Erinyes [or Furies] and the great Giants with gleaming armour, holding long spears in their hands....[6]

In summary, in the beginning was the unity of Heaven and Earth. Within this unity existed opposing principles, male and female. The male, Heaven, attempted to keep the offspring of the female, Earth, from emerging by covering her over completely with himself. This evil action eventually resulted in the separation of Heaven and Earth which in turn brought about the beginning of Chaos. From Chaos, Heaven and Earth first emerged as distinct entities. This is why Hesiod can claim that Earth came into being *after* Chaos; "for before Chaos came into being the form of earth was not yet visible as such, but was blended with the form of heaven in a single whole. It is their separation that marks the beginning of the creation of the world-order."[7]

2. The gods.

Following the creation of the world came the creation of the gods. Some of the gods arose from the union of the bloody drops that flowed from Heaven's mutilated body to Earth. Other gods emerged from the "rivers, and the boundless sea...and the gleaming stars, and the wide heaven above."[8] Thus, many of the gods were products of nature. Still other gods came to exist through the sexual activities of the already existent gods. This is how the greatest of the gods, Zeus, came to exist.

According to Hesiod, the god Cronos, through sexual intercourse with the goddess Rhea, fathered several children, including Zeus. Because of a prophecy that his own son would dethrone him as the king of the gods, Cronos ate his children as fast as they were born. When Rhea was about to give birth to Zeus, she devised a plan with "her own dear parents, Earth and starry Heaven," to have him hidden from Cronos. Upon the birth of Zeus, Rhea gave him to Earth "to nourish and to bring [him] up." To Cronos "she gave a great stone wrapped in swaddling clothes." Thinking that it was Zeus, Cronos took the stone "in his hands and thrust it down into his belly." After Zeus had time to grow in strength, Cronos was tricked by Earth to vomit up all the children he had eaten, including the stone. Zeus then led these regurgitated gods against the first generation of gods, the Titans, who were under Cronos' rule. Zeus defeated them and put them away forever in a place called Tartarus, which is "as far beneath the earth as heaven is above earth."[9]

After the defeat of the Titans, "the blessed gods . . . pressed far-seeing Olympian Zeus to reign and to rule over them by Earth's prompting."[10] Prior to the battle, Zeus had promised that the gods who fought with him would receive "the office" which they "had before amongst the deathless gods." Those who had been "without office or right under Cronos" would be "raised to both office and rights as is just." After the Titans were defeated Zeus honored all his promises and in return received the sovereign right to rule.[11]

Hesiod believed in a pantheon, or group, of gods, each one having jurisdiction over a specific aspect of life or the world. Besides those already mentioned, he spoke of gods of natural phenomena (like Boreas, the god of the cold wind) and the gods Day and Night. There were also gods of passion, such as Nemesis (Indignation), Deceit, Strife, Sorrows, Eros (Love), Desire, Panic and Fear. Hesiod even referred to the gods called Sleep, Death, and Hades ("the god of the lower-world"). All of the gods after the Titans were thought to live on Mt. Olympus.[12] They often had sexual relations among themselves and with human beings. The gods quarreled with one another, deceived one another, sought to overthrow one another, and could incur illness from Zeus as punishment for lying.[13] All the gods were considered to have a beginning but no end. That is, they came into existence but they could not cease to exist. They were "deathless." They also existed in the time-space universe, not outside of it. And although they were very powerful, they were prone to many of the same weaknesses that befall humans.

As mentioned before, the most powerful God was Zeus. Hesiod maintained that Zeus could not be deceived nor his will thwarted. He also believed Zeus to be all-wise, all-knowing, sovereign over the other gods and mankind, and true to his word.[14] Yet in other contexts Hesiod said that Zeus could be temporarily deceived and confused, and that he could deceive others.[15] In short, Zeus was elevated above all other beings, but he did not always live up to his exalted status.

3. The world.

The present world is finite and possibly symmetrical. The earth, which is surrounded by ocean, lies between the starry heaven and the "misty gloom" of Tartarus. Heaven or sky is as far above the earth as Tartarus is below the earth. Tartarus is separated from the earth by a "great gulf" which corresponds exactly to the gulf that separates the sky from the earth. The only difference between the two gulfs is that the one between Tartarus and the earth is always dark, dank, gloomy and beset by raging storms, while the one between the sky and earth is filled with light from the sun. The distance between the upper and lower limits of the entire world is so great that it would take an anvil 20 days to fall from the top of heaven to the bottom of Tartarus. Hence, it would appear that the sky has a descending dome and that Tartarus has a solid bottom that is curved to meet the heavenly dome.[16]

Although Hesiod did not distinctly say so, it would appear that he thought the primordial unity of Heaven and Earth had no beginning. If so, then before the severing of this union, the union itself was uncreated, thus eternal. It seems, then, that Hesiod considered two of the four elements—namely, earth and air—to be the materials from which the present world and the first generation of gods came to exist. Consequently, the present world is viewed as finite, while the world as undifferentiated is taken to be eternal, or at least preexistent to the present world-order.

4. Man.

Mankind is considered a creation of the gods. Hesiod believed that up to his day the gods had created five separate generations of human beings.

The first generation made by the "deathless gods who dwell on Olympus" was the "golden race of mortal men who lived in the time of Cronos when he was reigning in heaven." These humans "lived like gods without sorrow of heart, remote and free from toil and grief." They did not grow old. "They dwelt in ease and peace upon their lands with many good things, rich in flocks and loved by the blessed gods." And when "they died, it was as though they were overcome with sleep."[17]

The second generation made by the Olympian gods was the "silver" race, and it was by far less noble than the golden one. They matured very slowly and "could not keep from sinning and from wronging one another." Neither would they serve the gods, "nor sacrifice on the holy altars of the blessed ones as it is right for men to do wherever they dwell." As a result, Zeus became angry with them and "put them away."[18]

The third generation of humans was made by Zeus. They were "a brazen race, sprung from ash-trees." They were worse than the silver race for they were "terrible and strong." Hesiod describes them as a very militant group who "loved the lamentable works of Ares [the god of war] and deeds of violence." Eventually this race destroyed themselves.[19]

Zeus again created a fourth generation, "which was nobler and more righteous." They were "a god-like race of hero-men who are called demi-gods." Some of them died in military encounters, one of which was the long war over "Troy for rich-haired Helen's sake." The remainder of this race was given a place by Zeus to live apart from the rest of mankind and all the gods except Cronos, who was released from Tartarus to rule over them. In this place these god-like humans "live untouched by sorrow" in "honour and glory."[20]

The fifth generation was also made by Zeus. This was Hesiod's generation. Hesiod lamented that he had neither "died before [nor] been born" after the creation of this race. He called it "a race of iron." Those of the iron race "never rest from labour and sorrow by day, and from perishing by night." He claimed that the gods will bring trouble upon them, and when they degenerate so far that even a new-born child will show the marks of old age, then Zeus will destroy them. But before their final destruction many terrible things will happen among them. For example, children will dishonor their parents and speak harshly to them. "They will not repay their aged parents the cost of their nurture, for might shall be their right." Virtue will not be found in keeping promises or in doing what is just and good. Rather, "men will praise the evil-doer and his violent doing." Indeed, "strength will be right and reverence will cease to be." Eventually only "bitter sorrows will be left for mortal men, and there will be no help [from the gods] against evil."[21]

Even with this pessimistic view of the degeneration of mankind, Hesiod had a higher respect for men than for women. He considered women a "deadly race" who give "great trouble" to men and are good helpmates only in wealth, not in poverty. They were created by Zeus "to be an evil to mortal men, with a nature to do evil."[22]

Although Hesiod did not generally hold women in high esteem, he did believe that on rare occasions a mortal woman could become divine. One such occasion was when a mortal woman named Semele gave birth to an immortal son, named Dionysus. Semele became a goddess as a result. Another instance was when Dionysus took a mortal woman for his wife, and Zeus "made her deathless and unageing for him [Dionysus]."[23]

5. Evil.

Hesiod apparently believed that evil began with Heaven's hiding of his children in Earth. With the thwarting of Heaven's action by Earth and Cronos, the creation of the world began. Hence, the battle between good and evil produced a world that was a mixture of good and evil. This mixture is seen not only in the natural elements and mankind, but also in the gods. In all things, evil is a potential just waiting for the opportunity to be actualized.

Evil came upon man through the activity of the gods, especially Zeus. According to Hesiod, the god Prometheus deceived Zeus by stealing fire and giving it to man. In turn, Zeus "planned sorrow and mischief against men." He ordered some of the other gods to make a beautiful woman with a "shameless mind and a deceitful nature," whom Zeus called Pandora. The gods gave her a "great jar" filled with plagues. When she opened the jar she scattered all the plagues among mankind.[24]

6. Ethics.

The essence of Hesiod's value system is found in these words:

> ...listen now to right, ceasing altogether to think of violence. For the son of Cronos [Zeus] has ordained this law for men, that fishes and beasts and winged fowls should devour one another, for right is not in them; but to mankind he gave right which proves far the best. For whoever knows the right and is ready to speak it, far-seeing Zeus gives him prosperity; but whoever deliberately lies in his witness and forswears himself, and so hurts Justice and sins beyond repair, that man's generation is left obscure thereafter. But the generation of the man who swears truly is better thenceforward.[25]

The law-giver is Zeus. Whatever he declares to be right is right, and whatever he declares to be wrong is wrong. Zeus has given to man justice, and it is by justice that man should live.

Those who live according to what is right find reward for their action:

...they who give straight judgments to strangers and to the men of the land, and go not aside from what is just, their city flourishes, and the people prosper in it: Peace...is abroad in their land, and all-seeing Zeus never decrees cruel war against them. Neither famine nor disaster ever haunt men who do true justice....They flourish continually with good things, and do not travel on ships, for the grain-giving earth bears them fruit.[26]

On the other hand, those who practice injustice are punished by Zeus:

Often even a whole city suffers from a bad man who sins and devises presumptuous deeds, and the son of Cronos lays great trouble upon the people, famine and plague together, so that the men perish away, and their women do not bear children, and their houses become few, through the contriving of Olympian Zeus. And again, at another time, the son of Cronos either destroys their wide army, or their walls, or else makes an end of their ships on the sea.[27]

The reason one should do what is right is because justice *pays*. If the reverse were true, if injustice paid and justice did not, then one would be foolish to be just without any personal gain. In other words, one is not just because justice is good in itself, but because the way of justice is the will of Zeus who is able to reward justice and punish injustice.[28] In brief, the motivation for doing good is self-interest.

7. History and destiny.

From Hesiod's view of the five generations of human beings, it would seem that he had a generally pessimistic view of history. Mankind began at a very high and noble stage in life. But each subsequent generation, with the exception of the fourth one, became increasingly decadent and irreligious. For his own generation Hesiod saw only a gloomy future leading to its final destruction by Zeus.

It is important to notice that the history of man is intimately linked to the activity of the gods. When people obey the gods, they prosper. When they disobey the gods, they incur their wrath. Hence, Hesiod urged his fellow countrymen to live their days in accordance with the will of Zeus. Those who did so would be happy.[29]

As human history is wrapped up with the gods, so is human destiny. The way one lives determines where one will end up after death. For example, after death the golden race of man became "pure spirits dwelling on the earth." They now deliver others from harm, "keep watch on judgments and cruel deeds," and are "givers of wealth." After death the silver race became "blessed spirits of the underworld." The militant brazen race "passed to the dank house of chill Hades" and left no prosperity on the earth.[30]

Not all will pass on to another kind of life through death, however. Apparently those who were born gods can cause some men to become gods. Other men, like some from the fourth generation, continue to live forever in an earthly paradise prepared and ruled over by the gods. Therefore, it seems that man, if he dies, lives on in some state that either rewards or punishes him for the way he lived before death. The gods decide what man's destiny will be.

Hesiod did not speculate on whether there is a final goal of human history or the present world-order. But one thing is certain, if there is a goal, the gods will be the ones who will bring it about.

B. Mormonism.

One of the largest and fastest growing polytheistic religion in the United States today is Mormonism. At the start of the 20th century the Church of Jesus Christ of Latter-day Saints (LDS) had 250,000 members. By 1950 it had reached the one million mark, had doubled to two million by 1964, and had more than doubled again to five million members by 1982. Today the Mormons have about 30,000 missionaries in 83 countries.[31] Some have estimated their income to be about $3 million per day.[32]

The founder of the Mormon religion was Joseph Smith Jr. (1805-1844). In 1820 in Palmyra, New York, Smith claimed that he had a vision where two deities, God the Father and His Son Jesus Christ, told him that he was not to join any of the Christian denominations of his day. The two gods said that these denominations "were all wrong and their creeds an abomination to God." In 1823 Smith had more visions of an angel called Moroni. According to Smith, this angel led him to some gold plates that Smith later translated into what became known as the *Book of Mormon*.[33] On April 6, 1830, the Church of Jesus Christ of Latter-Day Saints officially began.[34] Allegedly it was the beginning of the restored Christian church.

1. The gods.

The Mormon apostle Orson Pratt claimed that there are an innumerable number of gods. He said that if we should take a million worlds like this and number their particles, we should find that there are more gods than there are particles of matter in those worlds. The second Mormon president, Brigham Young, though more modest in his claims, also a plurality of gods: "How many gods there are, I do not know. But there never was a time when there were not gods."[35] Indeed, in the long chain of gods there is no divine first cause that made all the rest of the gods. Rather, there is an infinite regress of gods making other (potential) gods. As Orson Pratt put it:

> ...our Father in Heaven was begotten on a previous heavenly world by His Father; and again, He was begotten by a still more ancient Father and so on, from generation to generation, from one heavenly world to another still more ancient, until our minds are wearied and lost in the multiplicity of generations and successive worlds, and as a last resort, we wonder in our minds, how far back the genealogy extends, and how the first world was formed, and the first Father was begotten. But why does man seek for a *first*, when revelation informs him that God's works are without beginning?...why...do you seek for a *first* personal Father in an endless genealogy? or for a *first* effect in an endless succession of effects?[36]

The gods are not created by other gods, but are offspring of the gods. Potential gods are begotten of male gods and born of female goddesses so that they might have an opportunity to become gods themselves. These potential gods are born as spirit beings who later become human beings. And man, said Brigham Young, "is the king of kings and lord of lords in embryo."[37] All people, said Joseph Smith ·Jr., need "to learn how to be gods . . . the same as all gods have done before" them. For "*God Himself was once as we are now, and is an exalted man, and sits enthroned in yonder heavens!*"[38] Hence, all the gods first began as "the spirit children of an *Eternal Father*" and "the offspring of an *Eternal Mother*."[39]

This procreative process suggests that the gods are not pure spirits, but are physical as well. Joseph F. Smith, a former Mormon president, confirmed this well when he said, "God is spiritual Himself, although He has a body of flesh and bone as [the resurrected] Christ has." Like man, the gods have both material and immaterial aspects to their nature, but theirs are perfect while man's are not.[40]

An exception to the flesh-and-bone aspect of the gods is the Holy Ghost. The "Holy Ghost does not possess a body of flesh and bones, as do both the Father and the Son, but is a personage of spirit." Although He lacks this material dimension, He is still "endowed with the attributes and powers of Deity, and not a mere force, or essence."[41]

2. Creation.

The Mormon Scripture entitled the *Book of Abraham* gives an account of the creation of the present world-order: "And then the Lord said: Let us go down. And they went down at the beginning, and they, that is the gods, organized and formed the heavens and the earth" (4:1). According to Mormonism, the gods counseled together and created the present world-order *ex-materia*, out of pre-existent material. Joseph Smith Jr. explained it this way:

> In the beginning, the head of the Gods called a council of the Gods; and they came together and concocted a plan to create the world and people it....
>
> Now, I ask all who hear me, why the learned men who are preaching salvation, say that God created the heavens and the earth out of nothing? The reason is, that they are unlearned in the things of God, and have not the gift of the Holy Ghost....If you tell them that God made the world out of something, they will call you a fool. But I am learned, and know more than all the world put together....
>
> ...Hence we infer that God had materials to organize the world out of chaos—chaotic matter, which is element....Element had an existence from the time he [God] had. The pure principles of element are principles which can never be destroyed; they may be organized and re-organized, but not destroyed. They had no beginning, and can have no end.[42]

Therefore the gods are organizers and shapers of the world, not creators or causes of its "primal existence," for "the ultimate elements of which the earth consists...'are eternal.'"[43]

Furthermore, at some unspecified time before the shaping of the material world "the Lord God, created all things...spiritually" (*Book of Moses* 3:5; cf. *Book of Abraham* 3:22-28). That is, "the earth and all life that was place upon it" were "first organized from spirit" before the "organizations and endowments" of matter were added to them.[44]

3. The gods and their relationship with the world.

Although there are countless gods and worlds, the gods that are of immediate importance to man and earth are "God, the Eternal Father, and...His Son, Jesus Christ, and...the Holy Ghost." God the Eternal Father, also called Elohim, "is the literal Parent of our Lord and Savior Jesus Christ, and of the spirits of the human race."[45] And though many contemporary Mormons reject it, the early Mormon teaching on the identity of the Eternal Father was that He was Adam. Brigham Young put the matter this way:

> How much unbelief exists in the minds of the Latter-day Saints in regard to one particular doctrine which I revealed to them, and which God revealed to me—namely that Adam is our father and God....Our Father Adam helped to make this earth, it was created expressly for him, and after it was made he and his companions came here. He brought one of his wives with him, and she was called Eve....
>
> ...Then he [Adam, after he had helped organize the earth] said, "I want my children who are in the spirit world to come and live here. I once dwelt upon an earth something like this, in a mortal state, I was faithful, I received my crown and exaltation. I have the privilege of extending my work, and to its increase there will be no end. I want my children that were born to me in the spirit world to come here and take tabernacles of flesh, that their spirits may have a house, a tabernacle or a dwelling place as mine has...."[46]

In an earlier sermon, Young said of Adam, *"He is our Father and our God, and the only God with whom we have to do."*[47]

Jesus Christ (Jehovah) is the literal Son of God the Eternal Father (Elohim). So Talmadge states, "Elohim is literally the Father of the spirit of Jesus Christ and also of the body in which Jesus Christ performed His mission in the flesh."[48] Jesus Christ received His physical body when the divine Father had intimate relations with the virgin Mary. There was nothing supernatural about Jesus' conception. As the Mormon apostle Bruce McConkie explained:

> Christ was born into the world as the literal Son of this Holy being; He was born in the same personal, real, and *literal sense that any son is born to be a mortal father. There is nothing figurative about His paternity; He was begotten, conceived and born in the normal and natural*

He was begotten, conceived and born in the normal and natural course of events. . . [49]

Jesus' mission on earth before He was resurrected was basically twofold: (1) through His substitutionary death on the cross He provided for all mankind "exemption from the penalty of the fall," and for individuals who obey "the laws and ordinances of the Gospel" He provided the way for the "remission of personal sins"; and (2) He gave a "great example to all mankind" on how they too can "become like the gods."[50]

The Holy Ghost is a "personage of spirit." He is "the minister of the Godhead, carrying into effect the decisions of the Supreme Council" (i.e., the council of the gods). Among the activities of the Holy Ghost are His direction and control of "the varied forces of nature." Such things as "gravitation, sound, heat, light and . . . electricity, are but the common servants of the Holy Ghost in His operations." The Holy Ghost is also involved in the giving of "prophecy and revelation" and the "enlightenment of the [human] mind, quickening of the intellect, and sanctification of the soul."[51]

The basic constituents of all the worlds are matter and intelligence. Both elements are eternal and both exist in space, which is boundless. Indeed, everything exists in space, including the gods. Furthermore, there are two major kinds of matter: (1) "gross matter"—"the more ponderous elements which man is capable of perceiving with his physical senses," and (2) spirit matter—"a substance" which is "material" but "more pure, elastic and refined matter" than is gross matter. Inherent in all matter is life or intelligence. However, spirit matter "possesses inherent properties of life to a far greater degree than does gross matter." Hence, "that which is organized from spirit is designed to act, whereas the gross organization, by the nature of the life therein, is but capable of being acted upon, or giving some form of intelligent response to a directing will. Initiative and direction come from the realm of spirit."[52]

In summary, then, the Mormon view of the gods and the world is:

The orderly cosmos is the product of divine powers acting through ordained laws upon eternal elements that possess certain innate and acquired properties of life or intelligence. The elements are able to respond to the will of God in such a way that they are sustained in their respective spheres of influence. Consequently, the universe is a living, moving system, not a static, stationary one.[53]

4. Man.

"Latter-day revelation declares that man existed as a conscious entity before his birth into mortality, and that the fundamental elements of life within man are coeval with God." According to Mormonism there were two stages to man's pre-earth life. The first stage was prior to man's organization as a human spirit. In this first stage existed "the central primal intelligence, or ego, of man." The properties man possessed at this time were "personality and individuality," the most basic properties "of an independent, uncreated, self-existing being." In this sense one can say that man has existed as long as any of the gods.

The second stage of man's pre-earth life was the uniting of his ego "with other life-possessing elements of spirit to make the pre-earth human spirit." This was "accomplished by a process of conception and birth. In that primeval birth, the organized spirit of man became literally the offspring of divine parents—the Man of Holiness [God the Eternal Father] and His glorified and exalted companion [the Heavenly Mother]."[54] Moreover, the "organized spirit of man" resembles "in form and stature the physical tabernacle which the spirit occupies on earth." The firstborn of the Father's spirit children was a noble son known as Jehovah, and also revealed as Jesus Christ."[55]

After His birth, each human spirit child is brought up to a level of maturity in the heavenly mansions of his divine parents. Eventually he leaves this environment "to dwell upon a spirit world adapted to [his] condition and state of progress." In this spiritual but pre-flesh stage, human spirits are "able to acquire a significant degree of glory" by "obedience to the laws of God." Eventually their development begins to level off, at which time it is "necessary for them to be clothed with physical tabernacles so that they might undergo a new series of experiences designed to elevate them further in the scale of life."[56]

Man's earthly existence begins when his human spirit acquires a physical, mortal body of flesh and bones. He receives this body through the natural processes of sexual intercourse. Once he has "received the endowments of physical life, man must adapt them by wisdom to their proper uses, and by sanctifying the body, mature in all the functions and expressions of the physical organism." This is accomplished by each person giving "of himself in service and dedication to others in doing the will of God."[57] The will of God is that each human being place faith in Jesus Christ as his Savior, repent of his sins, be baptized by immersion for the remission of sins, receive the gift of the Holy Ghost by laying on of hands, and for the rest of his life obey the laws and ordinances of the gospel. All of this is to be done in the manner prescribed by the LDS church.[58]

Implicit in the above is that man is personal, rational, and free. Indeed, he has always been like this and will remain so forever. Of course, mankind is capable of progressing through the various stages of existence until godhood is attained. Throughout this process man retains his personality, rationality and self-determination. Man attains higher degrees of perfection in these traits, but there is never a time when he loses or gains them.

5. Evil.

Evil or sin is anything that opposes the will of the gods. And although this opposition is not good in itself, it does serve a necessary purpose "in the divine plan of life." All forms of life need evil to help them to "exist and progress in intelligence and power" and thus become "independent in the spheres in which God has placed them." Hence, for man to "attain true independence" he "must obey freely the laws of life, and not succumb to the influence of opposing forces." But without evil there can be no progress. "Thus righteousness as well as wickedness is dependent upon the existence of opposition. So also is holiness as well as misery, and good as well as bad."[59]

The roots of evil in the earthly sphere began in the pre-earth spirit world. There, the spirit-brother of Jesus Christ, Lucifer, proposed to their divine Father that mankind be saved from sin by compulsion. His Father rejected his plan and instead adopted Jesus' plan to save mankind through the free response of their own wills. This prompted Lucifer's rebellion against the Father and the Son. A consequence of this rebellion was that Lucifer was cast out of Gods' presence.

When Adam and Eve were created as immortal earthly beings, Lucifer tempted Eve to disobey God's command to not eat of the tree of the knowledge of good and evil. Eve's disobedience made her become a "mortal" physical human being. She urged Adam to eat of the forbidden tree, a request that put Adam in an ethical dilemma. On the one hand, God had expressly commanded them not to eat of the tree. On the other hand, God had also commanded them to procreate and replenish the earth, which they could "not" do in an immortal spirit state. But since Adam was still immortal while Eve was now clothed in a mortal body, it was still impossible for them to fulfill the command to procreate as long as they were in two different states. So Adam "deliberately and wisely" decided to obey God's command to procreate by eating of the tree so that he too could receive a mortal body. Hence, sin came to earth through the disobedience of Adam and Eve. However, without their "fall" it would have been impossible for human spirits to acquire mortal bodies and thus continue to progress toward Godhood; thus Adam fell upward. The fall of man, then, was necessary for his continued progress toward divinity.[60]

The gods are not responsible for the continuation of evil. Rather, the free activity of their offspring is solely responsible. So states Joseph F. Smith:

> Sometimes we are prone to charge God [the Heavenly Father] with causing our afflictions and our troubles; but if we could see as God sees...we would unquestionably discover that our troubles, or suffering, or affliction are the result of our own indiscretion or lack of knowledge, or of wisdom. It was not the hand of God that put affliction and trouble upon us. [But rather] the agency that He has given to us ... to act for ourselves ....[61]

Since evil is a necessary constituent in the universe, it will never be totally eradicated. However, it will always be overcome by those who continue to progress toward the ever-perfectible state of deity.[62]

6. Ethics.

The gods are the givers of moral values in the respective spheres which they govern. The world or worlds populated by a given set of divine parents receive from those parents the laws by which they are to live. However, no moral law is given without the prior consent of those intelligent beings who will be required to live under it. "But having acquired their consent, God requires obedience to the law which is ordained."[63] On the other hand, since God's authority is dependent on the voluntary obedience of the intelligent beings He rules over, "it follows as a corollary that if He should ever do anything to violate the confidence or 'sense of justice' of these intelligences, they would promptly withdraw their support." And if this were to occur, then "the 'power' of God would disintegrate." In short, "if God should change or act contrary to truth and justice 'He would cease to be God.'"[64]

Although the moral laws that the gods ordain are freely consented to in the spirit world by all intelligences, including human spirits, earthly man again learns of these laws through divine revelation. This revelation is received by prophets and then written down for mankind. The standard written revelations of the LDS church are the Bible (as far as it is correctly translated), the *Book of Mormon*, the *Doctrine and Covenants*, and the *Pearl of Great Price*. Because the Mormons believe in "continuous revelation" through their prophets, they also accept other writings by their prophets as from God.[65]

7. History and goal.

Like space, time is endless. It has no beginning and it will have no end. However, like the histories of other worlds, this earth and its inhabitants did have a beginning and they do have a goal toward which they are moving. The earth itself is destined for a transfiguration by the Heavenly Father to a "celestial condition." In this state the earth will be "a fit abode for the glorified sons and daughters of our God."[66]

The eventual end of earthly human beings is decided by the Heavenly Father. All human beings will stand before His judgment seat to acquire what they deserve in accordance with their deeds. Those people who knew the truth of God but rebelled against it all their lives will be sent to a kid of purgatory, where they will receive their appropriate punishment. But "after the debt has been paid the prison doors shall be opened, and the spirits once confined in suffering, then chastened and cleaned, shall come forth to partake of the glory provided for their class." That is, they will progress to the lowest heaven, the telestial kingdom.

The next highest heaven is called the terrestrial kingdom. The inhabitants of this level will be those who "died without law"; those who rejected Mormonism in their earthly life but accepted it in "purgatory" (or spirit prison) after death; those who lived honorable lives on earth but did not accept Mormonism; and those who were members of the LDS church but were "not valiant" in their devotion to it.[67]

The third and highest heaven is the celestial kingdom. Within this level are three degrees of existence. The second and third degrees are for those who obeyed all the teachings of the LDS church but failed to be married in a Mormon Temple. The top or first degree is awarded to those who were completely obedient to Mormon teaching, including marriage in a Mormon Temple. Only at this highest degree does one attain actual godhood.[68] And once godhood is achieved, one gains "the kind of life that God possesses as a glorified being." One "may then see as God sees ... hear as God hears, move in space as God moves, and manifest his will in and through all things as God manifests His divine intelligence and power in and through universal space."[69]

Granted that godhood is the highest stage a person can achieve, once it is gained, advancement still does not end. All the gods are eternally progressing to higher stages of perfection, for eternal advancement *is* their perfection.[70]

C.   David L. Miller.

In 1974 David L. Miller (Associate Professor of Religion at Syracuse University) published a book entitled *The New Polytheism: Rebirth of the Gods and Goddesses.*[71] In this book Miller argues that polytheism is alive and well in contemporary society. He believes that this is a good thing. He urges people in Western society to get in tune with the gods in order to liberate themselves to be the kind of people they really are.

1.   The gods.

a. The rejection of monotheism.

Monotheism is the belief in one God above and beyond the world. Monotheistic thinking is the attempt to bring all man's "explanation systems, whether theological, sociological, political, historical, philosophical, or psychological" under one all-embracing system. This system operates "according to fixed concepts and categories" that are controlled by an either/or kind of logic—that is, something is "either true or false, either this or that, either beautiful or ugly, either good or evil." But this kind of thinking, says Miller, "fails a people in a time when experience becomes self-consciously pluralistic, radically both/and." This is what Western society is today—radically pluralistic. Contemporary Western man finds himself in a world where truth and morality are relative. His "life often feels anarchistic: no horizons, fences, boundaries, and no center to prove one securely close to home." (pp. 7, 9). The contemporary situation is so pluralistic that its modern interpreters "have

213

had to rely on a strange set of words" in their attempt to explain it. For example:

> In tracing our psychology Charles Baudouin speaks of *polyphonic* meaning and being. In speaking of the nature of thinking required for contemporary understanding Philip Wheelwright points to *plurisignificative* knowing and communicating. Norman O. Brown talks about *polymorphous* reality as a key to our history, and Ray Hart names the deepest aspect of our literature articulations of reality with the phrase *polysemous* functioning of imaginal discourse. If we try to make sense of our society Michael Novak suggests it will help to think of America as a *pluralistic* community of radically unmeltable ethnics. Concerning government and political science, Robert Dahl speaks of polyarchy (p.3).

This "poly" kind of thinking betrays the fact that "we have suffered a death of God." No longer is there "a single center holding things together." God is dead, as Friedrich Nietzsche so boldly declared. Western man has seen "the demise of a monotheistic way of thinking and speaking about God and a monotheistic way of thinking and speaking about human meaning and being generally" (p. 37). He has been "released from the tyrannical imperialism of monotheism." As a consequence,

> man has the opportunity of discovering new dimensions hidden in the depths of reality's history. He may discover a new freedom to acknowledge variousness and many-sidedness. He may find, as if for the first time, a new potency to create imaginatively his hopes and desires, his laws and pleasures (p. 4).

b. The revival of polytheism.

"The death of God gives rise to the rebirth of the Gods. We are polytheists" (p. 4). But what is polytheism? According to Miller, "polytheism is the name given to a specific religious situation," one which is "characterized by plurality, a plurality that manifests itself in many forms." For instance, socially speaking "polytheism is a situation in which there are various values, patterns of social organization, and principles by which man governs his poltical life." Sometimes these "values, patterns, and principles...mesh harmoniously, but more often they war with one another to be elevated as the single center of normal social order" (p. 4).

Philosophically polytheism "is that reality experienced by men and women when Truth...cannot be articulated reflectively according to a single grammar, a single logic, or a single symbol-system" (p. 4). Rather, "a philosophically polytheistic situation...will break forth with principles of relativism, indeterminacy, plural logic systems, irrational numbers; substances that do not have substances, such as quarks; double explanations for light; and black holes in the middle of actual realities" (p. 5).

Although "polytheism" carries these different meanings, "behind them is a *religious* situation. Religiously, polytheism is the worship of many Gods and Goddesses." These are not worshipped all at the same time. Rather, only one god or goddess at a time can be worshipped. In this way polytheism—the worship of many gods—includes monotheism—the worship of one God. "This implies that a polytheistic religion is actually a polytheistic theology, a system of symbolizing reality in a plural way in order to account for all experience, but that the religious practice is composed of consecutive monotheisms." And this "implies that our experience of social, intellectual, and psycholgocial worlds is religious—that is, it is so profound and far-reaching that only a theological explanation can account for it fully" (p. 6).

At one time polytheism reigned in Western culture. But when the Greek culture collapsed, polytheism died and was replaced by monotheism. Although polytheism remained "in the underground or countercultural tradition of the West" throughout the 2,000-year reign of monotheistic thought, it did not have any significant effect in the West.

Now with the death of monotheism, says Miller, polytheism may be resurrected again to its proper place. Indeed, the need to recall polytheism to help man deal with his pluralistic experience "may be behind the recent interest in the occult, in magic, in extraterrestrial life, in Hindu India and Buddhist Japan, in multidaemoned China, in sorcery, in new forms of multiple family life, in communes, in the 'new religions,' and many other alternative life-styles and meaning-systems which have been hitherto foreign" (p. 11).

According to Miller, the rebirth of polytheism is good because it has several advantages over monotheism. First, polytheism frees one from the monotheistic idea that one must "get it all together." Polytheism points "to the possibility that 'keeping it all apart' is a safe, a realistic, and an exciting way to 'go on.'" Second, poly-

215

theism better accounts for the nature of man. That is, man is not monotheistic in consciousness, but polytheistic. Hence, "only a polytheistic consciousness will account realistically for our lives" (p. 81). Third, polytheism will help man keep in touch with the richness and diversity of life. Monotheism does just the opposite, for it encourages thought about that which lies behind life, namely "the essence, or substance, or principle of being," rather than thought about life itself (pp. 27, 28).

What is needed, however, is not the rebirth of the old polytheism for old purposes, but for new ones. In this sense man needs a new polytheism—"a new function for the old Gods and Goddesses" (p. 81).

2. The world.

Miller suggests that this new polytheism has three aspects. First, the new polytheism "is a modern sensibility." It is not just that "our contemporary society is pluralistic, nor that our roles are many, nor that our morality is relativistic, nor even that our political ideology is fragmented." For these "are manifestations of something deeper and more fundamental. The more basic feeling is that the Gods and Goddesses are reemerging in our lives" (p. 64).

Second, the new polytheism is "a way of rethinking the past tradition of thinking, and especially the orthodox tradition of religious thinking" (p. 64). Since Western thought is rooted in the early Greek thinkers who were largely polytheistic, it follows that Western thought, even orthodox monotheistic thought, is dependent upon Greek polytheism for its "ideas, concepts, and categories, which were once the images of Gods and Goddesses," and for its "formal structures of thought or logic, which were once narrative processes in mythic tales" (p. 40).

And third, the new polytheism "is a discovery of the polytheism of the psyche." It helps one to see the "many potencies, many structures of meaning and being, all given to us in the reality of our everyday lives" (pp. 64, 65).

Given the death of monotheism and the rebirth of polytheism —even a new polytheism—who or what are the gods and goddesses of this polytheism?

Miller maintains that "the Gods and Goddesses are the names of powers, of forces, which have autonomy and are not conditioned or affected by social and historical events, by human will or reason, or by personal and individual factors" (p. 6). In other words, "the Gods are Powers" that transcend the personal, the historical and the social. Yet they are also immanent in the world as potencies "in each of us,in societies, and in nature" (p. 60). Indeed, "as they manifest themselves in life they are felt to be informing powers that give shape to social, intellectual, and personal behavior." They are the basic structure of reality, "the names of the plural patterns of our existence" (pp. 6, 7). These powers are "the Gods and Goddesses of ancient Greece—not Egypt, not the Ancient Near East, not Hindu India, not Ancient China or Japan. Greece is the locus of our polytheism simply because, *willy-nilly*, we are Occidental men and women" (pp. 80, 81).

Do these many different gods act harmoniously? Miller says no. They often act in "contention." Life may even be characterized as "a war of the Powers." (p. 60)

> Man—his self, his society, and his natural environment—is the arena of an eternal Trojan War. Our moods, emotions, unusual behaviors, dreams, and fantasies tell us those rough moments when the war is no longer a cold war or a border skirmish, but an all-out guerila conflict. These indicators also tell us, by feeling and intuition, when one God has absented himself and another has not yet rushed into the vacuum. We know the war well (p. 60).

Man's contemporary acknowledgement of these gods is important and functional. It will help him to infuse new life into old ways of seeing and thinking. It will provide the structure through which man may be able "to speak and to think appropriately concerning" his "deepest experience" (p. 62). Miller suggests many ways in which this new function of the gods and goddesses and the telling of their stories "all in terms of human reality" could work out (p. 66). For example, he proposes that the tremendous growth in technology coincides with the stories of Prometheus, Hephaestus and Asclepius:

> Prometheus steals the fire and ends trapped on a rock, gnawed at by the power he has himself supplanted by his knowledge. Hephaestus is the divine smith, the technologist supreme, who is the bastard of his mother and at a total loss for sensuousness and feeling. Asclepius is the technologist of the feelings; he is the psycotherapist whom technolgoy and its civilization will make into the high priest of a mental health culture (p. 66).

217

The story of the goddess Hera, who "tried to socialize Mount Olympus," is relived when "computers and statistical procedures come to be revered as true wisdom" and "consultants and experts must attend every decision in business and government" (p. 67). The work of the "ever-present god Pan ("All") is seen in the *ever-presence of outbreaks of the irrational,"* such as "in the violent forms of Vietnam or rape on college campuses, or in the subtler forms of compulsive participation in mystical movements and black magic groups" (p. 68).

At one time the view of the world was Ptolemaic. The earth was thought to be "an immovable sphere at the center of the universe, around which nine concentric spheres revolve." Thus, all that existed was "organized around a single center," the earth, with the end of the universe imagined to be "fixed and secure." This monotheistic view of the world collapsed with Copernicus (and subsequent scientists). Now the universe has no known center and its horizons are neither fixed nor secure. Instead, it is seen as an "infinitely expanding universe whose center is...unknown" (p. 9).

3. Man.

Man is "the playground" of the gods (p. 55). The gods parade "through our thoughts without our control and even against our will." Man does not possess the gods, but they possess him (p. 34). They "live through our psychic structures" and "manifest themselves always in our behaviors." We do not grab the gods, but the "gods grab us, and we play out their stories" (p. 59).

"Psychologically, polytheism is a matter of the radical experience of equally real, but mutually exclusive aspects of the self." In this situation the "person experiences himself as many selves, each of which is felt to have autonomous power, a life of its own, coming and going on its own and without regard to the centered will of a single ego" (p. 5).

But no one person can be gripped by more than one God at a time. In this sense man is a monotheist, "or at least a henotheist (that is, worshipping one God at a time in a large pantheon of gods)." However, in order for a person to think and speak about the God who has gripped him at that moment, "he will have to be polytheistic, since the story [about this temporary domination] may involve marriages with other Gods, parentage by still others, off-

218

spring by Godlings and maiden Goddesses." In brief, because life and meaning are pluralistic, man must be polytheistic in order to think and speak about it. "To think differently is self-deception, a self-deception perpetrated by monotheistic thinking" (p. 30; cf. p. 28).

Miller asks, "What do the Gods and Goddesses want with us?" His answer is that "our task is to incarnate them, become aware of their presence, acknowledge and celebrate their forms, so that we may better be able to account for our polytheism" (p. 55). This can occur only when we redivinize our thinking, remythologize our lives, in short, see our world through polytheistic glasses (pp. 63, 83).

4. Values.

All values, be they of truth, morality, beauty, or what have you, are relative. That is, "truth and falsity, life and death, beauty and ugliness, good and evil are forever and inextricably mixed together" (p. 29). The kind of thinking that separates values into either/or concepts and categories is monotheistic (p. 7). But this way of thinking does not adequately account for the many-sidedness of man's experience. What does is the polytheistic both/and sort of thinking, which recognizes the relativity of all values.

IV. Some basic beliefs of polytheism.

As with the other world views, there are differences among polytheists. However, their agreements allow one to see the essential elements of a polytheistic world view.

A. There are many finite gods in the universe.

In a polytheistic world view, the many gods in the world are finite. They have a beginning, although they have no end. Their beginning may have been a collective one with the cosmic mating of Heaven and Earth. Or each god may have acquired his divine station in life by obeying certain laws. Whatever the case may be, the gods had a beginning of some sort and thus are finite.

The gods are also changing. Unlike the God of theism, who has always been immutable and completely perfect, the gods of polytheism are always changing. Some polytheists hold that the gods are always changing toward greater degrees of perfection (à la Mormonism). Others depict the gods as changing in different directions, some toward good, some toward evil, and some vascillating between good and evil (à la Hesiod and Miller).

The gods are also viewed as forming a hierarchy that is often disharmonious. Often one god has power over the others. The kingship may be short-lived, even as brief as a momentary domination of a human action, but the gods are not seen as having equal power or as having equal rule. They compete for power over one another and over nondeities, such as human beings. This competition creates disharmony in the world.

Finally, the gods of polytheism are human-like. At times they represent what are usually considered some of the strengths of man—companssion, love, perseverance and hope. At other times they display what are often held to be some weaknesses of man—deceit, treachery, insubordination, tyranny and oppression. Some of the gods act like mothers, some like fathers, others like spoiled children, and still others like dictators. Some are virtuous and some are promiscuous. Some are wise while others are foolish.

B. The universe is alive and active.

The universe is generally understood to have the characteristics of life. For example, like living things, the universe changes. The universe may also be perceived as intelligent or at least as responsive to the varied wills of the gods. In this respect polytheism is not incompatible with some forms of pantheism that hold to mind or life pervading the whole universe. The world is a great multi-faceted, expanding organism that contains opposites which often war against each other, causing conflict and temporal states of chaos.

Furthermore, the universe is eternal. Although it has not always existed in its present state, there never was a time when the universe in some form did not exist. It has always existed and it will never cease to exist. The present condition of the universe was brought about either by the organizing, shaping power of the gods or by natural forces. In other words, the universe was created *ex materia* (out of some pre-existent stuff) by the gods or by itself.

C. The gods influence events in the world.

The gods exist in the universe. They may be beyond human history, even earthly history, but they do not exist outside of the space-time universe. They are in the world, and their activities influence those who exist with them in the world. Moreover, the gods

220

exercise some influence over the orderliness of the universe. Their behavior affects the world-process for better or worse. Further, the individual gods have their own specific spheres of influence in the world. Two or more may reign jointly over a given sphere, but they do not all rule over the same area. Indeed, conflict may arise when a god tries to extend his influence beyond his sphere and into that of another god.

D. Supernormal events occur.

Supernormal acts are possible. The gods may appear to man in visions, dreams, or even physical manifestations. They may reveal their desires to man through his intuitions and feelings (à la Miller) or through revelations (à la Mormonism and occult religions). Whatever they do, the gods have the ability to interfere in, work through, and influence human history by divine intervention.

However, there are no supernatural events in the theistic sense of a sovereign God acting from a transcendent realm beyond the natural (space-time) universe. There is no such supernatural being in polytheism.

E. Man is an immortal spirit in a mortal body.

Most polytheists understand man to be both a material and an immaterial being. They usually consider the nonphysical or spiritual aspect of man to be of a higher order than his physical aspect. This does not negate the importance of man's physical state, but merely places the focus on the spiritual, even mystical and experiential side of man. Indeed, the physical aspect of man is often viewed as a necessary vehicle for the progress of the spiritual side of man.

Man is also a free being who has some control over his destiny. However, he must consider the desires of the gods, for he is not totally independent of them. Although polytheists disagree on how much man must depend on the gods for his well-being, they all agree that he is dependent on them, perhaps even more so than he realizes.

Man is also an intelligent and religious being. He can and must reason about himself, others around him, the world and the gods. But many believe that for man's reasoning to be accurate to the pluralism of life, it must be polytheistic, not theistic.

F. Ethics generally are relative and localized, not universal.

Many polytheists hold that moral values transcend specific times, individuals and places. Other polytheists disagree. Like Miller, they maintain that all moral values are relative. Whatever is considered right or wrong by one person, in one place, at one time is not necessarily right or wrong for another person, in a different place, at another time. In fact, the whole universal kind of thinking that is necessary for an absolute ethic is grounded in monotheism, not polytheism. A consistent polytheist will tend to accept localized thinking and reject universal thinking. This will probably lead to the rejection of ethical absolutes and the acceptance of ethical relativism.

G. Man is destined for immortality.

Like the rest of man's life, his destiny is intimately related to the will of the gods. How the gods perceive a person's life will determine whether or not he is rewarded with an afterlife and, if so, what kind of experience he will have in that afterlife. If the gods consider one's earthly life to have been a model of obedience to the divine standard, exalted to godhood. However, if the gods look unfavorably on one's earthly life, then his afterlife may be spent in either everlasting or temporal punishment.

H. History is the outworking of the gods' activity.

Besides the belief that the gods influence and intervene in history, there is little else on which polytheists agree here. They do agree that the history of the universe is eternal and that human history (at least on earth) had a beginning. However, some are historical optimists and some are pessimists. Some polytheists (e.g., Mormonism) believe that human history is tending toward an end and thus is linear, while others (e.g. Miller) seem to hold that human history is cyclical, moving from polytheistic thinking to monotheistic then back to polytheistic. But most polytheists see history as an unfolding of the will of the gods.

V. An evaulation of polytheism.

A. Some commendations of polytheism.

Certain positive aspects of polytheism have been commended by many. Some of these are summarized below.

First, there is a widespread and growing recognition that man is not alone in the universe. Some people have persistently reported contacts with UFO beings or extraterrestrials. Even many scientists, such as Carl Sagan, believe that there are intelligent beings in outer space. Some non-polytheistic religions recognize the existence of superhuman beings, such as angels and demons.

Second, if there is a divine reality it follows that man should seek to discover what his relationship is to that reality and how he should respond to it. The emphasis that polytheists place on human beings getting "tuned in" to the divine reality and adjusting their behavior accordingly is commendable.

Third, polytheists are often praised for positing an analogy between man and the gods. If divine beings exist, and if they had something to do with the creation of man, then it would seem that human nature would in some way reflect deity. A cause cannot give characteristics to others it does not possess itself. As a painting displays some truths about its painter (e.g., the level of his skill, the breadth of his imagination, or the care he takes in his work), so man should display some truths about his Creator(s). Hence, if man is a creation of some divine reality, then he must possess some characteristics that resemble those of his Maker(s). Thus, it would appear reasonable to conclude that there is some analogy between man and the gods.

Fourth, polytheists have been commended for recognizing that there are various forces in the world, some within and others outside of man's control. Many scholars today have concluded that behind most myths, be they religious or not, lies a true story of man's encounter with forces that press in upon him. These may be forces of nature (e.g., wind, rain, earthquakes, tornadoes, or floods), forces prevalent in his own culture and psyche (e.g., greed, hope, love, or a desire for power), or forces that he believes lie behind the universe (e.g., gods, angels or demons). Polytheists, through various story forms, have managed to relate man's encounter with such forces very vividly.

B. Some criticisms of polytheism.

Many criticisms have been made against the polytheistic world view. Those that follow are a summary of some of the more significant ones.

First, some critics have maintained that if the natural elements, say heaven and earth, gave birth to the gods, then the gods are not really ultimate beings. Whatever is derived from something else is dependent on that something, at least for its origin. How could a being that received its existence from another be above its maker? This would be like a cookie claiming to be greater than its baker, or a computer declaring to be above its programmer. Similarly, if nature created the gods, then the gods are not ultimate beings; rather nature is ultimate. And if, as Paul Tillich thought, worship involves an ultimate commitment to an ultimate,[72] then the gods should not be worshipped, but nature should be worshipped. This would be true regarding whatever was believed to have given birth to the gods or to precede their existence. If the gods are derivative beings, then they are not ultimate beings. And if they are not ultimate beings, then they are not worthy to receive an ultimate commitment. Why worship something that has no ultimate worth?

Second, the idea of an eternal universe has met with many philosophical and scientific objections. One philosophical argument stems from the impossibility of an actual infinite series of events in time. An eternal universe would be a beginningless series of events in time. But how could such a series possibly exist? To illustrate, suppose there were a library with an infinite number of books on its shelves. Imagine that each book is numbered. Since there is an infinite number of books, every possible number must be printed on the books in the library. From this it would follow that no new book could be added to the library, for there would be no number left to assign. All the numbers have been used up. But this seems absurd, for all objects in reality can be numbered. Further, it would be easy to add to the library, since one could make a new book by tearing a page out of each of the first 50 books, adding a title page, binding them together and putting the finished product on the shelf. Hence, the idea of an actual infinite series of books appears to be impossible. For this same reason, an actual infinite series of events in time would also be impossible. Therefore, the polytheistic belief in an eternal universe [73] would appear to be impossible.

A scientifc argument against the idea of an eternal universe can be derived from the modern notion that the universe is expanding. An astronomer named Edwin Hubble concluded that the universe is expanding the same degree in all directions. If this were true, it would follow that at some point in the past the universe was only a single point from which it has been expanding. This single point would be one of "infinite density." However, no object could be infinitely dense, for if it contained any mass at all it would not be infinitely dense but finitely dense. Hence, a totally shrunken or contracted universe is really no universe at all. The concept of an expanding universe requires a point at which no universe existed. If this is so, then the universe could not be eternal, but must have begun from nothing.[74]

Third, if the universe is not eternal but came to exist from nothing, then it would seem reasonable to conclude that something other than the universe must have existed before it and created it. The only other two options are (1) that the universe came into existence out of nothing and by nothing, or (2) that the universe created itself from nothing. The first option is contrary to the widely held principle that only something can cause something. How can nothing cause anything? But if something caused the universe to exist, then something other than the universe must have brought it into existence. In this case, whatever caused the universe to exist must have also caused the gods of polytheism to exist, since they exist *in* the universe and not beyond it. Therefore, the Cause of the universe would also be the Cause of the gods. But if the gods of polytheism derive their existence from another, then this other is really the supreme God of monotheism. Thus, polytheism collapses into monotheism. Therefore, if the gods exist, they would ultimately be dependent on a Cause beyond them and beyond the universe. But this conclusion coincides with the claims of theism, not those of polytheism.

Fourth, the polytheistic analogy between man and the gods has been criticized as too anthropomorphic (interpreting what is not human on the basis of human characteristics). Certainly deity should bear some resemblance to man, and vice versa. On the other hand, to apply human imperfections to deity would seem to render the divine reality as less than worthy of our respect and worship. The gods of polytheism appear to be made in man's image rather than man being made in their image. This tends to give credence to the view that polytheism is a human invention or superstition rather than a depiction of what actually is.

VI. Summary and conclusion.

Discounting the differences among polytheists, they do agree that there is more than one god. These gods exist in the space-time universe, not beyond it. Each of the gods has his own sphere of influence, and in that sphere he exerts strong influence over the world. Like everything else, the gods are subject to change and process. Indeed, they have a beginning but have no end. The universe is eternal, yet the gods had some influence on the condition of its present order. Man is finite, intelligent and free. His life and destiny are intimately linked to the activity of the gods.

NOTES

1. Huston Smith provides helpful discussions of Hinduism, Confucianism and Taoism in his *The Religions of Man* (New York: Harper & Row, 1965). A succinct and sympathetic summary of Jainism is given by Swami Prabhavananda in his *The Spiritual Heritage of India*, with the assistance of Frederick Manchester (Hollywood: Vedanta Press, 1969 ed.), chapter 7.
2. Hesiod, *Theogony* 20-35; *Works and Days*, 1-10, 655-662.
3. Hugh G. Evelyn-White, "Introduction," in *Hesiod, the Homeric Hymns and Homerica* (Cambridge: Harvard University Press; London: William Heinemann, Ltd., 1964, first published 1914), p. xvi.
4. Hesiod, *Theogony*, 123-135.
5. F. M. Cornford, *From Religion to Philosophy: A Study in the Origins of Western Speculation* (New York: Harper Torchbooks, 1957), p. 66. Cf. Hesiod *Theogony*, 667-710.
6. Hesiod, *Theogony*, 154-185.
7. John Mansley Robinson, *An Introduction to Early Greek Philosophy* (Boston: Houghton Mifflin Co., 1968), p. 6.
8. Hesiod, *Theogony*, 108-112.
9. Ibid., 453-500, 664-723.
10. Ibid., 881-885.
11. Ibid., 390-404. See also Cornford, *From Religion to Philosophy*, pp. 25, 26.
12. Hesiod, *Works and Days*, 505-506; *Theogony*, 748, 211-228, 933, 767, 768.
13. Hesiod, *Theogony*, 378-380, 782-784, 793-800, 886-929, 967-968, 1019-1020.
14. Hesiod, *Works and Days* 104-105, 267-269; *Theogony* 403, 613-614.
15. Hesiod, *Works and Days* 47-53; *Theogony* 558, 886-929.
16. Hesiod, *Theogony* 719-729, 736-744; also see Robinson, *An Introduction to Early Greek Philosophy*, pp. 8-10.
17. Hesiod, *Works and Days* 109-120.
18. Ibid. 121-139.
19. Ibid. 143-155.
20. Ibid. 156-169b.
21. Ibid. 169c-201.
22. Hesiod, *Theogony*, 509-602.
23. Ibid. 945-949.
24. Hesiod, *Works and Days*, 47-105.
25. Ibid. 274-285.
26. Ibid. 225-237.
27. Ibid. 239-247.
28. Ibid. 267-273.
29. Ibid. 706-828.
30. Ibid. 122-126.
31. Rodney Clapp, "Fighting Mormonism in Utah," in *Christianity Today* 26 (July 16, 1982):30.

32. Jerald and Sandra Tanner, *The Changing World of Mormonism* (Chicago: Moody Press, 1980), pp. 19, 21. For additional information on the financial standing of the LDS church see Walter Martin, *The Maze of Mormonism*, rev. ed. (Santa Ana: Vision House Publishers, 1978), pp. 16-22.

33. Joseph Smith, Jr., "Writings of Joseph Smith," in the *Pearl of Great Price*, 2:19.

34. James E. Talmage, *A Study of the Articles of Faith*, 13th ed. (Salt Lake City: The Church of Jesus Christ of Latter-day Saints, 1924, first published, 1890), p. 15.

35. Tanners, *The Changing World of Mormonism*, p. 175.

36. *Where Does It Say That?* (Scottsdale: Christian Communications Inc., n.d.), p. 30.

37. Ibid.

38. Joseph Smith, Jr., *Teachings of the Prophet Josesph Smith*, ed. by Joseph Fielding Smith, 4th ed. (Salt Lake City: The Deseret News Press, 1943, first published, 1938), pp. 346, 345.

39. Bruce R. McConkie, *Mormon Doctrine—A Compendium of the Gospel*, rev. ed. (Salt Lake City: Bookcraft, 1966), p. 516.

40. Joseph F. Smith, *Gospel Doctrine*, 12th ed. (Salt Lake City: Deseret Book Company, 1961, first published, 1919), p. 70; and Hyrum L. Andrus, *God, Man, and the Universe* (Salt Lake City: Bookcraft, 1968), p. 111.

41. Talmage, *A Study of the Articles of Faith*, pp. 160, 159. Cf. *Doctrine and Covenants* 130:22.

42. Smith, *Teachings of the Prophet Joseph Smith*, pp. 349-52.

43. Talmage, *A Study of the Articles of Faith*, p. 466. Cf. *Doctrine and Covenants* 93:33.

44. Andrus, *God, Man, and the Universe*, p. 304.

45. Talmage, *A Study of the Articles of Faith*, pp. 1, 466.

46. Tanners, *The Changing World of Mormonism*, p. 197.

47. Ibid., p. 193.

48. Talmage, *A Study of the Articles of Faith*, p. 466.

49. McConkie, *Mormon Doctrine*, p. 742.

50. Talmage, *A Study of the Articles of Faith*, p. 87; and Smith, *Gospel Doctrine*, pp. 18, 19.

51. Talmage, *A Study of the Articles of Faity*, pp. 160, 163.

52. Andrus, *God, Man, and the Universe*, pp. 146-148, 150-151.

53. Ibid., pp. 156-57.

54. Ibid., pp. 170, 177.

55. Ibid., pp. 181, 179.

56. Ibid., pp. 187-91.

57. Ibid., pp. 195, 207.

58. Talmage, *A Study of the Articles of Faith*, pp. 89-91.

59. Andrus, *God, Man, and the Universe*, pp. 383, 384.

60. Talmage, *A Study of the Articles of Faith*, pp. 62-65. See also Andrus, *God, Man, and the Universe*, chapter 14; and the Tanners, *The Changing World of Mormonism*, pp. 192-93.

61. Smith, *Gospel Doctrine*, p. 57.

62. Andrus, *God, Man, and the Universe*, p. 388.

63. Ibid., p. 137.

64. W. Cleon Skousen, *The First 2000 Years* (Salt Lake City: Bookcraft, 1953), p. 65.

65. Talmage, *A Study of the Articles of Faith*, pp. 6-7.

66. Ibid., p. 371; cf., p. 378.

67. Ibid., pp. 148, 406-7; and McConkie, *Mormon Doctrine*, p. 784.

68. McConkie, *Mormon Doctrine*, p. 670. See also Talmage, *A Study of the Articles of Faith*, pp. 405-6.
69. Andrus, *God, Man and the Universe*, p. 199.
70. Talmage, *A Study of the Articles of Faith*, p. 430.
71. David L. Miller, *The New Polytheism: Rebirth of the Gods and Goddesses* (New York: Harper & Row, 1974). All subsequent references to this book will be noted by page references in the text of this chapter.
72. Norman L. Geisler, *Philosophy of Religion* (Grand Rapids: Zondervan Publishing House, 1974), pp. 36-39.
73. William Lane Craig, "Philosophical and Scientific Pointers to *Creatio ex Nihilo*," in *Journal of the American Scientific Affiliation* 32 (March 1980):6-7.
74. Ibid., pp. 8, 9.

9

Choosing
a World View

Shopping for a world view is not the kind of thing one does weekly. In fact, most people never shop for one; they simply inherit one. Few people ever make a deliberate decision to reject one world view and accept another. Most are not even aware that they have a world view. Like a pair of glasses, a world view is something we look through but do not often look at, unless, of course, something goes wrong.

I. How world views can go wrong.

Numerous things can go wrong with a world view (and with a pair of glasses).

A. A distorted vision.

One's world view may develop a distortion in its ability to reveal the world (reality). Of course, this distortion may be difficult to discover if one has his glasses on at all times. However, most people must remove their glasses to rub their eyes sooner or later. Even skeptic David Hume confessed to interrupting his skepticism long enough to play Backgammon.[1] In moments of relaxation, setting aside their normal viewing lenses, some people discover that their world view has been distorting their ability to see reality correctly. And sometimes they seek to correct their world vision.

Some agree that a world view is like a pair of glasses, but insist that these "glasses" are cemented to one's face. This seems unlikely for several reasons. First of all, people do change their world views. Some people experience a "conversion" from one world view to another. Or, to use other terminology, there are Copernican revolutions in world views just as there are in science. There are what Thomas Kuhn called "paradigm shifts," where one's prespective is radically altered and a very different one is adopted.[2]

Second, if one's world view glasses were cemented to his face, it would seem that world views would be inherited at birth. But there is no evidence that world views are hereditary. They seem to come from the environment, from the culture. World views can be taught, even though they seem primarily to be caught. But in either case they are acquired, not naturally transmitted.

Finally, even if world view glasses are naturally attached (and, hence, could be changed only by supernatural action), there is still a possibility of discovering a distortion in them before one is miraculously converted to another world view. Just as a person can detect an astigmatism in his own eye by noting that a distortion on a page moves as the eye moves, so too could a person detect a distortion in his world view. Such a discovery could awaken a person from his "dogmatic slumbers" to be more alert to other possibilities.

B. A crack in the glass.

Others have begun to contemplate the nature of their world view as a crack appears in it. Cracks may take several forms in the world view apparatus. Rational inconsistencies are common kinds of cracks. As one thinks more and more about the various premises of his world view, he may discover that some of them are inconsistent. Such a "crack" seems to be what contributed to the demise of deism as a widely held philosophy. For how can one consistently believe both of the following?:

(1) God created the world out of nothing.

(2) Supernatural acts are not possible.

Once one thinks about it, creation from nothing *is* a supernatural act of the first order. This crack in the deists' glasses is a serious one which would lead a sincere rational deist to reconsider his world view.

There is another kind of crack that appears in one's world view glasses: an inconsistency between a belief and a desired behavior. Few people can live with continual conscious tension between an essential belief and contrary (but desired) behavior. For example, one may hold to a world view that an absolute Law Giver has

232

decreed that adultery is evil. Yet as he begins to desire to have an affair, he may cast aside his world view in an effort to justify his behavior. Most normal persons seek peace between the mind and the will. A gap between these two can lead one to give up the belief (essential to a world view) in favor of a behavior. Of course, some determine that the world view is correct and choose to relinquish the behavior.

C. Shattered glasses.

A world view is not only what one thinks; it also involves the way one lives. It is not only a matter of the mind; it is also a matter of the will. It involves not only metaphysics but also ethics. It is concerned not only with truth but also with values. This being the case, some people are shocked into reconsidering their world view after a shattering experience. Those who are nearly blind and must depend completely on a pair of glasses know how disrupting it can be if their only pair breaks. And those who have lost their vision totally have experienced an even more dramatic upheaval in their lives.

Sometimes life-shattering experiences can cause people to rethink their values and the philosophical premises from which they stem. Sickness, disability, and death of a loved one can challenge a person to reconsider the fundamentals of life. It is through these breaks in the glass that the light of a new world view may penetrate.

But whatever the case—a crack, a blur, or a break—there are times when one re-examines his basic commitments. What is needed at such times is some reassurance that he is not discarding one inadequate world view for another inadequate view. This raises the important question: How should one choose a world view?

II.   How to choose a world view.

The previous chapters of this book have been devoted largely to explaining *what* basic world views are available and noting some of their chief proponents. Now we will concentrate our attention on *how* to decide among the world views available in the marketplace of ideas.

A.   How *not* to choose a world view.

First of all, some advice on how *not* to pick a world view is in order. This common-sense advice can save a lot of time and headache, as well as heartache.

1. You cannot read everything.

Life is not long enough to read everything on all these views. In fact, life is not long enough to read everything on even *one* of them, or even a significant fraction of the books on one view. You should read enough to understand the basic beliefs of each of them. If you have read the previous chapters in this book carefully, you probably have enough information to make a decision. If you are not yet sure of the essentials of the various views, then read some of the primary sources cited in the footnotes of each chapter. But remember what a wise man of old once said: "My son, be warned: the writing of many books is endless, and excessive devotion to books is wearing to the body" (Ecclesiastes 12:12). Sooner or later you must stop reading and start deciding.

2. Beauty is only skin deep.

Most would agree that it is not wise to pick a spouse simply because he or she is physically attractive. Those who marry *only* for sex appeal sometimes find that even *that* loses it appeal after they discover that a wretched personality came with it.

"All that glitters is not gold" is also true of world views. You should not choose a world view simply because, on the surface, it appeals to you. Like sex, certain aspects of the world view may appeal to your desires but will not fulfill your total human needs.

3. What works is not always true.

Simply because a belief system "works" does not make it true. Lies work very well for many people, but that does not make a lie true. Telling the boss that you're sick might "work" at getting you the day off, but the result does not validate the lie. Expedience is not a test for truth. Surely we could not determine the truth (and innocence or guilt) in a court of law were the witnesses to take the stand and say, "I swear to tell the expedient, the whole expedient, and nothing but the expedient. So help me, future results!"

If a world and life view is true it *will work* in life (if properly understood and applied), but simply *because* something works does not make it true. One can not determine truth by desired results any more than he can pick the best golf ball on the basis of which one made the hole-in-one. Success does not necessarily mean truth. Even swindlers are successful. Truth is determined by reality, not simply by results.

4. The majority can be wrong.

"All of my friends are doing it." So what! Columbus' friends were wrong, too. The truth of a world view is not decided by majority vote. Peer pressure is strong, but if it is pressing in the wrong direction, it should be resisted. Any dead fish can float down stream. It takes a live one to swim up stream.

Do not fall prey to the reverse error either: "the fewer the truer." "Everyone is wrong but me and thee, and sometimes I wonder about thee." Something is not necessarily true because only a select "enlightened" few believe it. On the other hand, something is not necessarily false because most people reject it. Truth is "telling it like it is," whether most people like it or not.

5. Difficulty should not prompt quick rejection.

Experience reveals that what has value often comes with great difficulty. Ask any great athlete or artist for confirmation. All great Olympians and musicians practice long and hard for their rewards. No pain, no gain.

It is true that some people fall into a fortune. However, many of them also fall out of it almost as easily. The fact that some discover the truth without difficulty does not mean that all will. It is a fact of life that truth is often discovered only after great questioning, conflict and difficulty. Major court cases are sufficient testimony to this.

6. The unexplained is not necessarily unexplainable.

We should not reject a view merely because it is difficult to understand or conceive. There are probably mysteries in all world views. No scientist rejects nature because of anomalies. For example, it is difficult to imagine how light can be both waves and particles, as physicists claim. Nevertheless, most scientists accept this as a limitation in our understanding, not a contradiction in nature.

The lack of ability to explain fully *how* all the pieces fit together is not adequate grounds for rejecting a world view. Were the truth told, all world views (being constructions of human minds) have this same problem. The important thing is that the view be able to show that all the pieces *can* satisfactorily fit together.

7. Absurdity does not guarantee truth.

"I believe because it is absurd" is the cry of an irrational mind, not the call for an intelligent truth-seeker. Beware of views that revel in paradox, that believe antinomy is the heart of reality. Socrates said that "the unexamined life is not worth living." Likewise, the irrational belief is not worth believing, nor a contradictory world view worth holding.

B. How to choose a world view.

Now for the positive advice. How *does* one decide on a world view? They cannot all be true, for they hold mutually exclusive views on many essential points. For example, atheism and theism cannot both be true, for atheism affirms that "God does not exist" and theism affirms that "God does exist." Likewise, God cannot be both finite (finite godism) and infinite (theism). Nor can miracles be possible (theism) and impossible (deism, atheism). The opposite of truth is falsehood. Hence, if one view is true, then the opposite must be false, unless, of course, one claims that there is no such thing as truth. But the problem with such a statement is that it claims to be true, thereby defeating its own claim that nothing is true.

Like it or not, we are stuck with the tough decision as to which one of the world views is true. Therefore, we must find a good way to test their claims to truth. We offer several criteria to test the truth or falsity of any particular world view.

1. A world view must be consistent.

If contradiction is a sign of falsity, then non-contradiction (or consistency) is a necessity for truth. Square circles do not exist since that would be contradictory. Therefore, we can eliminate a world view if it has actual contradictions in any of its essential premises. However, we must be sure that the contradictions are real and not merely apparent. That is, we must be dealing with real antinomies, not merely mysteries. A real contradiction occurs when two truth claims are given and one is the logical opposite of the other (they are logically contradictory, not merely contrary). For example:

(1) God is immutable (He does not change).

(2) God is not immutable (He changes).

No world view can hold these to be true simultaneously.

Further, the actual contradiction must be between *essential* premises of a world view. If either or both of the contradictory premises are non-essential, the contradiction does not necessarily falsify the world view. All one needs to do is discard the non-essential premises which occasioned the contradiction. Throwing away the non-essential will not affect the essential view.

All true views must be non-contradictory. However, simply because a view is consistent does not make it true. There may be more than one conceptually consistent world view. Indeed, it seems that several world views fit into this category. Some alleged inconsistencies are often created by comparing a premise from another person's world view with a premise from one's own view. For example, a theist may consider two premises he believes are held by pantheists:

(1) God is ultimate.

(2) I am not ultimate.

From these premises a theist would rightly conclude,

(3) I am not God.

This conclusion directly opposes pantheism, for a pentheist does claim "I am God" (*Atman* is *Brahman*). However, the contradiction is not inherent in pantheism, for the second premise is not a premise of pantheism but of theism. The theist did not *find* a contradication; he *made* a contradiction by evaluating the wrong series of premises.

2. A world view must be comprehensive.

It goes without saying that a *world* view should cover the whole "world" of reality. That is, it must encompass all of man's experience. If a world view is putting the whole picture together, then it must use all the pieces.

Unless a world view can encompass in some meaningful way all the data of the world, it is not a *world* view. Each world view must be evaluated in terms of how it assimilates the facts of experience. Here again, we must not be fooled by appearances. Often other people's world views *appear* to lack consistency and comprehensiveness because we comprehend the facts in a different way than they do. But it is unfair to ask a theist to understand all facts in the *same* way an atheist or a pantheist does. It is sufficient that they have *some way* to understand all facts. And in all fairness it seems that all the major world views do this, each of course, in its own way.

To understand this point, we should remember that what we take to be a "fact" is often determined by our world view. For example, Muslims take it as a fact that God gave revelations to Mohammad which he wrote in the Koran. Jews and Christians do not deny that Mohammad's teachings are in the Koran, but they do not accept it as fact that these teachings are revelations from God. Likewise, Muslims reject what Christians believe is the fact of Christ's resurrection. And atheists do not accept any miracles—Jewish, Muslim or Christian—as fact.

There are few hard "facts" which are crucial to one world view and which are accepted by all other world views, and even those are subject to different interpretations. Thus, we must be careful when we speak of a comprehensive view of all facts, since what is fact to one world view is often fiction to another. Or the same fact may be accepted by opposing world views because it is interpreted differently within each.

This leaves us with an important question: If more than one world view can consistently and comprehensively account for all the facts, then how do we know which one is true?

3. A world view must be liveable.

Another test for a world view is liveability. After all, a world and life view includes how one should live his life. Thus, if some views are not liveable, then they are not adequate.

There are several problems with offering this as a definitive test for the truth of a world view. First of all, like the pragmatic test for truth, it is fallacious to conclude that a view is true simply because it works in life. We can expect the reverse to be true, namely, that if the world view is true it will be liveable. But even in this case we can find difficulty in applying principles to life. Inconsistencies between deed and doctrine are part of any belief system.

Second, what is meant by "liveable" will be interpreted differently by different world views. For example, to a Christian, the pantheist (Buddhist) world view does not seem liveable, for the final end *(Nirvana)* is a cessation of all desire and a loss of personal life. Even before this final end, one is to learn to desire (crave for) less and less until at last he will thirst for nothing.

Yet how can the loss of individual personhood be personally satisfying? And how can the lack of all fulfillment ever be a satisfaction of all desires? The answer to these questions is: They cannot. But this does not mean that pantheism is "unliveable," at least not in pantheistic terms. Fulfillment *of all desires* is a Christian concept of

238

what "liveability" means. For the Buddhist, however, *cessation of all desire* is the goal of life. In other words, what the Buddhist "desires" is to *lose* all his desires. Therefore, to the degree he is achieving this goal, his view is liveable.

Finally, proponents of some world views have no desire to live at all. With them it is not a matter of *how* to live but *whether* one should live. For example, for nihilistic atheists, who believe that life literally holds *nothing* of value, suicide becomes the number one question. Some existential atheists (such as Jean-Paul Sartre) were willing to live without objective values by affirming their own values.[3] This, they deemed, gave value to life. But some nihilistic atheists deemed death to be the greatest value one could "live." For them, "liveability," or the fulfillment of their desires for life, is to initiate one's own death. Thus death becomes the ultimate in life for them.

In view of the problems of determining what is meant by "liveable," it is difficult to see how such a criterion can be used as a definitive test for a world view.

4. A world view must be consistently affirmable.

However, all is not lost. There is another way the premises of a world view can be tested. We can ask: Are the crucial premises consistently affirmable? You say, "Of course they are affirmable, since they have all been affirmed by these various world views." They have been affirmed, but have they been *consistently* affirmed? Let us give a few illustrations. Suppose one says, "I cannot utter a sentence in English." There is no question that this sentence is affirmable, for it was so affirmed right there on the previous line. However, is it *consistent* to make this statement? It is grammatically correct. It has no contradictions. It seems to say something. But still there is something wrong: It destroys itself. For in his very claim not to be able to utter a sentence in English the person utters this sentence in English. Therefore, the claim is self-defeating. It did what it claimed could not be done.

Not all truth claims refute themselves in this direct way. Some are self-refuting by presupposing what is contrary to the claim they make. For example, "Every statement ever made is absurd." If this is a serious truth claim, then the speaker is presupposing what is contrary to the statement (that is, "Not every statement is absurd, namely, this one"). Thus, there is a basic inconsistency between the two statements.

From this there emerges a test for the truth of a statement which can be applied to world view claims: *No statement is true if, in order to make it, the opposite would have to be true.*

In the light of this test let's examine statements *used by world views* to see if they are self-refuting. The following is a partial but significant list of statements made in different world views.

(1) "Reality cannot be known."

For one to make this statement, reality would have to be known. Otherwise, how could one know this about reality? "I know that I cannot know anything about reality" is self-defeating. For it claims to *know* that nothing can be known.

(2) "Be skeptical about everything."

If this is true, then one must be skeptical about this very statement; otherwise, it could not be true. Hence, if the claim is true, it must be false, for in order to be true, there cannot be *anything* about which one should not be skeptical, including this statement. But if this is so, then one should be skeptical about *everything*, including skepticism. Thus, total skepticism destroys itself.

(3) "Reality is not rational."

This claim says that reality goes beyond rational and logical thought. This means that reality could be contradictory.

The problem with this view is that the statement "reality is not rational" is offered as a rational statement about reality. And to claim that reality could be contradictory is to say that a statement about reality could be both true *and* false at the same time and in the same sense.

(4) "All truth is relative."

This means that statements are true at some time and in some place for some people, but no statement is true at all times and in all places for all people. However, the very claim that "all truth is relative [to certain times and places]" is offered as a statement that is true at all times and in all places and for all people. Thus, it is self-defeating.

(5) "Nothing exists."

This statement is clearly self-destructive. For if nothing existed, then no one could make this statement. One must exist in order to deny that anything exists. Hence, one's own existence is undeniable.

240

(6) "Nothing of value exists."

Total nihilism (the denial of all value) is self-destructive. For the statement implies by its very presence that someone thought it was valuable to make that statement. He no doubt valued his right to make such a statement. That is, he valued his freedom of thought and expression. So here too, the denial of all value presupposes some value.

(7) "Nothing can produce something."

Even the skeptic David Hume said such a statement is "absurd."[4] As a song in the film "The Sound of Music" puts it, "Nothing comes from nothing. Nothing ever could." But why is it self-defeating for one to claim that an event can occur without a cause? The very statement that "something can occur without a cause" assumes that there was a cause for that statement. Certainly the proponent of the statement assumes that there must be a cause for his statement. Statements like that do not appear willy-nilly out of nothing. But if one needs to presuppose there is a cause in order to deny there needs to be a cause, then he has destroyed his own argument.

(8) "Everything is based on something else."

This is another way of claiming that "everything has a cause." But if everything is caused, then what is causing it all? Something must be causing, otherwise nothing is being caused. If this statement is true, then the cause that is causing is also being caused to cause. Ultimately, the cause that is causing would have to be causing itself to exist.

But is it possible for everything to be caused and, hence, dependent? Does there not have to be at least one independent thing on which all else depends? Hence, this statement does not stand the test of rational thought.

III. Conclusion.

It is not our purpose to actually apply these principles to the various world views. But it is our conviction that when one takes the truths which cannot be successfully denied, they can be constructed into a valid world view. This we leave to each reader to do for himself. Truth is literally undeniable; however, truth is not always obvious. Only those who seek it find it.

NOTES

1. See David Hume, Appendix to *Treatise of Human Nature*, Selby-Bigge, ed. (Oxford, 1896, first published, 1739), p. 633.
2. Thomas Kuhn, *The Structure of Scientific Revolutions* (Chicago: University of Chicago Press, 1962), pp. 147, 149.
3. See Jean-Paul Sartre, *Existentialism and Humanism*, trans. by Philip Mairet (London: Methuen, 1948), pp. 29-32.
4. See David Hume, *The Letters of David Hume*, 2 vols., ed. by J. T. Greig (Oxford: Clarendon Press, 1932), I:187.

APPENDIX

SEVEN MAJOR WORLD VIEWS COMPARED *

*The features mentioned are not always true of everyone who holds that position but only generally true of the major representatives.

	THEISM	ATHEISM	DEISM
GOD	One, infinite, personal	None	One, infinite, personal
WORLD	Created *ex nihilo*	Uncreated	Created *ex nihilo*
	Finite, temporal	Eternal (material)	Finite, temporal
GOD/WORLD RELATION	God beyond and in world	World only	God beyond world and not in it miraculously
MIRACLES	Possible and actual	Impossible	May be possible but not actual
MAN'S NATURE	Soul-body, immortal	Body only, mortal	Body mortal, soul immortal
MAN'S DESTINY	Resurrection to reward or punishment	Extinction	Reward or punishment of the soul
ORIGIN OF EVIL	Free choice	Human ignorance	Free choice (and/or ignorance)
END OF EVIL	Will be defeated by God	Can be defeated by man	Can be defeated by man or God
BASIS OF ETHICS	Grounded in God	Grounded in man	Grounded in nature
NATURE OF ETHICS	Absolute	Relative	Absolute
HISTORY AND GOAL	Linear, purposeful, God appointed end	Linear or cyclical, purposeless, endless	Linear, purposeful, endless

FINITE GODISM	PANENTHEISM	PANTHEISM	POLYTHEISM
One, finite, personal	One, potentially infinite, actually finite, personal	One, infinite, impersonal	Two or more, finite, personal
Created *ex materia* or *ex nihilo*, eternal	Created *ex materia* and *ex deo*, eternal	Created *ex deo*, eternal (immaterial)	Created *ex materia*, eternal
God beyond and/or in world	God beyond world potentially and in it actually	God is world	Gods in world
May be possible but not actual	Impossible	Impossible	Not possible, supernormal events only.
Body mortal, soul immortal	Body mortal, soul immortal (some advocates)	Body mortal, soul immortal	Body mortal, soul immortal
Rewards and/or punishment	Live on in God's memory	Reincarnation, merging with God	Divine reward or punishment
In God's internal struggle	Necessary aspect of God	An illusion	In struggles between gods.
Can be defeated by man or God	Can't be defeated by God or man	Will be reabsorbed by God	Will not be defeated by gods
Grounded in God or man	Grounded in a changing God	Grounded in lower manifestations of God	Grounded in gods
Relative	Relative	Relative	Relative
Linear, purposeful, endless	Linear, purposeful, endless	Circular, illusory, endless	Circular, purposeful, endless

REFERENCES

ALTIZER, THOMAS. *The Gospel of Christian Atheism*. Philadelphia: The Westminster Press, 1966.

ANDRUS, HYRUM L. *God, Man, and the Universe*. Salt Lake City: Bookcraft, 1968.

ANSELM, SAINT. *St. Anselm: Basic Writings*. Translated by S. N. Deane. La Salle: Open Court Publishing Co., 1962.

AQUINAS, THOMAS. *St. Thomas Aquinas: Philosophical Texts*. Edited by Thomas Gilby. New York: Oxford University Press, 1964.

_____ . *Summa Contra Gentiles*. In *On the Truth of the Catholic Faith: Book One: God*. Translated by Anton C. Pegis. New York: Image Books, 1955.

_____ . *Summa Theologica*. Translated by Thomas Gilby. New York: McGraw Hill Book Co., 1968. Also in *The Basic Writings of St. Thomas Aquinas*. Translated by Anton C. Pegis. New York: Random House, 1944.

ARMSTRONG, A. H., ed. *The Cambridge History of Later Greek and Early Medieval Philosophy*. Chapter 12. Cambridge: Cambridge University Press, 1967; reprint ed., 1980.

AUGUSTINE, SAINT. *On the Trinity*. In *Nicene and Post-Nicene Fathers*. Edited by Philip Schaff. Grand Rapids: Wm. B. Eerdmans Publishing Co., 1956.

AYER, A. J. *Language, Truth, and Logic*. New York: Dover Publications, 1946.

BAYLE, PIERRE. *Selections from Bayle's Dictionary*. Translated by R. H. Popkin. Indianapolis: Bobbs-Merrill, 1965.

BENZ, ERNST. "Buddhist Influence Outside Asia." In *Buddhism in the Modern World*. Pages 305-322. Edited by Heinrich Dumoulin. New York: Macmillan Publishing Co., Inc., 1976.

BERGSON, HENRI. *Creative Evolution*. Translated by Arthur Mitchell. Westport: Greenwood Press, 1977; first published, 1911.

_____ . *Two Sources of Morality and Religion*. Translated by R. Ashley Audra and Cloudesley Brereton. New York: Doubleday, 1935.

BERTOCCI, PETER. *Introduction to the Philosophy of Religion*. New York: Prentice-Hall, Inc., 1953.

BHAGAVAD-GITA. Translated by Swami Prabhavananda and Christopher Isherwood. Bergerfield: The New American Library, Inc., 1972.

BLACK, MAX. *Models and Metaphors*. New York: Cornell University Press, 1962.

BRIGHTMAN, EDGAR S. *A Philosophy of Religion*. New York: Prentice-Hall, Inc., 1940.

BROWN, DELWIN, JAMES, RALPH E., JR., and REEVES, GENE, eds. *Process Philosophy and Christian Thought*. Indianapolis: Bobbs-Merrill Educational Publishing. 1971.

BRUCE, F. F. *The New Testament Documents: Are They Reliable?* Grand Rapids: Wm. B. Eerdmans Publishing Co., 1960.

BUTLER, JOSEPH. *The Analogy of Religion Natural and Revealed to the Constitution and Course of Nature*. 3rd ed. London: George Routledge and Sons, 1887; first published, 1872.

247

CHINMOY, SRI. "Revelation" on the *Birds of Fire* album cover. By the Mahavishnu Orchestra. New York: Columbia Records, n.d.

CLAPP, RODNEY. "Fighting Mormonism in Utah." *Christianity Today* 26 (July 16, 1982):30-32, 47-48.

CLARK, DAVID K. *The Pantheism of Alan Watts.* Downers Grove: Inter-Varsity Press, 1978.

CLARK, GORDON H. *Thales to Dewey: A History of Philosophy.* Reprint ed., Grand Rapids: Baker Book House, 1980.

CORDUAN, WINFRIED. "Transcendentalism: Hegel." In *Biblical Errancy: An Analysis of its Philosophical Roots.* Pages 81-101. Ed. by Norman L. Geisler. Grand Rapids: Zondervan Publishing House, 1981.

CORNFORD, F. M. *From Religion to Philosophy: A Study in the Origins of Western Speculation.* New York: Harper Torchbooks, 1957.

CORWIN, CHARLES. *East to Eden? Religion and the Dynamics of Social Change.* Grand Rapids: Wm. B. Eerdmans Publishing Co., 1972.

COUSINS, EWERT H., ed. *Process Theology: Basic Writings.* New York: Newman Press, 1971.

CRAIG, WILLIAM LANE. *The Kalam Cosmological Argument.* London: The Macmillan Press, Ltd., 1979.

_____ . "Philosophical and Scientific Pointers to *Creatio ex Nihilo*." *Journal of the American Scientific Affiliation* 32 (March 1980):5-13.

CRAIGHEAD, HOUSTON. "Non-Being and Hartshorne's Concept of God." *Process Studies* 1 (Spring 1971):9-24.

_____ . "Response." *The Southwestern Journal of Philosophy* 5 (Spring 1974): 33-37.

DEMAREST, BRUCE A. "Process Theology and the Pauline Doctrine of the Incarnation." In *Pauline Studies: Essays Presented to F. F. Bruce on His 70th Birthday.* Pages 122-142. Edited by Donald A. Hagner and Murray J. Harris. Exeter: The Paternoster Press, Ltd., 1980.

DUMOULIN, HEINRICH, ed. *Buddhism in the Modern World.* New York: Macmillan Publishing Co., Inc. 1976.

ELLWOOD, ROBERT S., Jr. "Polytheism: Establishment or Liberation Religion?" *Journal of the American Academy of Religion* 42 (June 1974):344-49.

The Enclyclopedia of Philosophy. 8 vols. Reprint ed. Editor in chief, Paul Edwards. 5.v. "Paine, Thomas," by Alfred Owen Aldridge, 6:17-18; s.v. "Parmenides of Elea," by David J. Furley, 6:47-51; s.v. "Jefferson, Thomas," by Ralph Ketcham, 4:259-60; s.v. "Pantheism" and "Spinoza, Benedict (Baruch)," by Alasdair MacIntyre, 6:32-35, 7:530-41.

FESPERMAN, FRANCIS I. "Jefferson's Bible." *Ohio Journal of Religious Studies* 4 (October 1976):78-88.

FEUERBACH, LUDWIG. *The Essence of Christianity.* New York: Harper Torchbooks, 1957.

FINDLAY, J. N. "Can God's Existence Be Disproved?" In the *Ontological Argument from St. Anselm to Contemporary Philosophy.* Pages 111-122. Edited by Alvin Plantinga. Garden City: Anchor Books, 1965.

FLINT, ROBERT. *Anti-Theistic Theories.* 3rd ed. Edinburgh and London: Wm. Blackwood and Sons, 1885.

FOOTE, HENRY WILDER. *Thomas Jefferson: Champion of Religious Freedom, Advocate of Christian Morals.* Boston: The Beacon Press, 1947.

FORD, LEWIS. "Biblical Recital and Process Philosophy." *Interpretation* 26:2 (April 1972):198-209.

FRAIR, WAYNE and DAVIS, PERCIVAL. *A Case for Creation.* Chicago: Moody Press, 1983.

FREUD, SIGMUND. *The Future of an Illusion.* Translated by W. D. Robson-Scott. New York: Doubleday & Company, Inc., 1957.

GARDNER, MARTIN. *The Whys of a Philosophical Scrivener.* New York: Quill, 1983.

GEISLER, NORMAN L., ed. *Biblical Errancy: An Analysis of its Philosophical Roots.* Grand Rapids: Zondervan Publishing Company, 1981.

_____ . *Christian Apologetics.* Grand Rapids: Baker Book House, 1976.

_____ . *Is Man the Measure?: An Evaluation of Contemporary Humanism.* Grand Rapids: Baker Book House, 1983.

_____ . *Philosophy of Religion.* Grand Rapids: Zondervan Publishing House, 1974.

_____ . "Process Theology." In *Tensions in Contemporary Theology.* Pages 237-284. Edited by Stanley N. Gundry and Alan F. Johnson. Chicago: Moody Press, 1976.

_____ . *The Roots of Evil.* Grand Rapids: Zondervan Publishing House, 1978.

_____ . ed. *What Augustine Says.* Grand Rapids: Baker Book House, 1982.

GEISLER, NORMAN L. and NIX, WILLIAM E. *A General Introduction to the Bible.* Chicago: Moody Press, 1968.

GLUT, DONALD F. *The Empire Strikes Back.* New York: Ballantine Books, 1980.

GRUENLER, GORDON R. *The Inexhaustible God: Biblical Faith and the Challenge of Process Theism.* Grand Rapids: Baker Book House, 1983.

GUINNESS, OS. *The Dust of Death.* Downers Grove: Inter-Varsity Press, 1968.

GUNDRY, STANLEY N. and JOHNSON, ALAN F., eds. *Tensions in Contemporary Theology.* Chicago: Moody Press, 1976.

GUTHRIE, DONALD K. *The Greek Philosophers from Thales to Aristotle.* New York: Harper & Row, 1975.

HACKETT, STUART. *The Resurrection of Theism.* Reprint ed. Grand Rapids: Baker Book House, 1982.

HARRISON, GEORGE. "My Sweet Lord." On the album *All Things Must Pass.* New York: Apple Records, Inc., n.d.

HARTSHORNE, CHARLES. "Abstract and Concrete Approaches to Deity." *Union Seminary Quarterly Review.* 20 (March 1965) :265-270.

_____ . *Aquinas to Whitehead: Seven Centuries of Metaphysics of Religion.* The Aquinas Lecture, 1976. Milwaukee: Marquette University Publications, 1976.

_____ . "Beyond Enlightened Self-Interest: A Metaphysics of Ethics." *Ethics.* 84 (April 1974):201-216.

_____ . *Creative Synthesis and Philosophic Method.* LaSalle: The Open Court Publishing Co., 1970.

_____ . "The Dipolar Conception of Deity." *The Review of Metaphysics.* 21 (December 1967) :273-289.

_____ . *The Divine Relativity: A Social Conception of God.* New Haven and London: Yale University Press, 1948.

_____ . "Efficient Causality in Aristotle and St. Thomas: A Review Article." *The Journal of Religion.* 25 (January 1945) :25-32.

_____ . "The Idea of God—Literal or Analogical?" *The Christian Scholar.* 34 (June 1956) :131-136.

_____ . "Idealism and Our Experience of Nature." In *Philosophy, Religion, and the Coming World Civilization: Essays in Honor of William Ernest Hocking.* Pages 70-80. Edited by Leroy S. Rouner. The Hague: Martinus Nijhoff, 1966.

_____ . "Is God's Existence a State of Affairs?" In *Faith and the Philosophers.*

Pages 26-33. Edited by John Hick. New York: St. Martin's Press, 1966.

———— . *The Logic of Perfection.* LaSalle: The Open Court Publishing Company, 1962.

———— . "Love and Dual Transcendence." *Union Seminary Quarterly Review.* 30 (Winter-Summer 1975) :94-100.

———— . *Man's Vision of God and the Logic of Theism.* Hamden: Archon Books, 1964; first published, 1941.

———— . *A Natural Theology for Our Time.* LaSalle: The Open Court Publishing Company, 1967.

———— . "The Necessarily Existent." In *The Ontological Argument from St. Anselm to Contemporary Philosophers.* Pages 123-135. Edited by Alvin Plantinga. New York: Doubleday, 1965.

———— . "Outlines of a Philosophy of Nature: Part II." *The Personalist.* 39 (Autumn 1958) :380-391.

———— . "Personal Identity from A to Z." *Process Studies.* 2 (Fall 1972) :209-215.

———— . "Two Levels of Faith and Reason." *The Journal of Bible and Religion.* 16 (January 1948) :30-38.

HARTSHORNE, CHARLES and REESE, WILLIAM L. *Philosophers Speak of God.* Reprint ed. Chicago and London: The University of Chicago Press, 1976; first published, 1953.

HEGEL, G. W. F. *The Phenomenology of Mind.* Translated by J. B. Baillie. New York: Macmillan, 1931.

HESIOD. *Hesiod, the Homeric Hymns and Homerica.* Translated and Introduction by Hugh G. Evelyn-White. Cambridge: Harvard University Press, 1964; first published, 1914.

HICK, JOHN, ed. *The Existence of God.* New York: The Macmillian Co., 1964.

———— . ed. *Faith and the Philosophers.* New York: St. Martin's Press, 1966.

HUDSON, LEE. "Deism: The Minimal Religion of Social Utility." *Dialog.* 16 (Summer 1977) :205-210.

HUME, DAVID. *Dialogues Concerning Natural Religion.* Indianapolis: Bobbs-Merrill, 1962.

———— . *Enquiry Concerning Human Understanding.* Indianapolis: Bobbs-Merrill, 1955.

———— . *The Letters of David Hume.* 2 vols. Edited by J. Y. T. Greig. Oxford: Clarendon Press, 1932.

———— . *Treatise of Human Nature.* Edited by Selby-Bigge. Oxford, 1896; first published, 1739.

JAMES, WILLIAM. *Essays in Pragmatism.* New York: Hafner Publishing Co., 1968.

———— . *Human Immortality: Two Supposed Objections to the Doctrine.* London: Archibald Constable & Co., Ltd., 1906.

———— . *A Pluralistic Universe.* London: Longmans, Green, and Co., 1909.

———— . *Pragmatism and Other Essays.* New York: Washington Square Press, Inc., 1963; first published, 1907.

———— . *Varieties of Religious Experience.* New York: A Mentor Book, 1958; first published, 1902.

KANT, IMMANUEL. *Critique of Pure Reason.* Translated by L. W. Beck. New York: Bobbs-Merrill, 1950.

KITCHEN, K.A. *Ancient Orient and the Old Testament.* Downers Grove: InterVarsity Press, 1966.

KUHN, THOMAS. *The Structure of Scientific Revolutions.* Chicago: University of Chicago Press, 1962.

KURTZ, PAUL, ed. *Humanist Manifestos I & II.* Buffalo: Prometheus Books, 1973.

LEWIS, C. S. *The Abolition of Man.* New York: Macmillan Publishing Co., 1947.

_____ . *Christian Reflections*. Edited by Walter Hooper. Grand Rapids: Wm. B. Eerdmans Publishing Company, 1967.

_____ . *God in the Dock: Essays on Theology and Ethics*. Edited by Walter Hooper. Grand Rapids: Wm. B. Eerdmans Publishing Co., 1970.

_____ . *The Great Divorce*. New York: Macmillan Publishing Co., 1946.

_____ . *Mere Christianity*. New York: Macmillan Publishing Co., 1953.

_____ . *Miracles: A Preliminary Study*. New York: Macmillan Publishing Co., Inc., 1947.

_____ . *The Problem of Pain*. New York: Macmillan Publishing Co., 1940.

LINDSEY, DUANE. "An Evangelical Overview of Process Theology." *Bibliotheca Sacra*. 134. (January-March 1977):15-32.

LONG, MARY. "Visions of a New Faith." *Science Digest*. 89 (November 1981) :36-42.

LOOMER, BERNARD. "A Response to David Griffin." *Encounter*. 36:4 (Autumn 1975):361-369.

McCONKIE, BRUCE R. *Mormon Doctrine — A Compendium of the Gospel*. Revised ed. Salt Lake City: Bookcraft, 1966.

McINERNY, RALPH M. *A History of Western Philosophy*. Notre Dame: University of Notre Dame Press, 1963.

MACHEN, J. GERSHAM. *The Virgin Birth of Christ*. Reprint ed. Grand Rapids: Baker Book House, 1977; first published, 1930.

MARTIN, WALTER. *The Maze of Mormonism*. Revised ed. Santa Ana: Vision House Publishers, 1978.

MAVRODES, GEORGE. *Belief in God: A Study of the Epistemology of Religion*. New York: Random House, 1970.

MILL, JOHN STUART. *Three Essays on Religion: Nature, Utility of Religion, and Theism*. London: Longmans, Green, & Co., 1885.

_____ . *Utilitarianism*. New York: Meridian Books, 1962.

MILLER, DAVID L. *The New Polytheism: Rebirth of the Gods and Goddesses*. New York: Harper & Row, 1974.

_____ . "Polytheism and Archetypal Theology: A Discussion." *Journal of the American Academy of Religion*. 40:4 (December 1972):513-20.

MORAIS, HERBERT M. *Deism in Eighteenth Century America*. New York: Russell & Russell, 1960; first published, 1934.

NASH, RONALD. *Christian Faith and Historical Understanding*. Grand Rapids: Zondervan Publishing House; Dallas: Probe Ministries International, 1964.

NIEBUHR, REINHOLD, ed. *Marx and Engels on Religion*. New York: Schocken, 1964.

NIETZSCHE, FRIEDRICH. *Anti-Christ*. Translated by H. L. Mencken. New York: Knopf, 1920.

_____ . *Beyond Good and Evil*. Cowan translation. Chicago: Henry Regnery Co., 1966.

_____ . *Joyful Wisdom*. Translated by Thomas Common. Frederick Unger Publishing Co., 1960.

_____ . *Thus Spoke Zarathustra*. Translated by Walter Kaufmann. New York: Viking Press, 1966.

OGDEN, SCHUBERT M. "Bultmann's Demythologizing and Hartshorne's Dipolar Theism." In *Process and Divinity: Philosophical Essays Presented to Charles Hartshorne*. Pages 493-513. Edited by William L. Reese. LaSalle: Open Court Publishing Co., 1964.

_____ . "The Meaning of Christian Hope." *Union Seminary Quarterly Review*. 30 (Winter-Summer 1975).

_____ . *The Reality of God and Other Essays*. San Francisco: Harper & Row,

Publishers, 1977; first published, 1963.

_____ . *Theology in Crisis: A Colloquium on the Credibility of "God."* New Concord: Muskingum College, March 20-21, 1967.

O'HIGGINS, J. "Hume and the Deists: A Contrast in Religious Approaches." *The Journal of Theological Studies.* 23:2 (October 1971):479-501.

ORR, JOHN. *English Deism: Its Roots and Its Fruits.* Grand Rapids: Wm. B. Eerdmans Publishing Company, 1934.

OWEN, H. P. *The Christian Knowledge of God.* University of London: The Athlone Press, 1969.

_____ . *Concepts of Deity.* London: Macmillan and Co., Ltd., 1971.

PADOVER, SAUL K. *Thomas Jefferson and the Foundations of American Freedom.* New York: Van Nostrand Reinhold Company, 1965.

PAINE, THOMAS. *Complete Works of Thomas Paine.* Edited by Calvin Blanchard. Chicago and New York: Belford, Clarke & Co., 1885.

PALEY, WILLIAM. *Natural Theology.* Indianapolis: Bobbs-Merrill Co., 1963.

PLATO. *Timaeus.* In *The Collected Dialogues of Plato.* Edited by Edith Hamilton and Huntington Cairns. New York: Pantheon Books, 1964.

PLOTINUS. *Plotinus: The Six Enneads.* Translated by Stephen MacKenna and B. S. Page. Great Books of the Western World. Editor in chief, Robert Maynard Hutchins. Chicago: Wm. Benton, 1952.

PRABHAVANANDA, SWAMI. *The Spiritual Heritage of India.* Hollywood: Vedanta Press, 1963.

RADHAKRISHNAN, SARVEPAIL. *The Hindu View of Life.* London: Allen & Unwin, 1927.

_____ . *The Principle Upanishads.* London: Allen & Unwin, 1958.

RAND, AYN. *For the New Intellectual.* New York: New American Library, 1961.

ROBINSON, JOHN A. T. *Redating the New Testament.* Philadelphia: The Westminster Press, 1976.

ROBINSON, JOHN MANSLEY. *An Introduction to Early Greek Philosophy.* Boston: Houghton Mifflin Company, 1968.

ROUNER, LEROY S., ed. *Philosophy, Religion, and the Coming World Civilization: Essays in Honor of William Ernest Hocking.* The Hague: Martinus Nijhoff, 1966.

RUSSELL, BERTRAND. "What is an Agnostic?" *Look,* 1953.

_____ . *Why I Am Not a Christian.* New York: Simon and Schuster, 1957.

RUSSELL, BERTRAND. and COPLESTON, F.C. "A Debate on the Existence of God." In *The Existence of God.* Pages 167-191. Edited by John Hick. New York: The Macmillan Co., 1964.

SAGAN, CARL. *Broca's Brain.* New York: Random House, 1979.

_____ . *Cosmos.* New York: Random House, 1980.

SARTRE, JEAN-PAUL. *Being and Nothingness.* Translated by Hazel Barner. New York: Philosophical Library, Inc. 1956.

_____ . *Existentialism and Humanism.* Translated by Philip Mairet. London: Methuen, 1948.

_____ . *The Flies.* In *No Exit and Three Other Plays.* New York: Vintage Books, 1947.

SATIN, MARK. *New Age Politics.* New York: A Delta Book, 1979.

SCHAEFFER, FRANCIS. *The God Who Is There.* Downer's Grove: Inter-Varsity Press, 1973.

_____ . *He Is There and He Is Not Silent.* Wheaton: Tyndale House, 1972.

SKINNER, B. F. *About Behaviorism.* New York: Alfred A. Knopf, 1974.

_____ . *Walden Two.* New York: Macmillan, 1976.

SKOUSEN, W. CLEON. *The First 2000 Years.* Salt Lake City: Bookcraft, 1953.

SMITH, HUSTON. *The Religions of Man.* New York: Harper & Row, 1965.

SMITH, JOSEPH, JR. *Teachings of The Prophet Joseph Smith.* 4th ed. Edited by Joseph Fielding Smith. Salt Lake City: The Deseret News Press, 1943; first published, 1938.

_____ . "Writings of Joseph Smith." In the *Pearl of Great Price.* 1974 ed.

SMITH, JOSEPH F. *Gospel Doctrine.* 12th ed. Salt Lake City: Deseret Book Company, 1961; first published, 1919.

SPINOZA, BENEDICT DE. *Ethics.* Translated by A. Boyle. New York: E. P. Dutton, 1910.

STOKES, WALTER E. "A Whiteheadian Reflection on God's Relation to the World." In *Process Theology: Basic Writings.* Pages 137-152. Edited by Ewert H. Cousins. New York: Newman Press, 1971.

SUZUKI, D. T. *An Introduction to Zen Buddhism.* Foreword by C. G. Jung. New York: Grove Press, Inc., 1964.

_____ . *Manual of Zen Buddhism.* New York: Grove Press, Inc., 1960.

_____ . *Outlines of Mahayana Buddhism.* New York: Shocken Books, 1963.

_____ . *Zen Buddhism.* Edited by William Barrett. Garden City: Doubleday Anchor Books, 1956.

TALMAGE, JAMES E. *A Study of the Articles of Faith.* 13th ed. Salt Lake City: The Church of Jesus Christ of Latter-day Saints, 1924; first published, 1890.

TANNER, JERALD and SANDRA. *The Changing World of Mormonism.* Chicago: Moody Press, 1980.

TINDAL, MATTHEW. *Christianity as Old as the Creation: or, the Gospel, a Republication of the Religion of Nature.* New York & London: Garland Publishing, Inc., 1978; first published, 1730.

The Upanishads: Breath of the Eternal. Translated by Swami Probhavananda and Frederick Manchester. New York: Mentor Books, 1957.

VAN BUREN, PAUL. *The Secular Meaning of the Gospel.* New York: Macmillan, 1963.

WATTS, ALAN. *Beyond Theology.* New York: Vintage Books, 1964.

_____ . *The Essence of Alan Watts.* Millbrae: Celestial Arts, 1977.

_____ . *The Spirit of Zen.* New York: Grove Press, Inc., 1958.

_____ . *The Way of Zen.* New York: Vintage Books, 1957.

Where Does It Say That? Scottsdale: Christian Communications, Inc., n.d.

WHITEHEAD, ALFRED NORTH. *Adventure of Ideas.* New York: The Free Press, 1967; first published, 1933.

_____ . *Process and Reality.* New York: Harper Torchbooks, 1960; first published, 1929.

_____ . *Religion in the Making.* New York: Meridian Books, 1967; first published, 1926.

WIEMAN, HENRY N. *The Source of Human Good.* Chicago: University of Chicago Press, 1946.

WILSON, CLIFFORD A. *Rocks, Relics and Biblical Reliability.* Grand Rapids: Zondervan Publishing House, 1977.

YOCKEY, HERBERT. "Self Organization, Origin of Life Scenarios and Information Theory." *The Journal of Theoretical Biology.* 91 (1981):13-31.

Subject Index

Abstract (primordial) pole, of God, 101, 109-110, 123, 127, 128

Actual entities
  in Hartshorne's thought, 113
  as a society, 107, 111
  in Whitehead's thought, 104, 107

Adventures of Ideas (Whitehead), 102

Aesthetics, as the basis of ethics in Hartshorne's thought, 116

Age of Reason (Paine), 144

Agnosticism, compared to atheism, 44

Analogy
  of mind-body in Hartshorne's thought, 111-12
  in religious language, 223

Analogy of Religion (Butler), 139

Anthropomorphic language, in polytheism, 225

Antinomy, in Ogden's critique of classical theism,
  of creation, 117, 130
  of service, 117, 130

Aseity, definitions of, 62-63

Atheism, 43-68
  basic beliefs of, 53-55
  case against theism, inconclusiveness of, 65
  compared to skepticism and agnosticism, 44
  contributions of, 55-56
  critique of, 56-65
  critique of theism, 52-53
  critique of theistic arguments, 51-52
  of Feuerbach, 47-48
  of Nietzsche, 45-47
  of Sartre, 48-50
  summary of, 15
  theistic reponses to arguments for, 62-65
  typology of, 44-45

Atman, in Vedanta pantheism, 73-74

Beatific vision, in Thomas Aquinas' thought, 30

Beatles, The, pantheistic influence on, 70

Becoming-Being, of God, in Hartshorne's thought, 110

Being and Nothingness (Sartre), 49

Bhagavad-Gita
  foundation for Vedanta pantheism, 72
  indifference to action explained in, 74-75

Bible
  in deism, 159-60
  in Jefferson's thought, 152
  in Mormonism, 212
  in Paine's thought, 147-48
  in Tindal's thought, 143

Book of Abraham, 206

Book of Mormon, 204, 212

Brahman, in Vedanta pantheism, 69, 72-76

Causality
  in Hume's thought, 58
  principle of explained, 57
  principle of noncontradictory, 62

Cause(s)
  difference between mathematical and infinite series of, 58
  impossibility of actual infinite series of, 224-25
  infinite series of, 39

Christian Science, pantheistic, 15

Christianity
  allegedly restored by Joseph Smith, Jr., 204
  in James' thought, 175, 176
  in Jefferson's thought, 151-52
  Nietzsche's rejection of, 46
  Paine's rejection of, 145
  theistic, 15, 21

Christianity as Old as the Creation (Tindal), 139

City of God, The (Augustine), 26

Common Sense (Paine), 143

Concrete (consequent) pole, of God,

109-110, 101, 123, 127, 128
Confucianism, polytheistic, 196
Contingent being, definition of, 27,59
Contradiction, definition of, 126, 236
Creation
  in Augustine's thought, 23
  in Bertocci's thought, 181
  in deism, 155
  in finite godism, 185
  in Hartshorne's thought, 112-13
  in Hesiod's thought, 197-98
  in Mill's thought, 168
  in Ogden's thought, 118-19
  in Paine's thought, 145
  in panentheism, 123-24
  in pantheism, 88
  in polytheism, 220
  in theism, 36
  in Thomas Aquinas' thought, 28
  in Tindal's thought, 140
Creativity
  and God in Whitehead's thought,
    104, 105-106
  in panentheism, 123
  as reality itself, in Hartshorne's
    thought, 114
Cunyata, as absolute Suchness or void,
  83
Declaration of Independence, The
  and Jefferson, 148- 149
  natural moral law in, 35
Deism, 137-63
  background of, 137-38, 158
  basic beliefs of, 154-57
  contributions of, 157-58
  critique of, 158-60
  of Jefferson, 148-54
  of Paine, 143-48
  summary of, 15
  of Tindal, 139-43
  typology of, 138-39
Demiurgos, in Plato's thought, 102
Destiny, human
  in atheism, 54, 55
  in Augustine's thought, 26
  in Bertocci, 182-83
  in deism, 157

  in Feuerbach's thought, 48
  in finite godism, 187
  in Hartshorne's thought, 114
  in Hesiod's thought, 203-204
  in James' thought, 178-79·
  in Jefferson's thought, 154
  in Lewis' thought, 35-36
  in Mill's thought, 172-73
  in Mormonism, 212-13
  in Nietzsche's thought, 47
  in Ogden's thought, 121-22
  in Paine's thought, 148
  in panentheism, 125
  in pantheism, 89
  in Plotinus' thought, 79-80
  in polytheism, 222
  in Sartre's thought, 50
  in Suzuki's thought, 86-87
  in theism, 37
  in Thomas Aquinas' thought, 30
  in Tindal's thought, 143
  in Vedanta pantheism, 75-76
  in Whitehead's thought, 108
Divine Light Mission, pantheistic, 71
DNA, indicates design, 58
Dualism
  Lewis' critique of, 33
  in Manichaenism, 22-23
  thought of, necessary to transcend,
    in Suzuki's thought, 84, 86-87
  polytheistic, 196
Egoism, in Suzuki's thought, 84
Eternal Father (Elohim), in Mormonism,
  207
Ethical essentialism, in Thomas Aquinas'
  thought, 30
Ethics
  in atheism, 54-55, 56
  in Augustine's thought, 25-26
  in Bertocci's thought, 183-34
  in deism, 156
  in Feuerbach's thought, 48
  in finite godism, 186-87
  in Hartshorne's thought, 115-16
  in Hesiod's thought, 202-203
  in James' thought, 177-78
  in Jefferson's thought, 153, 156

in Lewis' thought, 35
in Mill's thought, 171
in Miller's thought, 219
in Mormonism, 211-12
in Nietzsche's thought, 46
in Ogden's thought, 122-23
in Paine's thought, 147
in panentheism, 125
in pantheism, 89-90
in polytheism, 222
in Sartre's thought, 49
in Suzuki's thought, 84-85
in theism, 37, 38
in Thomas Aquinas' thought, 29-30
in Tindal's thought, 142-43
in Vedanta pantheism, 74-75
in Whitehead's thought, 108-109

Evil
in atheism, 54, 55-56
in Augustine's thought, 24-25
in Bertocci's thought, 182
in deism, 156
in finite godism, 165-66, 186, 189-91
in Hartshorne's thought, 114-15
in Hesiod's thought, 202
in James' thought, 177-78
in Jefferson's thought, 152
in Lewis' thought, 33-34
in Manichaen dualism, 25
in Mill's thought, 170-71
in Mormonism, 210-11
in Ogden's thought, 121
in Paine's thought, 147
in panentheism, 125
in pantheism, 89-90
in polytheism, 220, 221
in Suzuki's thought, 84-85
in Thomas Aquinas' thought, 29
in Tindal's thought, 142
in Vedanta pantheism, 74-75
in Whitehead's thought, 106

Evolution
in Bertocci's thought, 182-83
in finite godism, 186
in Hartshorne's thought, 115
in Whitehead's thought, 106

Existence, concept of, in the ontological

argument, 60

Existential repugnance, argument of, in Ogden's thought, 117, 130

Existentially necessary statements, possibility of, 59

Facts, as subject to different interpretations, 237-38

Finite godism, 165-93
basic beliefs of, 184-87
of Bertocci, 179-84, 189
compared to deism, 186
contributions of, 187-88
critique of, 188-91
influence of deism, 158
in James, 173-79
of Mill, 166-73
summary of, 15
typology of, 166

Force, The, in *Star Wars* film series, pantheistic, 71, 72

God(s)
in atheism, 52-53, 56, 62-65
in Augustine's thoughts, 23
in Bertocci's thought, 179-81
in deism, 154, 155
in Feuerbach's thought, 47
in finite godism, 185
in Hartshorne's thought, 109-111
in Hesiod's thought, 198-99, 219-20
in James' thought, 173-75
in Jefferson's thought, 149
in Lewis' thought, 31-32
in Mill's thought, 167-68
in Miller's thought, 213-16, 219-20
in Mormonism, 207-209, 219
in Nietzsche's thought, 45-46
in Ogden's thought, 116-18
in Paine's thought, 144-45, 146
in panentheism, 101, 123, 124
in pantheism, 88
in Plato's thought, 102
in Plotinus' thought, 76-79
in polytheism, 219-20
in Sartre's thought, 48-49
in Suzuki's thought, 82-83
in theism, 36, 37-38, 50-51
in Thomas Aquinas' thought, 23-24

in Tindal's thought, 139-40
in Unitarianism, 154
in Whitehead's thought, 102-104
Government, in Jefferson's thought, 150
Greeks, ancient, representatives of polytheism, 16, 196
Happiness, in deism, 156
Hare Krishna, religious group, pantheistic, 71
Hinduism
-certain forms of pantheistic, 15
-certain forms of polytheistic, 196
History
in atheism, 55
in Augustine's thought, 26
in Bertocci's thought, 184
in deism, 157
in Feuerbach's thought, 48
in finitie godism, 187
in Hartshorne's thought, 115
in Hesiod's thought, 203-204
in James' thought, 178-179
in Jefferson's thought, 153
in Lewis' thought, 35-36
in Mill's thought, 173
in Miller's thought, 222
in Mormonism, 212-13, 222
in Nietzsche's thought, 47
in Ogden's thought, 121-22
in Paine's thought, 147-48
in panentheism, 125
in pantheism, 90
in Plotinus' thought, 79-80
in polytheism, 222
in Suzuki's thought, 85-86
in theism, 37
in Thomas Aquinas' thought, 30
in Tindal's thought, 143
in Vedanta pantheism, 75-76
in Whitehead's thought, 106-107
Holy Ghost, in Mormonism, 205-206, 208
Humanism
atheistic, 56
religious, influence of deism on, 158
Humanist, ascription of, preferred by some atheists, 44

Humanist Manifesto, 55
Islam, theistic, 15, 21
Jainism, polytheistic, 196
Jesus Christ
in Jefferson's thought, 152, 153
in Mill's thought, 171
in Mormonism, 207-208
in Paine's thought, 148
in Tindal's thought, 142
Judaism, theistic, 15, 21
Karma
Buddhist concept of and place in Suzuki's thought, 85
in Vedanta pantheism, 75-76
Koan, in Zen Buddhism, 87
Krishna, in the Bhagavad-Gita, 74-75
Law
in deism, 155, 158-59
in finite godism, 185-86
in Thomas Aquinas' thought, 29-30
in Tindal's thought, 140-41
Life, purpose in, in theism, 38-39
Life and Morals of Jesus of Nazareth, The (Jefferson), 152, 154
Logic, necessary to transcend, in Suzuki's thought, 86-87
Logical positivism, 44-45
Mahavishnu Orchestra, The, pantheistic influence on, 70-71
Man
in atheism, 54
in Augustine's thought, 24
in Bertocci's thought, 182-83
in deism, 156
in Feuerbach's thought, 48
in Hartshorne's thought, 113-14
in Hesiod's thought, 200-202
in James' thought, 178
in Jefferson's thought, 149-50
in Lewis' thought, 34-35
in Mill's thought, 172-73
in Miller's thought, 218-19
in Mormonism, 209-210
in Nietzsche's thought, 46
in Ogden's thought, 119-21
in Paine's thought, 146-47
in panentheism, 124-25

in pantheism, 89
in Plotinus' thought, 79
in polytheism, 221
in Sartre's thought, 49
in Suzuki's thought, 84
in theism, 36-37, 38
in Thomas Aquinas' thought, 29
in Tindal's thought, 141-42
in Vedanta pantheism, 73-74
in Whitehead's thought, 107-108
Maya
    In Suzuki's thought, 84, 85
    in Vedanta pantheism, 73
Mere Christianity (Lewis), 31
Miracles
    in Augustine's thought, 24
    in deism, 155-56, 138-59
    in finite godism, 186
    in James' thought, 175-77
    in Jefferson's thought, 153
    in Lewis' thought, 32-33
    in Mill's thought, 169-70
    in Ogden's thought, 119, 124
    in Paine's thought, 148
    in panentheism, 124
    in pantheism, 88-89
    in polytheism, 221
    in theism, 36
    in Thomas Aquinas' thought, 28-29
    in Tindal's thought, 143
Modes of Thought (Whitehead), 102
Monotheism, Miller's rejection of,
    213-14
Mormonism, 204-213
    background and growth of, 204
    on the Bible, 212
    Book of Abraham, 206
    Book of Mormon, 204, 212
    on creation, 206
    on divine revelation, 212
    Doctrine and Covenants, 212
    on the Eternal Father (Elohim), 207
    on ethics, 211-12
    on evil, 210-11
    on the gods, 204-206
    on the gods and their relation to the
        world, 207-209, 219

on history and goal, 212-13
on the Holy Ghost, 205-206, 208
on human destiny, 212-13
on Jesus Christ, (Jehovah), 207-208
on man, 209-210
Pearl of Great Price, 212
Mount Rushmore, indicates design,
    57-58
"My Sweet Lord," song by George Har-
    rison, pantheistic influence on, 70
Naturalism, James' critique of, 176
Necessary being
    definition of, 27, 59
    difference between logical and actual,
        59
    in Ogden's thought, 118
Neo-platonism, pantheistic, 23
New Age movement, pantheistic, 71
New Polytheism, The (Miller), 213
Nihilism, in Nietzche's thought, 45
Nirvana, in Suzuki's thought, 84, 86
Omnipotence, meaning of, 187-88
Panentheism, 99-135
    background of, 102
    basic beliefs of, 123-125
    compared to pantheism, 99-100
    compared to theism, 100-101
    contributions of, 126
    critique of, 126-31
    of Hartshorne, 109-116, 127, 129,
        130
    of Ogden, 116-23, 130
    summary of, 15, 131
    typology of, 101-102
    of Whitehead, 102-109
Pantheism, 69-97
    background and contemporary in-
        fluence of, 70-71
    basic beliefs of, 88-90
    contributions of, 90-91
    critique of, 91-94
    James' critique of, 173
    James' view, similar to some forms of,
        176
    of Plotinus, 76-80
    summary of, 15, 94
    of Suzuki, 80-88

typology of, 71-72
of Vedanta, 72-76
Paul, the apostle, Jefferson's understanding, 157
Pearl of Great Price, 212
Polytheism, 195-229
anthropomorphic language in, 225
background and contemporary
influence of, 196
basic beliefs of, 219-222
commendations of, 222-23
compared with other world views,
195-96
critique of, 223-25
of Hesiod, 196-204
James' critique of, 174
of Miller, 213-19
of Mormonism, 204-213
summary of, 16, 225-26
typology of, 196
Pragmatism
of James, 173, 178
problems of, 234
Process and Reality (Whitehead), 102
Reality of God and Other Essays, The
(Ogden), 116
Reason
in deism, 156
in religion, 157
Redemption, in Ogden's thought, 121
Reincarnation, in Vedanta pantheism,
75-76
Relative perfection, of God, in Hartshorne's thought, 110
Religion
as natural, 141-42
in Ogden's thought, 122-23
"Report of Government for the Western
Territory" (Jefferson), 150
Revelation
in deism, 155, 159
in Jefferson's thought, 153
in Mill's thought, 171
in Mormonism, 212
in Paine's thought, 144-45, 147
in polytheism, 221
in Tindal's thought, 141, 143

Rights of Man (Paine), 143
Romans, ancient, representatives of
polytheism, 196
Salvation
in Ogden's thought, 121
in Paine's thought, 147
Samsara
in Suzuki's thought, 86
in Vedanta pantheism, 75-76
Satori, in Suzuki's thought, 87
Self-caused being,
atheistic objection to, 53, 56
in Whitehead's thought, 106
Shinto, polytheistic, 196
Skepticism, compared to atheism, 44
Slavery, abolition of, in Jefferson's
thought, 150
Space, Time and Deity (Alexander), 102
Spencer, Herbert, forerunner of panentheism, 102
Star Wars, film series, pantheistic, 71, 72
Subjective aim, in Whitehead's thought,
107
Tao
in Lewis' thought, 34-35
in *Star Wars*, film series, 71, 72
Taoism, polytheistic, 196
"Teaching of the Seven Buddhas, The,"
85
Tests for world views (or truth), validity
of,
absurdity, 235-36
compiling information, 234
comprehensiveness, 237-38
consistency in affirmability, 239-40
consistency in reason, 236-37
degree of difficulty, 235
liveability, 238-39
majority vote, 235
pragmatism, 234
surface appeal, 234
Theism, 21-42
arguments for, 50-51
of Augustine, 22-26
basic beliefs of, 36-37
classical, representatives of, 22
commendations of, 37-39

260

critique of, 39-40
James' critique of, 173
of Lewis, 30-36
major religions of, 21
summary of, 15
of Thomas Aquinas, 27-30
typology of, 22
Theistic arguments for God's existence
   atheistic objections to, 51-52
   cosmological argument, 50
   moral argument, 51
   ontological argument, 50-51
   teleological argument, 50
   theistic responses to atheistic objections, 57-62
Theogony (Hesiod), 196-97
Transcendental Meditation, pantheistic, 71
Trinity
   Jefferson's rejection of, 154
   Paine's rejection of, 154
UFO religions, polytheistic, 196
Unitarianism, deistic influence on, 154, 158
United States, deistic influence on, 139, 148, 149
Universe
   in atheism, 54
   in Augustine's thought, 23-24
   in Bertocci's thought, 181-82
   in deism, 155
   in finite godism, 185-86
   in Hartshorne's thought, 111-12
   in Hesiod's thought, 199-200
   in James' thought, 175
   in Jefferson' thought, 149
   in Lewis' thought, 32
   logical options of its origin, 224-25
   in Mill's thought, 169
   in Miller's thought, 216-18
   in Mormonism, 207-209
   in Nietzsche's thought, 46-47
   in Ogden's thought, 118-19
   in Paine's thought, 145-46
   in panentheism, 123-24
   in pantheism, 88

   in Plotinus' thought, 76-79
   in polytheism, 220
   in Sartre's thought, 49-50
   in Suzuki's thought, 82-83
   in theism, 36
   in Thomas Aquinas' thought, 28
   in Tindal's thought, 140-41
   in Vedanta pantheism, 73
   in Whitehead's thought, 104-105
Upanishads, 70, 72
Utilitarianism, of Mill, 171
Utopia, in atheism, 55
Vedanta pantheism, 72-76
   background of, 72
   on ethics, 74-75
   on God, 72-73
   on human destiny, 75-76
   on man, 73-74
   summary of, 76
   on the universe, 73
Vedanta Society of Southern California, pantheistic, 71
Vedas, part of the Hindu scriptures, 72
Virtue, in Thomas Aquinas' thought, 30
Voluntarism, in William of Ockham's thought, 30
Walden II (Skinner), 55
Whys of a Philosophical Scrivener, The (Gardner), 138
Works and Days (Hesiod), 196
World view(s)
   chart of, 243-44
   contrasted, 15-17
   definition and illustrations of, 11-14
   diagram of, 18
   how not to choose one, 233-36
   how one can fail, 231-33
   how to choose one, 236-41
Worship
   and a finite God, 189
   and polytheism, 224
Yoga, kinds of, 74-75
Zen Buddhism,
   nature of, according to Suzuki, 80-82
   pantheistic, 15

Biographical
Index

Alexander, Samuel
  early panentheist, 102
  Space, Time and Deity, 102
Altizer, Thomas, dialectical atheist, 44
Anselm St.
  classical theist, 22
  ontological argument of, 50-51
Augustine, St., 22-26
  background of, 22
  The City of God, 26
  classical theist, 22
  on ethics, 25-26
  on evil, 24-25
  on God, 23
  on history and goal, 26
  on man, 24
  on miracles, 24
  on the universe, 23-24
Bergson, Henri
  forerunner of panentheism, 102
  on God, 166
Berkeley, Bishop, idealistic theist, 22
Bertocci, Peter, 179-84
  background of, 179
  on creation, 181
  on ethics, 183-34
  on evil, 182
  on God, 179-81
  on history and goal, 184
  on man and his destiny, 182-83
  on the universe, 181-82
Bonaventure, St., on the origin of the
  universe, 22
Brightman, Edgar S.
  Bertocci's teacher, 179
  on God, 166
Bultmann, Rudolph, influence on Ogden, 116, 122, 124
Butler, Bishop, *Analogy of Religion*, 139
Cobb, John, on God, 101
Descartes, Rene, rational theist, 22

Eckhardt, Meister, on man's relation to
  God, 82
Epicurus, assessment of moral teaching,
  by Jefferson, 153
Ferkiss, Victor, on pantheistic influence
  in science, 70
Feuerbach, Ludwig, 44, 47-48
  background of, 47
  on ethics, 48
  on God, 47
  on history and goal, 48
  on man, 48
  traditional atheist, 44
Flew, Antony, traditional atheist, 44
Franklin, Benjamin, American deist, 138
Freud, Sigmund
  on theism, 39
  psychological atheist, 45
Gardner, Martin, *The Ways of a Philosophical Scrivener*, 138
Harrison, George, pantheistic influence
  on, 70
Hartshorne, Charles, 101, 109-116
  compared to Whitehead, 101
  on contradictoriness of panentheism,
    127
  on creation, 112-13
  on ethics and aesthetics, 115-16, 125
  on evil, 114-15
  on God, 109-111
  on history and goal, 115
  on human destiny, 114
  importance and influence of, 109, 116
  on impossibility of total non-
    being, 129-130
  on man, 113-14
  on personal identity, 113, 129
  on the universe, 111-12
Hegel, G.W.F.
  developmental pantheism of, 71
  forerunner of panentheism, 102

influence on Feuerbach, 47
influence of Western theism, 90
Heidegger, Martin, influence on Ogden, 116, 119, 120
Heraclitus, forerunner of panentheism, 102
Herbert of Cherbury, European deist, 138
Hesiod, 196-204
  background of, 196-97
  on creation, 197-98
  on ethics, 202-203
  on evil, 202
  on the gods, 198-99, 219-20
  on history and destiny, 203-204
  on man, 200-202
  Theogony, 196-97
  on the universe, 199-200
  Works and Days, 196
Homer, ancient Greek polytheist, 196
Hopkins, Stephen, American deist, 138
Hume, David
  importance to modern atheism, 44, 50, 51
  an inconsistent skeptic, 231
  objections to theistic arguments, 51-52
Humphreys, Christmas, influenced by Suzuki, 80
Isherwood, Christopher, on good and evil, 90
James, William, 173-79
  on Christianity, 175, 176
  on evil and morals, 177-78
  on God, 173-75
  on history and human destiny, 178-79
  on man, 178
  on miracles, 175-77
  on naturalism, 176
  on Nietzsche's view of weak saints, 178
  on pantheism, 173
  on polytheism, 174
  pragmatism of, 173, 178
  on theism, 173
  on theistic supernaturalism, similarity with Kant, 176
  on the universe, 175

view similar to pantheism, 176
Jefferson, Thomas, 148-54
  on abolition of slavery, 150
  background of, 148-49
  on the apostle Paul, 152
  on the Bible, 152
  on Christianity, 151-52
  considered himself a Christian, 152
  and the Declaration of Independence, 148, 149
  on Epicurus, 153
  on ethics, 153, 156
  on evil, 152
  on God and the universe, 149
  on government and religion, 150
  on history, 153
  on human destiny, 154
  influence of Isaac Newton, 149
  "The Life and Morals of Jesus of Nazareth," 152, 154
  on man, 149-50
  on miracles, 153
  on supernatural revelation, 153
  on the Trinity, 154
Jung, C.G., on influence of Suzuki, 80
Kant, Immanuel
  distinction between appearance and reality critiqued, 61-62
  importance of, to modern atheism, 44, 50, 51
  objections to theistic arguments, 51-52
Kierkegaard, Soren, existential theist, 22
Koestenbaum, Peter, phenomenological theist, 22
Kuhn, Thomas, on scientific revolutions, 232
Kushner, Rabbi Harold, on God and evil, 165-66
Leibniz, Gottfried, rational theist, 22
Lewis, C.S., 30-36
  background of, 30
  on the Bible, 159-60
  on ethics, 35
  on evil, 33-34
  on God, 31-32
  on history and goal, 35-36
  on man, 34-35

Mere Christianity, 31
on miracles, 32-33
moral argument of, 51
on the universe, 32
Long, Mary, on pantheism in science, 70
Marx, Karl
for communistic utopia, 55
influence of Feuerbach, 47
marxistic atheist, 45
rejection of divine creator or ruler,
43-44
Mill, John Stuart, 166-73
background of, 166-67
on creation, 168
on ethics, 171
on evil, 170-71
on God, 167-68
on Jesus Christ, 171
on man and his destiny, 172-73
on miracles, 169-70
similarity with Plato's thought, 168
on supernatural revelation, 171
on the universe, 169
Miller, David L., 213-19
background of, 213
on history, 222
on man, 218-19
The New Polytheism, 213
on rejection of monotheism, 213-14
on revival of polytheism, 214-16
on the universe, 216-18
on values, 219, 222
Newton, Isaac, influence on Jefferson,
149
Nietzsche, Friedrich, 45-47
background of, 45
on ethics, 46
on God, 43, 45-56
on history and destiny, 47
on man, 46
mythological atheist, 44
on the universe, 46-47
on weak saints, critiqued by James,
178
Ogden, Schubert M., 116-23
arguments against classical theism,
116-17, 130

on ethics, 122-23
on evil, redemption, and salvation,
121
on God, 116-18
on history and human destiny, 121-22
influence of Bultmann, 116, 122, 124
influence of Hartshorne, 116, 118
influence of Heidegger, 116, 119, 120
on man, 119-21
The Reality of God and Other Essays,
116
on the universe and creation, 118-19
Owen, H.P., on Hartshorne's view of
God, critique of, 127
Paine, Thomas, 143-48
The Age of Reason, 144
on the Bible, 147-48
on Christianity, 145
Common Sense, 143
on creation, 145
on ethics, 147
on evil, 147
on God, 144-45, 146
on God and universe, 145-46
on history and goal, 147-48
on human destiny, 148
importance and influence of, 143-44
on Jesus Christ, 148
on man, 146-47
on miracles, 148
Rights of Man, 143
on salvation, 147
on supernatural revelation, 144-45,
147
on the trinity, 154
Paley, William, teleological argument of,
50
Parmenides, absolute pantheist, 71
Pierce, Charles Sanders, pragmatic theist, 22
Plantinga, Alvin, analytic theist, 22
Plato, forerunner of panentheism, 102
Plotinus, 76-80
background of, 76
emanational pantheist, 71, 76ff.
on God and the universe, 76-79
on human destiny, 79-80

on man, 79
summary of his thought, 80
Prabhavananda, Swami
on eternal judgment, 76
on good and evil, 90
Radhakrishnan, Sarvepalli
multilevel pantheism of, 71-72
Rand, Ayn
capitalistic atheist, 45
for a capitalistic utopia, 55
Reid, Thomas, empirical theist, 22
Russell, Bertrand, critique of
cosmological argument, 54
Sagan, Carl, belief in extraterrestrials,
223
Sankara, on Brahman, 73
Sarte, Jean-Paul, 48-50
background of, 48
Being and Nothingness, 49
on ethics, 49
existential atheist, 45
on God, 48-49
on man, 49
on the universe and human destiny,
49-50
Skinner, B.F.
for a behavioral utopia, 55
behavioristic atheist, 45
Walden II, 55
Smith, Huston, on *Karma,* 75
Spinoza, Benedict de, modal pantheist,
71
Suzuki, D.T., 80-88
background and influence of, 80
on ethics, 84-85
on God and the universe, 82-83
on history, 85-86
on human destiny, 86-87
on man, 84
on the nature of Zen Buddhism, 80-82
summary of his thought, 87-88
Thomas Aquinas, St., 27-30
classical theist, 22
cosmological argument of, 50
on creation, 22

on ethics, 29-30
on evil, 29
on God, 27-28
on history and goal, 30
on man, 29
on miracles, 28-29
on the universe, 28
Tillich, Paul, on worship, 189, 224
Tindal, Matthew, 139-43
on the Bible, 143
Christianity as Old as the Creation,
139
on creation, 140
on ethics, 142-43
on evil, 142
on God, 139-40
on God and the universe, 140-41
on history and goal, 143
on human destiny, 143
importance and influence of, 139
on Jesus Christ, 142
on man, 141-42
on miracles, 143
on natural law, 140-41
on natural religion, 141-42
on natural revelation, 143
Van Buren, Paul, semantical atheist, 44
Voltaire, French deist, 15
Watts, Alan
influence of Suzuki, 80
pantheist, 71
Whitehead, Alfred N., 102-109
Adventures of Ideas, 102
compared to Hartshorne, 101
on creation, 105-106
on ethics and values, 108-109
on evil, 106
on God, 102-104
on history and goal, 106-107
on man, 107-108
Modes of Thought, 102
Process and Reality, 102
on the universe, 104-105
Wieman, Henry, on God, 166
Woolston, Thomas, European deist, 138

Glossary

Absolutism. The belief that there are universals; truths and moral norms that are applicable to all times, places, and peoples.

Abstract. That which has no extra-mental or external existence in the world, but only exists in the mind; the conceptual, not the objective.

Absurd. In logic, a contradiction, as in a "rectangular triangle" or "round square." In existentialism, the impossibility of objective or ultimate meaning or purpose.

Aesthetics. The study of beauty.

Agnosticism. The belief that one either cannot or does not know reality or certain aspects of it, like God.

Anthropomorphism. The assigning of human charracteristics to that which is non-human.

Antinomy. The denial and affirmation of the same thing at the same time and in the same sense or respect; a contradition.

Being. That which is or exists; that which is real.

Brahman. In Hinduism, the Ultimate Reality; that which is formless, unknowable, inexpressible, and beyond all categories, whether moral, immoral, or amoral. Brahman is all and all is Brahman.

Causality. The principle which holds that every finite, contingent, changing thing needs a cause for its existence.

Cause. The necessary and sufficient condition for an effect.

Concrete. That which has extra-mental or external existence in the world.

Contingent. Dependent on another for its existence or function; that which can *not* be or cease to exist.

Contradiction. See *Antinomy* above.

Cosmological argument. The argument from a changing, finite world (cosmos) to the existence of God.

Demiurgos. Plato's (the ancient Greek philosopher's) concept of a god who created the world out of pre-existing material (*ex materia*).

Dualism. The polytheistic world view that teaches the existence of two ultimate realities, such as God or Good and Evil, or Spirit and Matter.

Emanation. In the pantheism of Plotinus, the necessary flowing of the world out of God, as a flower flows out of a seed or as rays flow from the sun.

Empiricism. The theory of knowledge which holds that all knowledge begins in sense experience.

Epistemology. Theory of knowledge or how we know.

Ethics. The study of right and wrong, of what one ought to do and ought not do.

Ex Deo. Creation of the world out of God.

Ex materia. Creation of the world out of pre-existent material or 'stuff.'

Ex nihilo. Creation of the world out of nothing (i.e., not out of something).

Existentialism. A movement that stresses existence is prior to essence; the concrete and individual is over or more important than the abstract and universal.

Finite. Having limits or boundaries; having the potential to cease to exist or change.

Humanism. The belief that human beings have the highest value in the universe.

Immanent. Indwelling. In relation to God, his presence *in* the universe.

Immortality. The teaching that human beings will live forever.

Infinite. Without boundaries or limits.

Infinite regress. The idea that there is no first cause in the infinite line of causes extending into the past; causes are infinitely dependent on dependent causes.

Karma. The belief that whatever one sows one reaps; every act, word, or thought produces or causes an inevitable effect.

Krishna. In Vedanta pantheism, one of the many manifestations of Brahman; also presumed to be one of the reincarnations of the Hindu God Vishnu (the Preserver).

Logic. The study of valid and sound thinking and argument.

Materialism. The belief that all that exists is material only; there are no spiritual or non-material realities such as God, souls, or angels.

Maya. The pantheistic idea that the material world does not actually exist but only appears to; the universe is an illusion, a superimposition on the one true reality, Brahman.

Metaphysics. The study of reality or being.

Moral argument. The argument from moral laws to a divine moral Law-Giver.

Natural law. In ethics, the belief that there are innate or natural moral laws discoverable and/or known by all human beings.

Naturalism. The view that the universe is all there is, the "whole show," and that what exists operates by natural law; no supernatural beings exist whatsoever, thus miracles are impossible.

Necessary being. An existent that *cannot* not exist; a must-be being whose nonexistence is impossible; a being whose very essence is existence.

Necessity. That which must be or cannot be other than it is.

Nihilism. The idea that there is no value in the universe or no value in being in it.

Nirvana. In Hindu and Buddhist thought, nothingness; the extinction of personal or individual existence through union with God, the All.

Noncontradiction, law of. A proposition or statement cannot be both true and false at the same time and in the same sense or respect.

Ontological argument. The argument that from man's idea or concept of God it can be concluded that God must actually exist.

Pluralism. The belief that reality is many rather than one (as in absolute pantheism).

Pragmatism. The view which makes what works the test for truth and/or moral norms.

Relativism. The belief that there are no absolutes; truth and morals vary among times, places, and people.

Samsara. The wheel or cycle of birth, death, and rebirth, escapable only through union with the Absolute One.

Skepticism. The belief that one should doubt or suspend all judgment on reality.

Teleological argument. The argument from the design or purposiveness displayed in the world to the existence of a cosmic Designer (God).

Transcendent. That which goes beyond or is more than human experience of the world. As applied to God in theism, the idea that God is outside of or beyond the universe.

Utilitarianism. In ethics, the view that a person should act to bring about the greatest measure of good for the greatest number of people.

Yoga. The practice designed to bring about a trance-like state which presumably allows the practitioner to unite in spirit with Brahman.